Caribbean Connections
Moving North

Other titles in the *Caribbean Connections* series:

Puerto Rico

Jamaica

Overview of Regional History

Teaching about Haiti

Caribbean Connections
Moving North

Edited by
Catherine A. Sunshine and Keith Q. Warner

Network of Educators on the Americas
Washington, D.C.

For Cynthia, Jade and Billy

For permission to reprint other portions of the book, contact:

Network of Educators on the Americas
P.O. Box 73038
Washington, DC 20056
(202) 238-2379 or (202) 429-0137
e-mail: necadc@aol.com

Book design by Free Hand Press, Washington, D.C.

Printed in the United States of America

Library of Congress Cataloging-in-Publication Data

Caribbean connections : moving north / edited by Catherine A. Sunshine
    and Keith Q. Warner.
        p.   cm.
    Includes bibliographic references (p. 233).
    ISBN 1-878554-12-3
    1. American literature—Caribbean American authors. 2. Caribbean
Area—Emigration and immigration—Literary collections. 3. West
Indies—Emigration and immigration—Literary collections. 4. West
Indian Americans—Literary collections. 5. Caribbean Americans—
Literary collections. 6. West Indian Americans. 7. Caribbean
Americans. I. Sunshine, Catherine A. II. Warner, Keith Q.
PS508.C27C37 1998
810.9'9729--dc21
                                                            98-28600
                                                              CIP

Contents

Read

Might want to Read These P.R. personal accounts

Part Three:
FICTION, MEMOIRS AND POETRY

not necessary unless interested

Part Four:
CARIBBEAN CROSSROADS

Part Five:
RESOURCES

U.S. PR relations

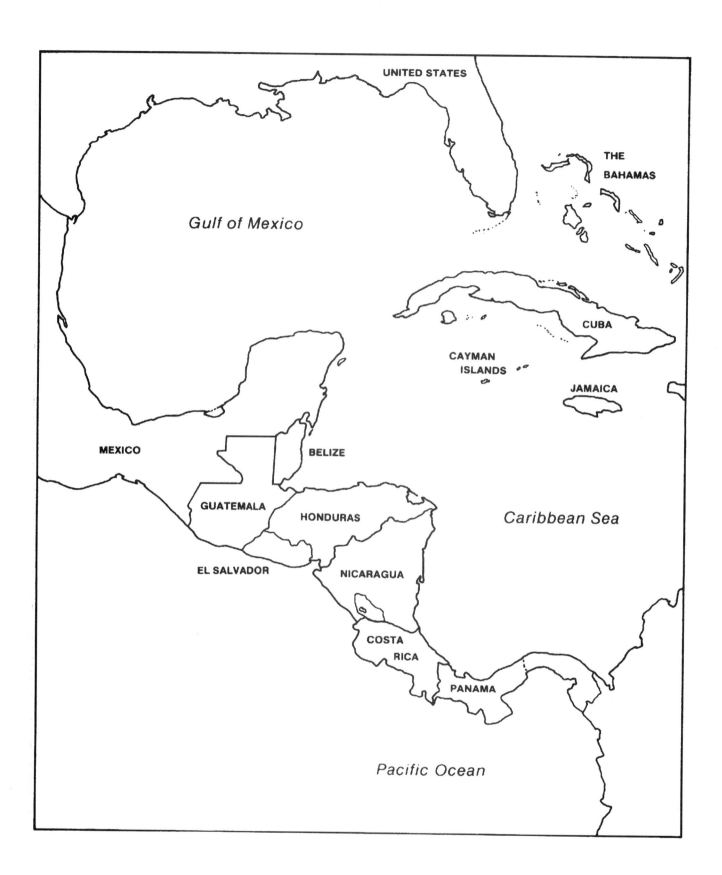

UNITED STATES

THE BAHAMAS

Gulf of Mexico

CUBA

CAYMAN
ISLANDS

JAMAICA

MEXICO

BELIZE

GUATEMALA

HONDURAS

Caribbean Sea

EL SALVADOR

NICARAGUA

COSTA
RICA

PANAMA

Pacific Ocean

The Caribbean

TURKS and CAICOS

Atlantic Ocean

U.S. VIRGIN ISLANDS

PUERTO RICO

ANGUILLA

ST. MARTIN

ST. BARTHELEMY

HAITI

DOMINICAN REPUBLIC

SABA

ST. EUSTATIUS

ST. KITTS-NEVIS

MONTSERRAT

ANTIGUA and BARBUDA

GUADELOUPE

DOMINICA

MARTINIQUE

ST. LUCIA

ST. VINCENT
and the Grenadines

BARBADOS

GRENADA

ARUBA

CURACAO

BONAIRE

TRINIDAD
and TOBAGO

VENEZUELA

GUYANA

SURINAME

FRENCH GUIANA

COLOMBIA

Acknowledgements

This book would not have been possible without the generous cooperation of the writers whose work is presented here. Our warmest thanks to all those who wrote for this volume, gave oral narratives, or gave permission for their published work to appear.

Eight humanities scholars with expertise in different areas of the Caribbean provided guidance to the project. Members of this advisory board are:

Dr. Roy S. Bryce-Laporte, MacArthur Professor of Sociology, Colgate University

Dr. Merle Collins, Department of English, University of Maryland at College Park

Mr. E. Leopold Edwards, National Coalition on Caribbean Affairs

Dr. Aida Heredia, Department of Modern Languages, Howard University

Dr. Julio Morales, School of Social Work, University of Connecticut

Dr. Sonia Nieto, School of Education, University of Massachusetts at Amherst

Dr. Marie Racine, Department of Languages and Communication Disorders, University of the District of Columbia

Dr. Elizabeth Mahan, Center for Latin American & Caribbean Studies, University of Connecticut

Dr. Ruth Glasser, an independent historian based in Waterbury, Connecticut, played a major role in the project. She coordinated the research in Connecticut and wrote the chapters on Caribbean communities in that state, even while seeing her own book on Puerto Ricans in Connecticut into print.

We are grateful to the following people for their efficient and timely assistance: Liz Hottel for research, Jenna Moniz for photography, Anne Sunshine and Amanda Wheeler-Kay for proofreading, and Paige Billin-Frye for cover art. Special thanks to Willy Packard and Sarah Carter of Free Hand Press for their fine work on book design.

A number of organizations opened their resource libraries or photo collections to us, or helped in other ways. They include the Caribbean Research Center at Medgar Evers College; Centro de Estudios Puertorriqueños at Hunter College; City Lore; Dominican Studies Institute at City College of New York; *El Diario-La Prensa;* Haitian Bilingual Education Technical Assistance Center at City College of New York; National Coalition for Haitian Rights; Washington Office on Haiti; and West Indian Social Club of Hartford, Connecticut.

We gratefully acknowledge funding assistance from the Connecticut Humanities Council, an affiliate of the National Endowment for the Humanities. The views expressed in this book are those of the individual authors and editors and do not necessarily reflect the views of the funding agencies or board of advisors.

Catherine A. Sunshine
Keith Q. Warner
Editors

Deborah Menkart
Project Director

Introduction

Nostrand Avenue cuts through the Flatbush section of Brooklyn, one of the five boroughs of New York City. Long the hub of the city's West Indian community, Flatbush today is becoming increasingly Haitian. From its studios on Nostrand Avenue, Radio Soleil broadcasts in Haitian Creole to listeners eager for news from Haiti. A few doors down the street is the office of *Everybody's,* "the Caribbean-American magazine." Many of the small businesses along Nostrand are Caribbean-owned and cater to the immigrant community. Pelican Shipping and Trading will ship household effects to destinations in the Caribbean and worldwide. Alken Tours offers chartered flights to Trinidad at Carnival time. Haitian Transfer Express helps immigrants send money to their families back home. Caribbean Taste, Isle of Spice, and dozens of other eateries cook up dishes such as curry goat and callaloo greens. Allan's Bakery offers Jamaican meat patties and coconut buns. You can even get your hair cut in a Haitian ambiance at the Charlemagne Péralte barber shop.

Across the river in northern Manhattan, travel agencies boast cheap fares to Santo Domingo. Restaurants serve *sancocho,* a savory meat and vegetable stew. The Dominican Republic is the leading source of legal immigrants entering New York City, and the Washington Heights/Inwood neighborhood is the heart of the city's burgeoning Dominican community.

Along Park Street in the Frog Hollow section of Hartford, Connecticut, businesses draw customers with names that recall hometowns in Puerto Rico. Caguitas Market. Aibonitos Restaurant. Corozal Grocery. You can buy a muffler at Borinquen Auto Parts, and religious articles at Botánica Changó. Yet for most Park Street shoppers, however nostalgic, Hartford has become home. A popular restaurant on the street says as much in its name: "Aquí Me Quedo" (I'm Here to Stay).

New York City and Hartford are centers of Caribbean life in the United States. But they are not the only ones. In Miami, Boston, Philadelphia, Chicago and other cities, and in small towns from New Jersey to California, immigration from the Caribbean is reshaping the ethnic and cultural landscape.

This collection presents the voices of women and men of Caribbean background living in the United States. Some came to this country from the Caribbean as adults. Others arrived as children or teenagers with their families, and grew up here. Still others were born in the United States to parents who had immigrated from the Caribbean. There are important differences between the various Caribbean immigrant groups, and each person's history is unique. Yet their narratives and writings reveal many common experiences and feelings about the migration experience.

The Readings

The readings fall into three broad categories: (1) oral narratives and memoirs; (2) fiction and poetry; (3) nonfiction articles and interviews.

In **oral narratives**, a person speaks to an interviewer who records the session. The audio tape is then transcribed, translated if necessary, and edited into a shorter written statement. The "life stories" in Part Two are oral narratives by

Aquí Me Quedo restaurant on Park Street in Hartford, Connecticut.

Caribbean immigrants or their descendants, most of whom were interviewed especially for this project. In **memoirs** a person writes about his or her life, usually in book form. An example is the excerpt in Part Three from Nicholasa Mohr's *Growing Up Inside the Sanctuary of My Imagination.*

Fiction and poetry in this book are mostly autobiographical, based on or inspired by events in the author's life. An example is the short story by Paule Marshall, "To Da-duh, in Memoriam."

Nonfiction articles and interviews in this collection are by writers who have personal knowledge of their topics. In Part Four, for example, Victor Morisete, director of a Dominican community agency, discusses Dominican life in Washington Heights.

The Writers

Speakers and writers in this book represent the largest Caribbean-origin groups in the United States. They trace their roots to one or more of the following areas: Puerto Rico; the English-speaking countries (sometimes called the West Indies); the Dominican Republic; Haiti; and Cuba.

By choosing to focus on these five groups, we have excluded those that are present in much smaller numbers, such as Surinamers. There are only a few Caribbean territories that have *not* sent a significant share of their population to North America. These territories are current or former colonies of France or the Netherlands, and their emigrants go mainly to Europe.

Puerto Ricans occupy a special position. As U.S. citizens, they are not immigrants. The quasi-colonial relationship between the United States and Puerto Rico makes the Puerto Rican migration unlike any other. Nonetheless, Puerto Ricans who have moved to the United States share some experiences in common with others who have come from the Caribbean. They are the largest Caribbean-origin group in the 50 states and form one of the earliest and strongest connections between the United States and the Caribbean. As such, they feature prominently in this book.

Some of the selections in *Moving North* are excerpted from the published works of well-known authors. Others are essays written for this volume, or interviews with people from various walks of

Lloyd Patterson, Everybody's Magazine

Metro Steel, a local steelband, warming up to play in the Labor Day Carnival in Brooklyn, New York.

life. In all cases, deciding what to include was difficult. There is a rich and growing literature of fiction, poetry and memoirs by U.S. writers of Caribbean heritage; to keep the book a manageable size, we were forced to choose only a few examples and omit a number of prominent authors. Part Five suggests further reading for those who wish to explore this literature in greater depth.

Focus on Connecticut and New York

Although the readings are drawn from various communities, New York City and Connecticut are areas of emphasis. Both have had immigration from the Caribbean since the nineteenth century. Both currently have large populations of Caribbean origin, especially Puerto Ricans, Dominicans, and West Indians. And the Caribbean population in both Connecticut and New York is growing steadily as newcomers continue to arrive.

Caribbean cultural influence on the New York urban scene is unmistakable. Who could imagine the city without salsa, without merengue, without the West Indian Carnival procession through Brooklyn each Labor Day? Less well known is the marked Caribbean presence in many Connecticut cities and towns. Puerto Ricans make up at least 27 percent of Hartford's population, the highest concentration of any large city in the United States, and are a rapidly growing presence in smaller cities such as Waterbury. West Indians in the Hartford area may number as many as 40,000, and 12 West Indian social clubs enliven the city's cultural scene.

For all these reasons, New York City and Connecticut make good case studies of Caribbean immigration when one book cannot do it all. Other cities and states could equally well have been chosen, and it is our hope that this glimpse of Caribbean life in the United States will encourage readers to discover and appreciate the Caribbean presence in other communities, beginning with their own.

Organization of the Book

Part One, by the editors, begins with an overview of Caribbean history and a look at the migration experience of each of the five featured groups. A summary of U.S. immigration law is presented, along with a brief discussion of our nation's changing attitudes toward immigrants.

Part Two consists of personal narratives by 15 women and men of Caribbean heritage living in the United States. Their stories, told in their own words, bring to life the economic and political forces behind immigration. Their occupations—trade unionist, lawyer, factory worker, doctor, student, farm worker and musician, among others—suggest the wide range of talents Caribbean immigrants have brought and the kinds of contributions they have made.

Part Three contains selected fiction, poetry and memoirs by writers of Caribbean heritage in the United States. All the readings deal in some way with the migration experience and life in this country; works set principally in the Caribbean are not included, even if their authors have emigrated. Themes include homesickness, divided families, culture conflict, school experiences, language issues, generational issues, stereotyping, and construction of ethnic, national, racial and gender identities.

The title of Part Four, "Caribbean Crossroads," has a dual meaning. U.S. communities where many Caribbean immigrants have settled are a crossroads where American and Caribbean cultures meet. At the same time, these diaspora communities have become a crossroads for the meeting of people from different parts of the Caribbean, bringing their cultures into contact with each other. Articles and interviews provide a glimpse of Caribbean life in four cities: Miami, Washington D.C., Philadelphia and New York. The section concludes with a case study of one state, Connecticut, where Caribbean immigration has had a broad impact on community life.

Part Five outlines resources that groups can use to explore the Caribbean presence in their own communities, and gives suggestions for further reading. ❖

Martha Cooper, courtesy of Rockland County Historical Society

Caribbean Voices

Lesa Thomas

I'm from Trinidad and Tobago, and I came to the United States when I was 17. I really didn't want to come. But my mother wanted me to go to college here, and my father was living in Washington, D.C. at the time. So I had to leave my mom and come to a new country to live with a dad that I hardly knew at all.

I cried the entire plane ride. I would picture leaving the airport, waving to my mother and my brothers, not knowing where I was going, or if I would ever see them again.

At the University of the District of Columbia, I was the only person in my English class from another country. When I first came I had a heavy accent, and people would say, "How did you come over, on a banana boat?" Or they would joke, "Are you legal or illegal?" I arrived in February, and at first my dad didn't realize I would need heavier clothes. I wore skirts with socks folded over and tennis shoes, and I was cold. Nothing really matched. People would say, "You must be from the islands!" And they would joke about that.

At first I withdrew and was just kind of quiet. Finally, though, I got over it. In my college chemistry class I was getting good grades, but the instructor would still pick on me, ask absurd questions and put me on the spot. One day I really lost it. I stood up and said, "Are you judging me based on my accent or on my capabilities?" And I just went off, started talking.

People might still make fun of the way I speak but I'm past that now. But when you're not yet at the point where you can take it as a joke, it hurts. I don't think people understand how much it hurts. Dealing with it as an adult, I really feel for the kids who are coming here now and going through that.

I now have two master's degrees and teach both middle-school students and adults, but I still sometimes feel I have to justify myself. When I'm leading a workshop, I might start by saying, "If I'm talking too fast just let me know, because I'm from Trinidad and I have an accent." It's funny, but I still feel I have to do that.

My husband is from Jamaica. He has his own carpentry business, and as a hobby, he collects cars and fixes them up. But he worries about having so many cars around. He says, "I wonder if the neighbors on the block think we're doing drugs." He can't get that out of his head—the whole stereotype of being Jamaican. It's still there, no matter how hard you work.

There are positive stereotypes too. Someone might tell you, "I want to hire you, because people from the islands work harder." When someone says that, I feel it's really putting me down. It hits me like a ton of bricks.

Lesa Thomas teaches seventh grade in the Washington, D.C. public schools. She was interviewed by Catherine Sunshine on July 12, 1997.

Claude

When I left my country, I went by boat with a group of people. I ended up at Guantánamo Bay [the U.S. naval base in Cuba where Haitian refugees were sheltered temporarily.] I don't like talking about this time in my life; it was difficult.

It's hard to live in a new place without your family. My family is still in Haiti. I have five sisters and one brother. Sometimes I get homesick. Lately, it's been difficult to contact them by phone, because the phone lines are down, but I can still reach them by letter.

I left Haiti because of the military. I didn't want them to get me, so I had to leave. I had to keep on the move. If they catch you, they kill you.

I would like to go back to Haiti someday, but only if things there are cool again. It's not good there right now. My biggest wish for Haiti is that things settle down there. I'd like to finish my education in the U.S. and go back to Haiti, if the situation improves. I'd like to see my family again.

Some American teenagers don't understand my situation. They haven't had to experience what it's like to want peace so much. Some of them only think of the dollar, and that's all they know. They think they know a lot because they live in the United States, but they haven't experienced the kinds of things I have.

Claude fled Haiti at age 17. After being admitted to the United States from Guantánamo, he was resettled in Massachusetts by a Catholic organization. Only his first name is used here to protect his family in Haiti. Reprinted by permission from Valerie Tekavec, ed., Teenage Refugees from Haiti Speak Out *(New York: Rosen Publishing, 1995).*

Elba Tirhado-Armstrong

I don't have a typical Spanish name—my name's not Carmen, my name's not María, and my last name is not Hernández, Fernández, Pérez or García. I'm talking to people on the phone, they have no idea that I'm Puerto Rican because I'm not giving off anything that says I'm not like them. But when they meet me, all of a sudden it's like, "Are you Puerto Rican?" And I'm like, "Yeah, I am! I'm Dominican too!" "Really? You don't sound it." Not only do I not have the accent, but in many people's minds, what it's like to sound Puerto Rican is not very flattering. On the echelon of minorities we're not too far from the bottom for many people.

There are blond, blue-eyed Puerto Ricans. There are Puerto Ricans who look like African-Americans, who are very dark-skinned and have curly hair. Others may be café au lait with green eyes and light brown hair. I don't have what everybody assumes are typical Puerto Rican features— whatever those are! I haven't fit into that mold and people frequently make it a point to tell me.

I always thought of myself as very Latina. I didn't necessarily think I was more Puerto Rican or more Dominican because I really thought I was a good mixture of both. I'm a Latina woman, Dominican and Puerto Rican, with a husband who's not Hispanic, in a society that looks at most Latina women as "Are you on welfare? How many kids do you have?" That is the first assumption. That sometimes is hard to swallow, but it's a reality and I've accepted it. I haven't accepted it as my own personal philosophy but I've accepted that people will judge me by those criteria. That's unfortunate and I do everything I can to change that and dispel the myth.

Elba Tirhado-Armstrong is a visiting nurse in Waterbury, Connecticut. Reprinted by permission from Ruth Glasser, Aquí Me Quedo: Puerto Ricans in Connecticut *(Middletown, Conn.: Connecticut Humanities Council, 1997).* ❖

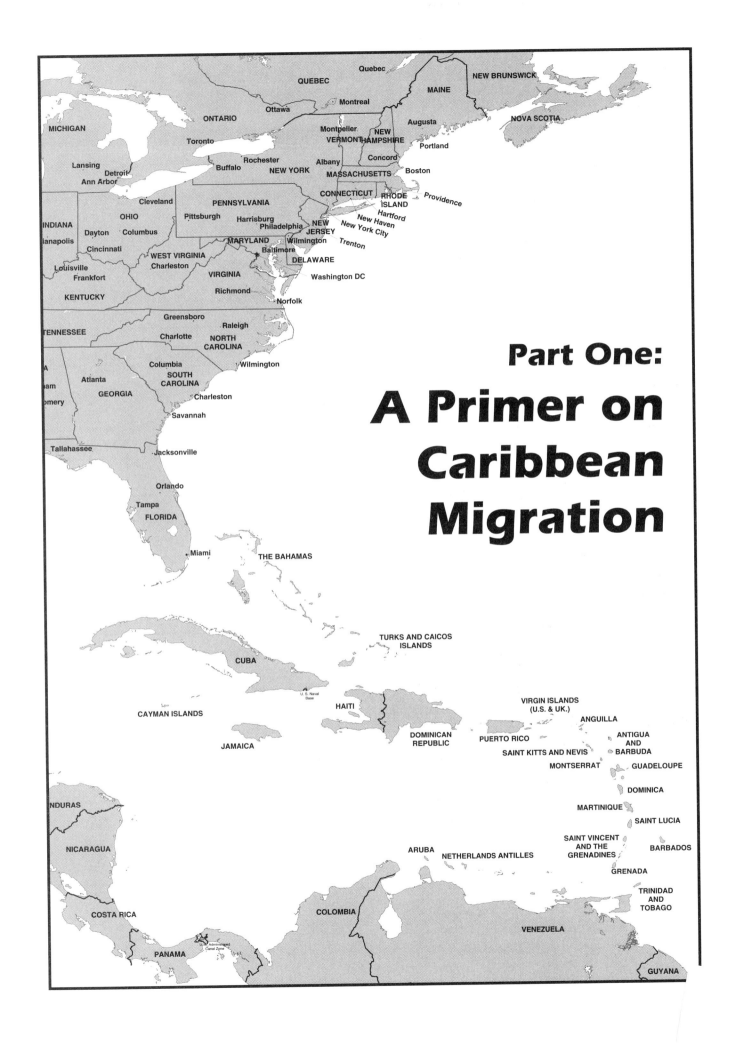

Part One:
A Primer on Caribbean Migration

Countries and Territories of the Caribbean

Independent States

COUNTRY BY DATE OF INDEPENDENCE	CAPITAL	POPULATION (1998 PROJECTED)
French & Creole–speaking		
Haiti (1804)	Port-au-Prince	6,781,000
Spanish-speaking		
Dominican Republic (1844)	Santo Domingo	7,999,000
Cuba (1902)	Havana	11,045,000
English-speaking		
Jamaica (1962)	Kingston	2,635,000
Trinidad and Tobago (1962)	Port-of-Spain	1,117,000
Barbados (1966)	Bridgetown	259,000
Guyana (1966)	Georgetown	708,000
Bahamas (1973)	Nassau	280,000
Grenada (1974)	St. George's	96,000
Dominica* (1978)	Roseau	66,000
St. Lucia (1979)	Castries	152,000
St. Vincent and the Grenadines (1979)	Kingstown	120,000
Antigua and Barbuda (1981)	St. John	64,000
Belize (1981)	Belmopan	230,000
St. Kitts and Nevis (1983)	Basseterre	42,000
Dutch-speaking		
Suriname (1975)	Paramaribo	428,000

Dependent Territories

TERRITORY AND AFFILIATION	CAPITAL	POPULATION (1998 PROJECTED)
U.S. Territories		
Puerto Rico (Spanish-speaking)	San Juan	3,861,000
U.S. Virgin Islands	Charlotte Amalie	118,000
British Territories		
Anguilla	The Valley	11,000
Bermuda	Hamilton	63,000
Cayman Islands	Georgetown	38,000
Montserrat	Plymouth	13,000
Turks and Caicos	Grand Turk	15,000
British Virgin Islands	Road Town	14,000
French Territories		
Guadeloupe	Basseterre	416,000
French Guiana	Cayenne	163,000
Martinique	Fort-de-France	407,000
Dutch Territories		
Netherlands Antilles	Willemstad	213,000
Aruba	Orangestad	68,000

Source of population estimates: International Data Base of the U.S. Census Bureau.

* The Commonwealth of Dominica (pronounced DominEEka), an English-speaking country, should not be confused with the Spanish-speaking Dominican Republic.

Migration in Caribbean History

The Caribbean Sea is a body of water southeast of the Gulf of Mexico. It's easily found on a map. The more difficult question is how to define the *region* we call the Caribbean. The usual image is of a group of islands in the Caribbean Sea, but that is not exact. In fact, definitions of the Caribbean region have varied over time.

The region clearly includes the chain of islands arcing across the Caribbean Sea, from Trinidad and Tobago in the south to the Bahamas in the north. Bermuda, in the Atlantic, is sometimes included as well because of its historical ties to the West Indian islands. Most definitions also take in four mainland territories: Belize, Suriname, Guyana, and French Guiana. Although located in Central and South America, they have strong historical and cultural connections to the islands. The inclusion of both islands and mainland territories is one reason the Caribbean isn't an easy concept to define.

The more important divider, however, is language. Four European powers colonized the region: Spain, England, France and Holland. Each organized its Caribbean possessions into a self-contained grouping linked primarily to the European "mother country" rather than to neighboring Caribbean territories. As a result, Caribbean countries fall into four broad groups, speaking Spanish, English, French or Dutch, as well as related Creole languages. Even now, in the age of independence, the region remains largely divided along these same lines. Contacts across the linguistic barriers are relatively few.

Yet another divider is political status. In the last quarter-century, most of the Caribbean colonies have gained independence and become sovereign nations. But a few are still dependent territories of England, France or the Netherlands. Puerto Rico is a special case, a self-governing "commonwealth" linked to the United States; many Puerto Ricans say the island is a colony in all but name.

Given this complexity, is it still possible to speak of a Caribbean region? The answer is a qualified "yes." Caribbean societies share historical experiences of colonial rule, of slavery and indentureship, and of struggles for freedom and national independence. These linger in the collective memory of the region's people. Each people and country in the region has its own history, but there are many parallels and connections between them.

Migration is one such connector. Since precolonial times, the movement of people into, within, and out of the region has been an integral part of the Caribbean experience. It has linked Caribbean societies to one another, and with the outside world.

Yet a word of caution is in order. Just as the diversity of Caribbean societies makes it difficult to generalize about the region, so too with Caribbean immigrant communities. Patterns of migration for Cubans, for example, are entirely different from those of Puerto Ricans. Dominicans and West Indians in the United States have some interaction, but not necessarily a great deal. Haitian-Americans share some experiences with other Caribbean immigrants, yet have a unique identity rooted in Haiti's history, language and culture. Understanding Caribbean migration means looking for shared themes and experiences while appreciating the important differences between the various immigrant groups.

Migration into the Caribbean

The first inhabitants of the Caribbean were indigenous peoples from South America and Central America. They moved into the Caribbean islands more than a thousand years ago, migrating north and east in their dugout canoes. First came the Ciboneys and other groups who lived by hunting and gathering. They were followed by the Arawaks, a peaceful farming people. Finally, Carib warriors pushed up the island chain from the south, raiding Arawak settlements and forcing the Arawaks to retreat to the northern islands.

The arrival of Europeans in the region, beginning with Christopher Columbus and his gold-seekers in 1492, resulted in the near-complete destruction of the native populations. Although the Arawaks and Caribs tried to resist, they died in great numbers as a result of conflicts with the Spanish, forced labor in Spanish mines and ranches, and new diseases.

Claiming possession of the land, the governments of Spain, England, France and Holland set up colonies on the Caribbean islands. They used these colonies to grow profitable crops, especially sugar cane, on large plantations.

To provide labor for the plantations, the colonial powers organized a slave trade that brought six million Africans to the Caribbean region. This massive, forced migration from Africa laid the basis for contemporary Caribbean societies. The majority of Caribbean people today trace their roots wholly or partly to Africa, and African influences have shaped the development of Caribbean languages, religions and cultures.

Slavery was abolished in the British colonies in 1834, and in the French colonies in 1848. As the freed slaves moved away from the plantations, the planters looked for new sources of cheap labor. They found it in distant lands. Agents of the planters recruited laborers from India, China and other parts of the world. These "indentured" workers signed contracts to work on the sugar estates for five or ten years.

All these peoples—Native Americans, Africans, Asians and Europeans—mingled to form the Caribbean populations of today.

Early Emigration

Caribbean people began emigrating to Europe and North America during the colonial era, but in small numbers. Some of the first migrants went seeking employment, others to further their education. Notable examples included Prince Hall, who moved from Barbados to Boston and established the black Freemasonry movement in the 1700s. Jean Baptiste Pointe du Sable, born in the French colony of St. Domingue, founded the settlement that would become the city of Chicago. Alexander Hamilton, from the island of Nevis, helped draft the U.S. Constitution.

During the nineteenth century, revolution swept the Caribbean as people in the larger territories revolted against slavery and colonial rule. These upheavals resulted in the first major emigration from the region.

The first uprising came in 1791 in the French colony of St. Domingue. The enslaved Africans in the colony rose up, claimed their freedom and overthrew French rule, proclaiming the independent Republic of Haiti in 1804. During and after

West Indian laborers building the Panama Canal, October 10, 1913. More than 100,000 men and women from the Caribbean islands traveled to Panama to work on the canal between 1881 and 1914. Here, workers load holes with dynamite at the Culebra Cut.

the Haitian Revolution, thousands of St. Domingue plantation owners fled to the United States. They settled throughout the American South, where slavery was still entrenched. Some brought slaves with them, and these black men and women from St. Domingue helped spread the message of freedom, taking part in revolts that hastened the end of slavery in the United States.

By the mid-1800s, nationalists in Cuba and Puerto Rico were challenging Spanish rule. In movements that were jointly planned and closely coordinated, rebels in both territories fought for the abolition of slavery and independence from Spain. Some were expelled from the colonies and went to the United States, especially New York City, where they continued to organize and raise

funds to support the cause. Jose Martí, the "father of Cuban independence," was a member of this exile community. So was Arturo Schomburg, a black Puerto Rican who arrived in 1891. His extensive collection of books, manuscripts, prints and pamphlets about people of African descent became the basis for the Schomburg Center for Research in Black Culture in New York City.

The United States Looks South

As Spain's grip weakened, a new economic and military power was poised to move in to the region. Many influential Americans believed that the United States, having reached its western limit, should expand south. Military strategists argued that the country needed naval bases in the

Caribbean from which to project its power. At the same time, American business interests wanted new lands and markets. By the 1890s, U.S. sugar and banana companies were investing heavily in Cuba, Jamaica, and other territories of the region.

The end of slavery in the British and French colonies 50 years earlier had set people adrift, searching for paid employment. Laborers from around the region were drawn to the new economic projects undertaken by U.S. firms. Thousands of men from the British and French colonies traveled to Cuba, the Dominican Republic and Puerto Rico to cut sugar cane on U.S.-owned plantations. Others worked on the banana plantations and railroads of the United Fruit Company in Central America. The biggest project of all was the building of the Panama Canal between 1881 and 1914 under first French, then American direction. More than 100,000 men from the British and French islands went to Panama to hew the canal through solid rock and pestilent swamps; tens of thousands died in the effort.

American business leaders, politicians and military men dreamed of a "Caribbean empire" that ultimately would enable the United States to dominate the hemisphere. But first, the European powers had to be edged out of the region. In 1898 pro-independence rebels in Cuba were on the verge of victory against Spain. Suddenly, the United States entered the war. U.S. Marines invaded Cuba and Puerto Rico, and Spain quickly surrendered.

Instead of the independence the rebels had fought for, Puerto Rico and Cuba came under U.S. military rule. In 1900 the U.S. Congress declared Puerto Rico a United States territory. Cuba became nominally independent, but under the "Platt Amendment" that U.S. officials wrote into Cuba's constitution, the United States retained the right to intervene militarily in Cuba and to build two naval bases on the island.

Over the next 30 years, U.S. gunboats and troops invaded independent countries of the Caribbean and Central America dozens of times. Five countries came under lengthy U.S. military occupation: Cuba, Nicaragua, Panama, the Dominican Republic, and Haiti. The U.S. occupation forces wrote new laws that helped American investors take over land. By the time the last troops were withdrawn in 1934,

U.S. firms had extensive holdings and influence in all the major Caribbean and Central American countries. When the troops departed, they left in place U.S.-trained military "guards" and U.S.-allied dictators to protect those interests.

Moving North

The projection of American power into the Caribbean in the nineteenth and twentieth centuries had far-reaching consequences. It linked the two regions in a web of economic, political and military relationships that brought increasing cultural contact. European colonialism, while not gone, was on the way out. As the United States reached south, the people of the Caribbean increasingly looked north.

Foreign investment in the islands provided jobs for some people while destroying the livelihood of many. Small farms were swallowed up by vast U.S.-owned plantations. Displaced rural people drifted to the cities, searching for work.

The steamships that carried bananas from the United Fruit Company's plantations to New York City and other U.S. ports also had room for passengers. More and more people made the trip. Between 1900 and 1930, some 40,000 immigrants from the British Caribbean colonies settled in New York City. Smaller West Indian communities formed in other cities such as Boston, Philadelphia and Washington.

The United States imposed U.S. citizenship on Puerto Ricans in 1917. One result was increased emigration. The Puerto Rican population in the mainland United States grew rapidly, reaching about 50,000 by 1930.

Several factors slowed emigration to a trickle during the 1920s and 1930s. The Panama Canal project came to an end, and new investment dried up during the Great Depression. A new U.S. immigration law in 1924 established national quotas that restricted Caribbean immigration; these quotas did not, of course, affect the migration of Puerto Ricans. Poverty deepened throughout the region, and pressure built for renewed emigration.

Release came with the outbreak of World War II. With most able-bodied men fighting overseas, England, Canada and the United States were desperately short of labor. Caribbean men were recruited to work on farms and in factories and in the British armed forces. After the war, England, France and Holland, in need of labor to rebuild war-torn economies, opened their doors to immigrants from their overseas colonies. The island economies were stagnant and large numbers of people seized the chance to work abroad. The era of mass migration had begun.

People departed by the boatload, steelbands playing at the pier. Jamaican poet Louise Bennett joked that Jamaicans—who had been colonized by England—were now "colonizing England in reverse."

> *What a joyful news, Miss Mattie*
> *I feel like me heart goin' burst*
> *Jamaica people colonizin'*
> *England in reverse.*
>
> *By de hundred, by de thousand*
> *From country and from town*
> *By de ship-load, by de plane-load*
> *Jamaica is England-bound.*

Similarly, Puerto Ricans were encouraged to migrate to the United States to fill postwar jobs in factories and on farms. Puerto Ricans remember the 1950s, when hundreds of thousands of Puerto Ricans moved north, as the time of the "great migration." By 1970 there were 1.4 million people of Puerto Rican birth or parentage in the 50 states.

A second major flow came to the United States from Cuba. After 1959, hundreds of thousands of Cubans left when it became clear that the Cuban Revolution would be socialist. The first wave included Cubans who had ties to the old regime, or affluent families who had lost property and influence under the new government. The U.S. government welcomed them as refugees from communism and provided resettlement aid.

The next turning point came in 1965. New laws in the United States and Canada changed the way immigrants were admitted. National quotas favoring Europeans were eliminated. Instead, the new U.S. law gave preference to people who had family members already living in the United States and to people whose job skills were in demand.

Britain and France, meanwhile, were tightening their immigration laws to keep more people out. As a result, the bulk of Caribbean migration shifted from Europe toward Canada and the United States—a pattern that continues today.

Motives for Migration

Why do Caribbean people move north?

Each person who migrates has a story to tell. At one level, migration is an individual or family decision. Often there is not just one reason for that decision, but several interconnected ones.

It would be a mistake, however, to explain the movement of large populations as *only* the sum of these individual decisions. When hundreds of thousands of people from one "sending" country migrate to a single "receiving" country, one needs to look at the relationship *between those two countries.*

In the Caribbean, the largest flows have come—and continue to come—from Puerto Rico, the Dominican Republic, Jamaica, Cuba and Haiti. These territories have the largest populations in the region and, therefore, more people to send. But there are other reasons as well for the large numbers who trek northward. These territories, ringed along the U.S. periphery, are the ones that have had the closest political and economic relations with the United States over many years. All but Jamaica experienced U.S. military occupation and/or U.S.-supported dictatorial regimes. All had their economies restructured by U.S. investment, and with the exception of Cuba, continue to depend upon U.S. aid, trade and tourism. Although distant from the periphery, Trinidad and Tobago, another major source of immigrants, also has U.S. ties. During World War II, the construction of a huge U.S. naval base on Trinidad employed many Trinidadians, while the thousands of American soldiers stationed at the base infused American influences into Trinidadian culture.

All these linkages—economic, political, cultural—can be seen as "bridges" encouraging migration. Within this larger framework, one can point to various factors that may be involved in an individual's decision to migrate.

Recruitment

There is a popular perception that immigrants come seeking personal gain even though "we don't really want them." The fact is that many people come to the United States, from the Caribbean and elsewhere, because there is a demand for their labor. This demand has sometimes been expressed through formal recruitment. During World War II the federal government brought in temporary workers, mostly from the English-speaking islands, to harvest sugar, tobacco and other crops. After the war, employers sent delegations to Puerto Rico to recruit workers for farm and factory jobs.

The government also set up a special "H-2" visa program for farm workers that continues to bring in some 20,000 seasonal workers each year, mostly from the Caribbean. In recent decades Florida sugar growers have recruited almost all their cane cutters from the West Indies, mainly Jamaica. Although an increasing proportion of the cane is harvested by machine, West Indian cutters are still the backbone of the Florida sugar industry.

During the 1960s and 1970s, middle-class American women entered the work force in large numbers. As they did, jobs were created for housekeepers and nannies. The U.S. Labor Department certified "domestic help" as a category in need of workers, and many women were recruited from the Caribbean to fill these jobs.

Today, the sectors of the U.S. labor market that are expanding most rapidly are those at either extreme: low-wage jobs that pay poorly and high-tech jobs that require specialized skills. To employers at the low end, an influx of immigrants is a welcome source of cheap labor. At the same time, immigrants with high-level skills such as scientists and computer programmers are sought after by employers in specialized fields.

Economic progress
The countries of the Caribbean are mostly small, and some are tiny. There is limited land for farming. Caribbean economies historically have depended on one or two major export products, such as sugar or bananas, which bring low prices on the international market. Tourism, the other mainstay, creates some jobs but most of the profits go to foreign investors. Throughout the region, wages are low and unemployment staggeringly high. Joblessness rates of 30 percent, 50 percent and higher are not uncommon.

U.S. policy-makers have argued that foreign investment, by energizing Caribbean economies, helps keep people at home. In actual practice this does not appear to be true. Over the past few decades most Caribbean governments have followed the dictates of international lenders and have reorganized their economies to emphasize exports. This has meant neglecting small-scale agriculture in order to give priority to large mechanized farms and factories—often foreign-owned—that produce goods for markets abroad.

These large farms and factories create a certain number of jobs. But as small farms become uneconomical and obsolete, many more people are uprooted from their rural homes. Many migrate to the cities, where they may join the ranks of the urban unemployed or eke out a meager living as peddlers or day laborers. The lucky ones who land a factory job typically make as little as $4.00 per day. Now that they are no longer farmers but wage workers, common sense dictates going where wages are highest. It takes little imagination to see how emigration to the United States would appear an attractive option.

The manual worker who migrates and earns the U.S. minimum wage of $5.15 an hour is making more in one hour than he or she might have earned in a whole day at home. By working several jobs and living frugally, workers can send home money every week or month to relatives in the Caribbean.

These "remittances" are a lifeline for people in the region. They pay for new houses, land and school tuition. Migration thus becomes an economic strategy for families, who may arrange for one member to migrate in the expectation that he or she will contribute to the support of all those left behind. The millions of dollars in remittances from nationals abroad have become a crucial source of foreign exchange for virtually every Caribbean nation.

Academic and professional advancement
Not all migrants are manual laborers or farmers. A fair proportion are already highly educated and skilled when they arrive in the United States. They come to attend college, graduate school or medical school, or to pursue a career. The Caribbean has a relatively large number of university graduates who

must compete for the very small number of professional jobs in the region. Furthermore, the average salary of a doctor in the Caribbean, for example, is nowhere near what a doctor with equivalent qualifications could earn in the United States. The heavy emigration of physicians, nurses, college professors, writers, artists and other highly trained persons has robbed the region of some of its most skilled and creative workers, generating alarm about a "brain drain."

Family reunification
Whatever an individual's reasons for migrating, he or she often wants family members to follow, if not immediately, then perhaps after some years. U.S. law also recognizes the importance of keeping families together. Under the 1965 immigration law, naturalized U.S. citizens and legal permanent residents may petition to obtain visas for their close family members (children, spouses, parents and siblings). Immigrants typically send for their relatives one by one, often having to wait months or even years for the necessary visas. These relatives in turn bring in others, until extended families are completely or partially reunited in the United States. This "chain migration" is one reason why immigrants from particular countries, regions or towns tend to cluster in specific places in the United States.

Political conditions
There is seldom a clear distinction between "economic" and "political" migrants, although U.S. policy-makers have insisted that such categories exist. A few people—in recent years, mainly Haitians—do leave their countries primarily because they fear persecution. But it is far more common for the decision to migrate to involve a mix of economic and political considerations.

Cuba, the Dominican Republic, and Haiti have all sent large numbers of emigrants to the United States. In all three countries, U.S. political involvement helped create the conditions that caused people to leave.

For years the United States propped up the brutal and corrupt Batista dictatorship in Cuba. After he was toppled by a revolution in 1959, the United States encouraged Cubans to abandon the island and welcomed all who reached U.S. shores. Washington imposed a trade embargo that cut Cuba off from critical supplies of food, medicine, raw materials and spare parts. Today, ordinary Cubans, frustrated with the beleaguered island economy, compare their lot to the comfortable lives of their relatives in Florida. For many, dissatisfaction with political conditions and with the standard of living in Cuba go hand in hand.

In the Dominican Republic the United States supported another notorious strongman, General Rafael Trujillo. After his assassination in 1961, Dominicans elected a new president, Juan Bosch. But the Dominican military ousted Bosch only seven months later. When a popular rebellion broke out demanding the return of democratic government, the Johnson Administration sent in 22,000 U.S. Marines to crush the uprising. In the invasion's aftermath thousands of Dominicans, many of them Bosch supporters, fled to New York, beginning an exodus that continues today.

The United States also helped maintain dictatorship in Haiti. Beginning in 1957, Washington supported first François Duvalier, then his son Jean-Claude, and finally a series of murderous military regimes. Haitians have streamed out of the country over the last four decades, impelled by poverty and political persecution.

Political conditions have played a significant if less dramatic role in emigration from other Caribbean nations. Even in countries with regular multi-party elections, the ruling party frequently keeps a tight grip. Jobs and other opportunities, scarce to begin with, may be reserved for the favorites of whoever happens to be in power.

An example is Guyana between 1964 and 1992 under the People's National Congress. Holding power through elections that many believed to be fraudulent, the ruling party dominated every aspect of Guyanese society. Thousands of Guyanese, demoralized and seeing no future for themselves if they stayed, opted to migrate to the United States and Canada.

Expectations, hopes and dreams
Although economic hardship is widespread in the Caribbean, the countries of the region, with a few exceptions, are located near the middle of the

world economic ladder. Yet the Caribbean sends many more people to the United States than do a number of more deeply impoverished nations.

This becomes easier to understand when one visits or lives in the Caribbean and feels the looming presence of the giant to the north. Pervasive U.S. influences shape the expectations and aspirations of people in the region. U.S.-made products line store shelves for those who have money to buy. Seductive images of "the good life" come via American movies and television programs. Remittances from family members who have already migrated are a constant reminder of the economic opportunities up north. The sight of free-spending tourists fosters the myth that all Americans are wealthy.

Perhaps most important, there is a steady flow of return migrants heading back to the Caribbean to visit or to stay. They come laden with gifts, cash, and tales of success, real or exaggerated. Returnees also tell of the high cost of living and the crime, unemployment, and racial discrimination in U.S. society. But to many people, the potential rewards appear well worth the risks. ❖

Ken Martin, Impact Visuals

Puerto Ricans

Two facts distinguish the migration of Puerto Ricans from that of other Caribbean groups. First, Puerto Ricans are U.S. citizens, and therefore not "immigrants" at all in the eyes of the law. Like all U.S. citizens, they have the right to live anywhere in the United States and its territories. They can travel freely between the island of Puerto Rico and the 50 states, a fact that gives many Puerto Ricans a foothold in both worlds.

Nonetheless, although they hold U.S. passports, virtually all who trace their origins to the island feel a strong identity as Puerto Ricans. Taking a plane from San Juan to New York doesn't require one to clear customs. But it does mean leaving a Spanish-speaking Caribbean society with its own history and culture, and entering an English-speaking nation that is culturally different. In this sense, Puerto Ricans who move to the United States share experiences in common with others who have come from the Caribbean.

The second distinguishing characteristic of the Puerto Rican migration is its size. No Caribbean group has had a greater impact on U.S. society. The 2.7 million Puerto Ricans living in the 50 states are the country's second-largest Latino population, after Mexican-Americans. They remain the predominant Spanish-speaking group in most cities of the U.S. Northeast and Midwest, although other Latino groups are growing fast.

Puerto Rico itself has been deeply affected by the exodus. Nearly as many Puerto Ricans now live in the 50 states as in Puerto Rico, which consists of the main island plus the offshore islets of Vieques, Mona and Culebra. The colonial relationship between the United States and Puerto Rico has influenced Puerto Rican culture and language. Yet pride in being Puerto Rican remains strong, generation after generation.

Why They Come

Puerto Rican communities began forming in the United States more than 100 years ago as artisans, tradespeople and a few professionals came north, mainly to New York City. Some of these late-nineteenth-century migrants were political exiles who had been expelled from the island for

Playing dominoes in El Barrio (East Harlem).

their involvement in the revolt against Spain. Together with exiles from Cuba, they formed revolutionary support groups in New York that continued plotting strategy and raising funds for the independence struggle. Among the most dedicated activists were the *tabaqueros*, or cigar makers—skilled men and women who rolled cigars by hand in the small cigar factories of New York City and Tampa, Florida.

In 1898, the United States forced Spain out of the Caribbean in the Spanish-American War and seized Spain's colonies. The main object was Cuba, a territory that U.S. businessmen and politicians had long coveted. Puerto Rico was taken as "compensation for the expenses of war." The U.S. Congress assumed control of Puerto Rico's laws, courts, currency, customs, immigration, defense, foreign relations and trade. In 1917 Congress passed the Jones Act, imposing U.S. citizenship on Puerto Ricans; one consequence was that Puerto Ricans could be and were drafted into the U.S. armed forces. Citizenship also made the prospect of national independence for Puerto Rico seem even more remote.

U.S. corporations arrived to take over vast tracts of land on the island for U.S.-owned sugar plantations. Many Puerto Rican farmers lost their land and became poorly-paid laborers, or unemployed. Deepening poverty drove tens of thousands of people from the island to search for work as far away as Hawaii.

A movement of nationalists who favored independence for Puerto Rico strongly challenged U.S. domination. While suppressing the nationalists by force, U.S. authorities also tried to reduce the movement's appeal by allowing Puerto Ricans more self-government. In 1952 the island became a United States "commonwealth"—neither a state of the union nor a separate nation, but a territory "associated" with the United States. Commonwealth status was a compromise that in the end pleased neither statehood supporters nor those advocating independence.

U.S. and Puerto Rican officials together mapped out a strategy to ease poverty on the island. Under the plan, called Operation Bootstrap, U.S. firms built factories in Puerto Rico that provided some jobs. At the same time, "surplus" Puerto Rican workers were encouraged to migrate. The U.S. economy was expanding rapidly after World War II and there were many low-wage jobs to be filled.

A massive northward movement began. U.S. steel manufacturers, automakers, and garment firms sent delegations to Puerto Rico to recruit workers. Many Puerto Ricans were also recruited to work on farms and orchards in the eastern states. Whereas the early migrants had come by steamship, the hundreds of thousands of postwar migrants arrived by air.

Operation Bootstrap did not solve the problem of unemployment in Puerto Rico. Labor-intensive assembly factories were later replaced by other industries, such as pharmaceuticals, that needed fewer workers. Migration from the island to the mainland continued, slowing in the recession-plagued 1970s, but surging again in the 1980s.

Where They Live

The migrants of the 1940s, 1950s and 1960s settled mainly in the large cities of the East and Midwest. New York City, Chicago and Philadelphia received the largest numbers. But quite a few Puerto Ricans

Top Ten Cities with Largest Concentrations of Puerto Ricans in the United States

City and State	PR pop., 1990
New York City, New York	896,763
Chicago, Illinois	119,866
Philadelphia, Pennsylvania	67,857
Newark, New Jersey	41,545
Hartford, Connecticut	38,176
Jersey City, New Jersey	30,950
Bridgeport, Connecticut	30,250
Paterson, New Jersey	27,580
Boston, Massachusetts	25,767
Springfield, Massachusetts	23,729

Cities with Population at Least 20% Puerto Rican

City and State	% of total city pop. that is PR, 1990
Hartford, Connecticut	27
Camden, New Jersey	26
Bridgeport, Connecticut	21
Lawrence, Massachusetts	21
Passaic, New Jersey	20
Paterson, New Jersey	20

Source: Francisco Rivera-Batiz and Carlos Santiago, "Puerto Ricans in the United States: A Changing Reality" (Washington, D.C.: National Puerto Rican Coalition, 1995). Based on 1990 census data.

went to smaller industrial cities, such as the steel town of Lorain, Ohio, or to agricultural areas in New England, New Jersey and Pennsylvania.

In 1960 nearly two-thirds of all Puerto Ricans in the 50 states lived in New York City. Puerto Ricans who arrived in the early part of the century had formed core communities in Brooklyn and in Manhattan, particularly East Harlem (known as *El Barrio*) and the Lower East Side. The postwar migrants expanded these settlements to other parts of Manhattan, Brooklyn and the Bronx. Over time, some people moved from the inner city to the suburbs and to nearby states such as New Jersey,

Connecticut and Massachusetts. There they joined the farm and factory workers who had migrated to these areas directly from Puerto Rico.

By the late 1980s the pattern had changed. Rather than concentrating in New York, recent arrivals from Puerto Rico dispersed to states as far-flung as California, Connecticut, Florida and Texas. Jobs in these areas were generally more plentiful, and housing more affordable, than in the traditional "gateway" cities. At the same time, significant numbers of Puerto Ricans who arrived years ago were moving out of New York and other big cities, seeking a more tranquil lifestyle in smaller communities.

Today, less than a third of mainland Puerto Ricans live in New York City. The most rapid Puerto Rican population growth is in smaller cities such as Holyoke, Massachusetts; Waterbury, Connecticut; Lancaster, Pennsylvania; and Tampa, Florida. But the nearly 900,000 Puerto Ricans in New York City are still the city's largest ethnic community, accounting for one-half of all Latinos in New York.

Life in the U.S.

The early Puerto Rican migrant communities were closely knit. People from the same island hometowns formed clubs and civic groups where they could meet, enjoy their culture, and support each other in the alien world of the big U.S. cities. Puerto Rican workers, especially the cigar-makers, were also active in American labor organizations and political parties. The writings of Jesús Colón and Bernardo Vega, cigar workers and essayists, give a glimpse of this early Puerto Rican community life.

The post–World War II migrants found jobs in many types of factories and sweatshops. New York City's garment industry, for example, depended on Puerto Rican labor. In the 1960s, however, industries began abandoning the northern cities, seeking cheaper labor in the southern states and overseas. The loss of manufacturing jobs was disastrous for Puerto Ricans. Many were forced into the poorly-paid service sector, becoming hotel maids or hospital janitors. Unemployment rose. As other groups gradually moved from the blighted inner cities, Puerto Ricans remained.

Osvaldo Pérez, El Diario/La Prensa

Spectators enjoy the Puerto Rican Day parade in the Bronx.

During the 1960s, new organizations sprang up to provide social services and education as a route out of the ghetto. The most important was ASPIRA, which began as a small education and youth leadership agency in 1961. Now a national association with branches in six states and Puerto Rico, ASPIRA has worked for three and a half decades to promote higher education and leadership development for Puerto Rican youth.

By the late 1960s conditions were desperate for many Puerto Ricans in the inner cities. No longer newcomers, they were increasingly treated by the larger society as yet another despised "minority group." But a new generation of Puerto Ricans, born or raised in the United States, was coming of age. Angered by racism and poverty and inspired by the African-American civil rights movement, they formed organizations to fight discrimination and empower their communities.

The best known of these groups was the Young Lords, which had chapters in Chicago, New York and Philadelphia. The Lords organized community-based programs such as free breakfasts and lead screening for poor children, and demanded that city agencies meet the Puerto Rican community's needs. They also made a direct connection between the oppressed situation of mainland Puerto Ricans and the colonial status of the island. The young radicals challenged the older Puerto Rican leadership that worked mainly within the Democratic Party and had done little, the youth felt, to confront the racism and other harsh realities facing Puerto Ricans in the 50 states.

After the Young Lords disbanded in the mid-1970s, many of the group's leading members became active in new organizations such as the National Congress for Puerto Rican Rights. Although direct protest and grassroots organizing were not abandoned, there was growing awareness that the ballot box was a tool too important to ignore. Former Young Lords were among the first Puerto Ricans elected to school boards, city councils and state legislatures in various localities.

In the last decade the economic picture has brightened—at least for some. Mainland Puerto Ricans as a group made substantial economic progress in the 1980s. However, Puerto Ricans in the 50 states are still far more likely to be poor than are non-Hispanic whites. Furthermore, there are sharp and growing inequalities within the

Puerto Rican population. One group, composed largely of U.S.-born Puerto Ricans, has acquired higher education, professional jobs and middle-class status. The other group, accounting for a large segment of the Puerto Rican population, has not shared in this prosperity. Without the education or skills demanded by an increasingly high-tech economy, these families remain trapped in poverty.

In the 1990s, Puerto Ricans are working to defend their rights in the United States through grassroots organizing, trade unionism, and

Osvaldo Pérez, El Diario/La Prensa

"Here as well as there, we are Puerto Ricans." Contingent led by New York city councilman José Rivera marches in the Bronx Puerto Rican Day parade in 1990. The banner demands that Puerto Ricans living outside the island be allowed to vote in a plebiscite on Puerto Rico's political future (statehood, Commonwealth or independence).

At Rincon Criollo, a casita in the South Bronx, children learn to play traditional plena music using hand drums called panderetas. Most of the members of Rincon Criollo are artists and musicians who work to pass on Puerto Rican folk traditions.

electoral politics. They have been a political force in New York City for several decades as voters, candidates and elected officials, and are gradually increasing their participation in other localities. As of 1998, three Puerto Ricans serve in the U.S. House of Representatives. Congressman José Serrano and Congresswoman Nydia Velázquez represent districts in New York City; Congressman Luis Gutiérrez represents a district in Chicago.

This increasing participation goes hand in hand with an enduring cultural identity, symbolized by the Puerto Rican Day parades held in New York, Hartford, Philadelphia and other cities. Music is an important expression of this culture, from the traditional *bomba* and *plena,* to the urban Latin hybrid known as *salsa,* to the contemporary emergence of Latino rap. The effort to nourish

Puerto Rican culture in the inner cities can be seen, too, in the *casitas,* small clubhouses tucked into vacant lots in some of New York City's toughest neighborhoods. Built by groups of neighbors and friends who raise funds and donate their labor, the casitas provide a refuge from urban problems and a place where members can tend gardens, cook traditional foods, play music, party and relax in an atmosphere reminiscent of the island homeland.

Cultural pride is also reflected in the use of Spanish, generation after generation, even as most younger Puerto Ricans have become more fluent in English than Spanish. Puerto Rican writers born or raised in the 50 states have produced an abundant bilingual literature that explores the complex question of what it means to be Puerto Rican within U.S. society today. ❖

16   A PRIMER ON CARIBBEAN MIGRATION

West Indians

arry Belafonte, whose renditions of West Indian calypsoes and folk songs helped shape the American image of the Caribbean, sings in the chorus to "Jamaica Farewell":

Sad to say, I'm on my way
Won't be back for many a day
My heart is down, my head is turning around
I had to leave a little girl in Kingston town.

Virtually all West Indian immigrants could identify with Belafonte's regret at having to leave the region for an indefinite, but most likely lengthy, stay in a foreign land.

The West Indian–American experience is unique in several respects. First, the term "West Indian" does not refer to nationals of a single country, but to people from any of the 19 Caribbean countries and territories where English is the official language. These territories are linked by much shared history and culture, as well as by language. Nonetheless, all have separate and strongly defined national identities. Within the context of U.S. society, this has complicated the evolution of West Indian–Americans into a cohesive "ethnic group."

Secondly, West Indians are the only Caribbean immigrant group to enter U.S. society as native English speakers. As a group, they arrive with relatively high educational levels. Further, most have some familiarity with U.S. culture because of the pervasive presence of American television, films and other media in the English-speaking Caribbean. All these factors contribute to the relatively smooth incorporation of West Indians into U.S. society and the labor force.

This in turn poses complex questions of identity, especially for the second generation, those born or raised in the United States. These young people do not automatically identify with the Caribbean cultures of their parents. Perceived by the larger society simply as "black," they often socialize with African-Americans, yet are aware of fundamental differences between themselves and their African-American peers. As a result,

A Jamaican family in their shoe repair business in Brooklyn.

From 1881 to 1914 the major destination was Panama, where tens of thousands of laborers worked to build the giant Panama Canal. After the United States took over the project from France in 1904, an estimated 25,000 to 30,000 men from the English-speaking islands, mainly Barbados, provided the labor in the Canal Zone. Wages were 10 cents a day for digging out rock with a pick and shovel. As meager as these wages were, many workers were able to save, and "Panama money" helped some people later pay their passage on boats bound for the United States.

The early U.S.-bound emigrants, both women and men, went mainly to New York City. There the stream of incoming West Indians converged with that of African-Americans moving up from the South to create an urban black community centered in Harlem. Caribbean immigrants were prominent among the writers, journalists, trade unionists and political organizers who gave Harlem its vitality in the 1920s. Marcus Garvey, a Jamaican, based his Universal Negro Improvement Association in Harlem. Another Jamaican, Claude McKay, was a leading literary figure in the black cultural movement known as the Harlem Renaissance.

Many of the migrants from the English-speaking Caribbean had been manual laborers or farmers, but a significant number were skilled workers, students or professionals. As early as the 1940s, top students from the West Indies enrolled at Howard University in Washington, D.C., some later returning to become leaders in their countries.

Following World War II, West Indians emigrated to England by the thousands. Two things happened to shift the flow to North America. First, the larger British colonies gained political independence: Jamaica and Trinidad in 1962, Barbados and Guyana in 1966. This made them eligible to send immigrants to the United States under national quotas. Second, in 1962 Britain enacted racist legislation that barred most nonwhites from entry. The door to Britain swung shut.

West Indian–Americans may identify with African-Americans when practical but choose to emphasize their Caribbean heritage at other times.

Why They Come

In *Pilgrims from the Sun*, Ransford Palmer writes that migration from the English-speaking Caribbean began as flight from the legacy of slavery. After emancipation in the British colonies in 1834, the newly freed workers began a determined movement away from the plantations. Some became independent farmers. Others set out in search of paid work, moving to nearby towns, to other Caribbean territories, and eventually out of the region, to Britain and North America.

Workers from the West Indian islands built railways and planted bananas in Central America. They cut sugar cane on U.S.-owned plantations in Cuba, the Dominican Republic, and Puerto Rico.

The United States, meanwhile, needed workers for a booming economy. The 1965 immigration law allowed legal permanent residents to petition for visas for family members, setting up migration "chains" in which members of an extended family would arrive one by one. The law also set aside visas for people whose job skills were in demand. Thousands of West Indian nurses, doctors and teachers answered the call. Caribbean women from all walks of life went north to become housekeepers, child care workers and health care aides.

Today, the economies of the English-speaking Caribbean countries are still depressed. The region's main export commodities—sugar, bananas and bauxite—face weak and unstable markets. Foreign-owned assembly factories provide some jobs, but even these are declining as the North American Free Trade Agreement (NAFTA) encourages a shift of U.S. investment out of the Caribbean.

Meanwhile, growing numbers of people in the English-speaking Caribbean are well educated. They aspire to more than working in a factory for low wages or carrying baggage for tourists. Few young people want to scratch a meager living from a family farm, returning to the hardships of their grandparents' day.

Compared to other Caribbean immigrants in the United States, those coming from the English-speaking countries are more likely to be students, professionals, technicians or business persons. Indeed, emigration has left certain job areas in the Caribbean, such as health care, deprived of skilled workers. Although the money emigrants send back is a source of foreign exchange, the "brain drain" is a serious concern for virtually every country in the English-speaking Caribbean. Highly skilled immigrants have been educated at least in part at their home country's expense. But it is the adopted society, in this case the United States, that reaps the benefits of this training.

Four countries dominate the flow of West Indians to the United States: Jamaica, Guyana, Trinidad and Tobago, and Barbados. Jamaica, with the largest population in the English-speaking Caribbean, has sent by far the greatest number. The 1990 census recorded nearly half a million persons of Jamaican descent in the United States.

Where They Live

The great majority of West Indians coming to the United States have headed to the nation's large cities and their near suburbs. The largest concentrations are in and around New York City, Miami, Hartford, Washington, D.C., Chicago, Philadelphia, Detroit and Baltimore.

New York City has been a magnet for West Indians. They have seen it as a welcoming city, a place of economic opportunity where they can feel at home among diverse racial and ethnic groups. More than 72,000 Jamaicans settled in New York City during the 1980s, accounting for 44 percent of all Jamaicans who came to the United States during that period. Sixty percent of Barbadian immigrants, 70 percent of those from Guyana, and 49 percent of those from Trinidad and Tobago also chose New York.

Accordingly, immigration into New York City in recent decades has had a strongly Caribbean flavor. Between 1982 and 1989, four of the top five

Ian Edwards

Celebrating the Reggae Boyz: Jamaican-American soccer fans greet a Washington, D.C. transit employee following the World Cup qualifier match between Jamaica and the U.S. in 1997. Jamaicans from across the United States and Canada converged on Washington to witness the historic match, which qualified Jamaica to enter the 1998 World Cup finals in France. Jamaica's "Reggae Boyz" became the first team from the English-speaking Caribbean to make it to the finals.

"source" countries sending legal immigrants to the city were Caribbean: the Dominican Republic, Jamaica, Guyana, and Haiti. (Immigration figures do not include Puerto Ricans, who are U.S. citizens.) By contrast, immigration to the United States as a whole is dominated by Mexico and several Asian countries.

The West Indian preference for New York abated somewhat in the first half of the 1990s. Although the city still gets a disproportionate share of new West Indian immigrants, increasing numbers are heading to towns and suburbs of the surrounding region, or to other parts of the country.

A separate, seasonal flow of West Indian workers takes place under the farmworker program. The U.S. sugar industry and other agricultural interests recruit more than 10,000 West Indian workers each year, the majority of them Jamaicans, to cut sugar cane and pick tobacco and fruit. These workers go home at the end of their six-month contract period, although some sign up again year after year.

Some longer-term immigrants also return to the Caribbean. They may alternate periods of residence in North America and the Caribbean, or they may go back for good. A few work for decades in the United States and then move back home for a comfortable retirement—although many more dream of such an outcome than actually achieve it.

Life in the U.S.

West Indians in the United States have typically held two over-arching goals: owning a house and getting an education, if not for themselves then for their children. A great many have succeeded through talent, persistence and sheer hard work. Most adults arrive with at least some years of high school, and as English speakers they are well able to take advantage of opportunities for further education in the United States. This has helped them advance in academia, the professions, the service industries and government work. But even those with less schooling, such as domestic workers, have in many cases managed to see their children through high school, college and beyond.

As a result, the second generation has prospered. U.S.-born children of West Indian immigrants have, on average, more years of schooling and higher incomes than whites born in the United

States. West Indian–Americans have emerged as a significant component of this country's black middle class. They have helped revitalize rundown inner-city neighborhoods through home and business ownership, for example in Brooklyn, Queens and the Bronx.

This economic strength forms a potential basis for political empowerment. Since the 1930s, men and women of West Indian background have played active political roles in New York City and nationally. Among the best known are former Congresswoman Shirley Chisholm, Black Power leader Stokely Carmichael, former Congressman Mervyn Dymally, and General Colin Powell, former chairman of the Joint Chiefs of Staff.

Until recently, West Indians participated mainly within the framework of African-American politics rather than as a distinct ethnic group. Culturally and socially, West Indians maintain a strong ethnic identity and frequently have emphasized their separateness from African-Americans. Nonetheless, white society for the most part overlooks these differences, and West Indians have therefore understood their prospects as tied to the larger struggle for racial justice in American society. This has led to a dynamic relationship with African-Americans and to alliances, as well as some tensions, over the years.

Quite a few West Indian immigrants have simply kept their distance from the U.S. political system. Compared to some other immigrant groups, smaller numbers have chosen to become U.S. citizens; as noncitizens they cannot vote in most U.S. elections. This reluctance relates in part to the nearness of the Caribbean and the ease with which people maintain strong ties to "home." Elsa Chaney writes in *Caribbean Life in New York City:*

> Cheap airfares facilitate frequent comings and goings of island peoples and goods ... On Sundays and holidays, the international telephone circuits are clogged with the relatively inexpensive direct-dial service to and from Area Code 809. That particular "space" in New York City where each Caribbean group first established its center becomes like a distant province of the homeland ...

West Indians in the United States remain keenly interested in the politics and well-being of their countries of origin. Many continue to be actively involved, such as by fundraising for island-based political parties or by sending relief supplies after a hurricane. Radio programs catering to the West Indian community play a key role in marshalling these efforts.

To some extent, these continuing ties to home reinforce social divisions among people from different countries of the English-speaking Caribbean. In West Indian social circles, nationality matters: one identifies first as Jamaican or Guyanese or Trinidadian, and secondly as West Indian or Caribbean. In cities with large West Indian populations almost every nationality has its own social club. Hartford, for example, has a Barbados-American Society, a St. Lucia–American Society, a Trinidad and Tobago–American Society, and various others. There is even a Jamaica Ex-Police Association, a reflection of the large number of Jamaicans in the Hartford area.

These national ties have to some extent discouraged West Indian–Americans from speaking with a single voice. At the same time, there is evidence that a "pan-Caribbean" consciousness is gradually emerging to complement (not replace) national affiliation. Plunged into the alien world of American cities, English-speaking Caribbean immigrants have often found that their similarities outweigh their differences. They come together in Caribbean-American social clubs, business groups and student groups, in cricket leagues and in "mas bands" at Carnival time. Carmen Boudier, a Jamaican-born resident of Hartford, describes the social scene in that city:

Just about every island in the Caribbean has its own club. Interesting though that we do work together. And this week [the West Indian independence celebration] is an example of all the different organizations and different Caribbean islands coming together. People come together not just for this week but constantly. I remember in 1988 when we had a hurricane in Jamaica. Everyone was

The National Coalition on Caribbean Affairs was formally launched with a reception at the Organization of American States on February 7, 1998. Among the guests were (l-r): Dr. Alston Meade, president of NCOCA; Ms. Joyce C. Hamilton of Hartford, Connecticut; Dr. Alred Dyce, a member of the Bloomfield, Connecticut town council; and Ambassador Lionel Hurst of Antigua and Barbuda.

fundraising for hurricane relief. So people come together and we work very well.

As the number of West Indians in the United States increases, they are showing a greater tendency to pursue their interests as a distinct ethnic group. Members of this community are increasingly aware that they have a special stake in certain issues such as U.S. immigration law, eligibility of legal immigrants for federal programs, and U.S. aid, trade and political relations with Caribbean countries. West Indian–Americans will be most able to have an impact in these and other areas if they speak with a unified voice.

In the 1990s, the passage of new laws denying federal benefits to many legal immigrants has lent urgency to this effort. West Indian–American organizations are encouraging their members to naturalize as U.S. citizens, both to ensure their eligibility for benefits and to enable them to vote. There are renewed efforts to build an influential Caribbean-American umbrella group, a goal that has long been elusive. In 1998 a group of prominent West Indian–Americans launched the National Coalition on Caribbean Affairs (NCOCA). This advocacy group will seek to offer a Caribbean perspective on public policy issues and promote the participation of Caribbean-Americans in civic affairs at the local, state and national levels. ❖

Cubans

The migration experience of Cubans differs fundamentally from that of other Caribbean groups. Cubans are the only Caribbean nationality whose large-scale immigration was initially welcomed and subsidized by the U.S. government. They receive special treatment under U.S. immigration law, and sectors of the Cuban-American community enjoy access to the White House and Congress far beyond that of other immigrant groups.

Another difference is Cubans' own perspective on their sojourn in the United States. Through the 1960s and 1970s at least, most considered themselves not immigrants but political exiles from Cuba, who would eventually return. A single-minded focus on securing the fall of the Castro regime initially provided the community with strong internal cohesion.

In the 1990s these dimensions of the Cuban experience are still present. But they are becoming less sharply defined. Changes in U.S. immigration policy have removed some of the special privileges for Cubans. Although the 1960s exodus from Cuba was overwhelmingly political, recent emigrants from the island express a mix of economic, political and personal motives, much like other migrant groups. A younger generation of Cuban-Americans is firmly grounded in the United States and contributing to a greater diversity of views.

Why They Come

When the Cuban Revolution of 1959 set off the contemporary emigration from the island, Cubans already had a century of close ties with the United States. In the late 1800s, as rebels on the island fought for independence from Spain, many Cubans fled north or were expelled by the Spanish. They settled in New York, Philadelphia, New Orleans and other cities, and in Florida. Cuban influence was particularly strong in Key West and Tampa, centers of the hand-rolled cigar industry that was owned and worked by Cuban émigrés.

After the Spanish-American War and Cuba's independence, many Cubans remained in the United States. While Miami attracted new migrants, New York City was the center of Cuban culture in exile. During the 1940s and 1950s, Cuban influences spilled over into American pop culture. Desi Arnaz, starring with Lucille Ball in the popular situation comedy *I Love Lucy*, introduced a generation of television viewers to the idea of Cuban-Americanness. Cuban bandleaders playing at New York City dance halls set off the dance craze known as the mambo, made famous by Pérez Prado, the original Mambo King.

New waves of exiles continued to arrive. Each time a Cuban president was overthrown his supporters fled to Florida, there to await a change of regime that would allow them to return.

The ouster of Fulgencio Batista's U.S.-supported dictatorship in 1959 initially fit this pattern. In the weeks after the revolutionary forces swept into Havana, many Batista collaborators fled the island. The new government headed by Fidel Castro undertook radical reforms that soon alienated most upper-class Cubans. Large private property holdings were transfered to the state in an effort to boost production and provide revenues to develop the country. Over the next year and a half, affluent landowners and business people left with their families when their lands, businesses or bank accounts were nationalized. Many wealthy Cubans already had connections in the United States. They gathered in Miami, expecting to return as soon as Castro fell.

Relations between Havana and Washington deteriorated swiftly. In 1961 the Central Intelligence Agency mounted an invasion of Cuba to remove Castro from power, using Cuban exiles from Miami as foot soldiers. The invasion at the Bay of Pigs failed, and Cuba stepped up its turn toward socialism and the Soviet bloc. Most trade between the two countries had already ended. Washington imposed a formal trade embargo on Cuba on February 6, 1962.

While most wealthy Cubans left within a few years after the revolution, many middle-class professionals such as doctors and teachers initially remained. Encouraging them to emigrate and deprive Cuba of their skills became part of the U.S.

Jack Kurtz, Impact Visuals

Worker rolls cigars in El Credito Cigar Factory in Miami's Little Havana section. El Credito is one of the businesses that moved to the United States from Cuba after the Cuban Revolution.

strategy to undermine Castro. The U.S. government gave special treatment to Cubans seeking to resettle in the United States. Would-be immigrants from other countries had to seek visas under the regular immigration system or else obtain refugee status by proving a personal risk of persecution. Most arriving Cubans, by contrast, were simply "paroled" into the United States with no questions asked. In 1966 Congress passed the Cuban Adjustment Act, allowing Cubans to become permanent U.S. residents after just one year in the country—an opportunity offered to no other national group.

Between 1965 and 1973, special "freedom flights" ferried large numbers of Cubans to Miami. The federally funded Cuban Refugee Program helped arriving Cubans with job placements and financial assistance.

For Cubans who remained in Cuba, the early years of the revolution were extremely hard. Although education and health care improved and became available to everyone, food shortages were widespread. The U.S. embargo cut Cuba off from vital supplies of food, medicine, raw materials and spare parts. Attempts at industrialization foundered, and the country remained dependent on sugar exports and on Soviet aid. The poorest Cubans saw their standard of living rise as the country's resources were distributed more evenly.

But for many others, asked to sacrifice for a better future, the frustrations were too grinding, the progress too slow.

Through harassment and imprisonment of dissidents, the Castro government made clear that it would tolerate no organized political opposition. Discontented Cubans had few options but emigration.

By the late 1960s the outflow from Cuba had become more diverse, including many working-class people. As the class composition shifted, so too did the mix of motives for leaving. Increasingly, the desire to seek economic opportunity and reunite with family members played a role. Despite the revolution's achievements in some areas, Cuba remained underdeveloped compared to the United States. Just 90 miles away in Miami, hundreds of thousands of émigrés enjoyed a level of affluence that island Cubans could only dream of. As the Cuban colony in the United States grew and prospered, it exerted a magnetic pull.

In 1979 an agreement between the U.S. and Cuban governments allowed Cuban-Americans

for the first time to visit their families in Cuba. The impact was enormous and unforeseen. The arrival of some 100,000 well-heeled Miami Cubans, bringing sought-after consumer goods to their relatives, sharpened the yearning of many to leave the island.

The visits were among the factors that led to the chaotic departure of 125,000 Cubans, most of them young men, through the port of Mariel in 1980. Although it was Castro's decision to allow the exodus, U.S. actions had set the stage for Mariel. For years, Washington had refused visas to most Cubans who applied through legal channels. But Cubans arriving on U.S. shores illegally, typically by boat or raft, were allowed to stay. If rescued at sea by the U.S. Coast Guard, they were escorted to the United States. The policy provided an obvious incentive to take to the seas. It also stood in striking contrast to the treatment of Haitian refugees rescued by the Coast Guard, most of whom were forcibly returned to Haiti.

Of the 125,000 Cubans who arrived in the United States from Mariel, 2,700 were deemed ineligible to remain because of criminal backgrounds or other problems. They were sent to U.S. detention facilities. In 1984 Cuba agreed to take back these "excludables" in return for a pledge by the United States to accept up to 20,000 legal immigrants from Cuba per year.

As it turned out, the United States admitted nowhere near 20,000, but only about 1,300 yearly. Meanwhile, emigration pressures mounted in Cuba. The collapse of the Soviet Union in 1991 plunged the already troubled Cuban economy into crisis. As the standard of living plummeted, the number of illegal rafters surged upward, peaking in the summer of 1994.

Alarmed by the prospect of another Mariel, the Clinton Administration abruptly announced a change. Cubans rescued at sea would no longer be brought to the United States; instead, they would be sheltered at the U.S. military base at Guantánamo Bay, Cuba. Within weeks, an enormous and costly tent city sprawled across Guantánamo, yet the stream of rafters continued.

In September 1994, Cuba and the United States began talks to resolve the migration crisis. The two countries soon announced an accord under which

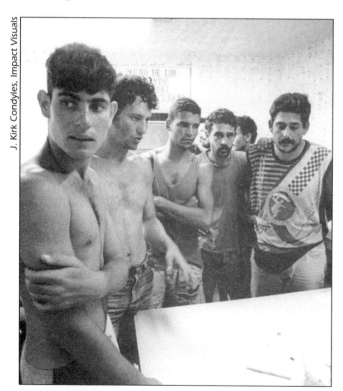

These Cuban rafters were picked up by the U.S. Coast Guard in August 1994 and brought to a transit center for Cuban refugees in Key West, Florida. They were among the last Cubans to enjoy automatic entry to the United States before the change in policy.

J. Kirk Condyles, Impact Visuals

Exiles wave Cuban and American flags at an anti-Castro rally in Miami's Orange Bowl.

Washington agreed to accept a *minimum* of 20,000 Cuban immigrants through normal channels each year. Cuba for its part pledged to discourage rafters from setting sail. Under a second accord in 1995, most of the approximately 30,000 Cubans waiting at Guantánamo were admitted to the United States, but U.S. officials announced that future rafters would be returned to Cuba.

Where They Live

A unique aspect of Cuban immigration is the community's concentration in south Florida. Cubans are the only Caribbean group for whom New York City is *not* now a primary destination, although there is a secondary Cuban enclave in northern New Jersey, across the Hudson River from New York.

The 1990 census counted just over one million people of Cuban origin in the United States. More than 60 percent of them lived in the Miami area. Other Florida cities, notably Tampa, also had significant Cuban populations. Although refugee agencies initially resettled many Cubans in other parts of the country, many of them eventually made their own way back to south Florida where they had relatives and where the climate and cultural ambiance were the next best thing to home. Cubans arriving from the island in recent years have also headed to Miami.

In northern New Jersey, Cubans are concentrated in the towns of Union City, North Bergen and West New York. The Cuban enclaves in Florida and New Jersey are closely linked. Two bus lines make daily trips between Union City and Miami, a 26-hour ride. Many New Jersey Cubans move to south Florida when they reach retirement age.

Cubans in Miami at first clustered in the southwest part of the city in an area that came to be called Little Havana. Cuban-owned businesses, some of them transplanted directly from Cuba, lined *Calle Ocho* (Eighth Street). Through Cuban restaurants and clubs and domino games in the park, homesick exiles tried to recreate the Havana they had left.

By the 1980s the enclave had expanded far beyond the limits of Little Havana as many Cubans moved to suburbs such as Hialeah, Coral Gables, Kendall and Perrine. Little Havana is now populated mainly by recent immigrants, including Mariel Cubans, Nicaraguans, and people from other Latin American countries.

Life in the U.S.

The early years of exile were dominated by the dream of *regreso*—return to Cuba. This did not at first seem an unreasonable hope. The CIA was working to overthrow Castro, and quite a few Miami Cubans were on the agency's payroll in the early 1960s. Exile paramilitary groups trained in the Florida Everglades for a future strike against the island.

But the years went by and Castro remained. Meanwhile, Cuban exiles drew on their entrepreneurial skills and access to capital to build a successful economic enclave in greater Miami. Cuban-owned firms came to dominate construction and other key sectors of the local economy. With economic influence came a cultural impact that transformed Miami into perhaps the most bilingual and bicultural city in the United States.

Cuban business success was the result in part of the community's cohesiveness, based in turn on shared political views. The core ideology was, and remains, support for the embargo and refusal to engage in any dialogue with Castro.

Yet while the Cuban-American community may appear monolithic, it has never actually been so. Since the 1970s, a quiet minority of the community has called for dialogue between the U.S. and Cuban governments. A small number of young Cuban-Americans have even traveled to Cuba to show support for the revolution. Taking such positions publicly, however, has often brought ostracism and harassment from the anti-Castro majority.

In the 1970s, frustrated by the failure to unseat Castro, militant exile groups carried out a series of violent attacks. The targets ranged from Cuban diplomats in New York to Cuban-Americans who had organized in support of dialogue. In 1976 a bomb exploded aboard a Cuban passenger jet bound from Venezuela to Cuba, killing all 73 persons aboard; a Venezuelan court later found three prominent anti-Castro exiles guilty of planting the bomb. Cuban-Americans later cemented an alliance with the Reagan Administration that drew militant exiles into various anti-communist foreign policy ventures.

Over the last two decades, the violence has subsided. Instead, Cuban-Americans increasingly have pressed their agenda through political participation. They dominate local government in what is now called Miami-Dade County. A voting bloc in the swing states of Florida and New Jersey, Cuban-Americans are courted by nearly every presidential hopeful; three members of the U.S. Congress are of Cuban descent. A powerful Cuban-American lobby is influential in shaping official U.S. policy toward Cuba. The Cuban American National Foundation, led by millionaire businessman Jorge Mas Canosa until his death in 1997, has been a key force in securing passage of embargo-tightening laws. Its political action committee has given more than $1 million in campaign contributions.

Especially in Miami, Cuban-Americans who express moderate views may still be vilified and threatened. But several trends suggest that those who favor a broader debate have time on their side.

The early exiles, passionate defenders of the anti-Castro cause, are passing from the scene. As a result, an increasing proportion of the Cuban-American population consists of two groups: recent immigrants from Cuba, and the American-raised children of the early exiles.

Cubans arriving from the island in recent years tend to be more concerned with gaining an economic foothold than with ideological goals. For many, especially those who came through Mariel or Guantánamo, adjustment has not been easy. As a group, they lack the personal wealth, connections and business experience that helped the early exiles prosper. A higher proportion are black or mulatto, and they confront the racial prejudices not only of white Americans but also of the predominantly white Cuban-American old guard.

Children of the early émigrés were raised in the culture of exile, and many are politically conservative. But they do not as a group share the obsession with Castro that marked their parents' generation. In their introduction to *Little Havana*

Blues, Virgil Suárez and Delia Poey reflect on the change. "For many Cuban-Americans, particularly those who left the island as children and those born in the United States, Cuba has become a creation of the imagination, a fictional space pieced together from recollections, fading photographs and family anecdotes." The dream of a permanent return to the island is unlikely to last beyond the first generation.

These demographic shifts are gradually enlarging the space for alternative approaches to Cuba. While hardliners still dominate the debate, other voices increasingly are heard. The strategy of ever-harsher sanctions, in place for more than 35 years, has failed to eliminate the regime, and more Cuban-Americans seem willing to ask whether negotiations might be a more effective means of fostering political and economic reforms in Cuba.

Many worry that the embargo is causing greater suffering for their relatives on the island. Indeed, Cuban-Americans themselves have effectively weakened the embargo's hold by sending an estimated $800 million yearly in remittances to family members. Some want increased contact between the two countries in order to ease the pain of divided families. Several Cuban-American advocacy groups now lobby the U.S. government to end the embargo and enter into a dialogue with Cuba. ❖

Performers in the Cuban Day parade wait to march down Madison Avenue in New York City.

Jack Kurtz, Impact Visuals

Haitians

A well-to-do doctor in suburban New Jersey, U.S.-educated and fluent in English, French, and Haitian Creole. A farm worker in Florida—recently arrived, barely literate, and monolingual in Creole. An American-born college student who speaks only English and has never been to Haiti, the land of her parents' birth.

These are a few of the faces of Haitian America. The stereotype of Haitian immigrants as poverty-stricken "boat people" is deeply etched, but the reality is far more complex.

Although Haitian-Americans occupy every rung of the socioeconomic ladder, members of the community point to common underlying values. "Work, work, work, church, school and more work. That is the life of Haitians in this country," commented one Haitian man who came to Miami 14 years ago.

The other common thread is the role of political persecution, as well as economic need, in driving people to leave Haiti. Beginning in 1957, three decades of U.S.-backed dictatorship were followed by a series of brutal military regimes. A climate of terror, together with widespread impoverishment, spurred hundreds of thousands to flee the country. Only in the 1990s, with a legitimate government at last in place, did the exodus begin to slow.

Under the circumstances, Haitians would seem as deserving of a refuge in the United States as any other group. Yet more than any other nationality, they have been systematically excluded. Classified as "economic migrants" by the U.S. government, most Haitian asylum-seekers have been swiftly deported.

Through the 1980s, U.S. authorities welcomed the Cuban boat people as refugees from communism. But Haitians were fleeing a government seen in Washington as an anticommunist ally, despite its shocking human rights record. Many observers believe that racism has also played a role in the discriminatory treatment of this majority-black people whose culture reflects African and European roots.

Why They Come

Throughout the first part of the twentieth century, a small number of Haitians moved north to seek work or an education. After World War II an increasing number arrived, many of them women recruited for domestic work.

Large-scale migration began in 1957 after an army-controlled election in Haiti brought François Duvalier to power. With the help of 22,000 henchmen known as Tontons Macoutes, "Papa Doc" exiled, tortured, imprisoned or killed thousands of people to eliminate potential rivals. The first wave of exiles consisted of opposition politicians and their close supporters, many of them professionals from Haiti's small upper class. They emigrated to French colonies in the Caribbean, to French-speaking African nations, and to Canada, France and the United States. As Duvalier tightened his reign of terror in the 1960s, declaring himself "President for Life," the exodus broadened to include skilled workers and members of the lower middle class.

In 1971 François Duvalier passed on the life presidency to his son Jean-Claude. Under the younger Duvalier, arbitrary imprisonment, torture, and political killings continued. At the same time, guided by U.S. and international aid agencies, the Haitian government pursued an economic strategy that emphasized exports at the expense of the traditional farming sector. Poverty deepened, and the stream of refugees began to include many peasant farmers and unskilled urban workers.

Most of the early exiles had arrived by plane as legal immigrants. Many of the newer refugees, lacking immigrant visas, overstayed tourist visas or attempted the 800-mile ocean crossing to Florida in small boats. Setting sail in barely seaworthy craft, an unknown number drowned in the shark-infested waters. Those who reached shore found a cold welcome. The United States

Haitian students of Spring Valley Senior High School in Rockland County, New York, with artifacts they brought from home for an exhibit of Haitian folk art.

Haitian-Americans demonstrate their support for President Aristide outside United Nations headquarters in New York City. The exiled Haitian president addressed the U.N. in August 1992.

is required by law to give political asylum to persons at risk of persecution in their home country. But the U.S. government argued that the Haitians were merely seeking work, and therefore did not qualify.

Haitians who managed to enter the United States unauthorized, if caught, were jailed in federal detention centers until their applications for asylum could be heard. Almost all were eventually deported. In 1981, under an agreement with the Duvalier government, the Reagan Administration ordered the Coast Guard to seize boatloads of Haitians at sea and return them to Haiti by force. Over the next decade, 23,000 boat people were intercepted. Of these, 11 were admitted to the United States; the rest were forcibly repatriated without ever getting the chance to apply for asylum.

In Haiti, meanwhile, members of peasant organizations, grassroots religious communities, and students led mounting resistance to Duvalier. Jean-Claude was overthrown by a popular revolt in 1986. But the military juntas which replaced him continued to abuse human rights, using weapons

shipped from Washington. Although some Haitian exiles returned home after Duvalier's fall, most left again when it became clear that little had changed.

New hope dawned on February 7, 1991, when Jean-Bertrand Aristide took office as Haiti's first legitimately elected president. A former Catholic priest with strong ties to Haiti's poor, he enjoyed overwhelming popular support. But hopes were dashed only seven months later when the Haitian army overthrew Aristide in a bloody coup on September 30, 1991.

The army sent Aristide into exile and targeted his supporters with arbitrary arrests, beatings, rape and assassination. Up to 3,000 people were killed. Many of the abuses were the work of a paramilitary terrorist group known as FRAPH, which had been built up with the help of U.S. intelligence agencies seeking to counterbalance Aristide's influence. Meanwhile, an international embargo against the coup regime caused prices to skyrocket, increasing the desperation of Haiti's poor.

The bloodbath in Haiti triggered a new outpouring of refugees. In the next 20 months some 35,000 Haitians were picked up by the Coast Guard at sea. Of those, 11,000 were allowed to enter the United States to apply for political asylum; the rest were sent back to Haiti. Later, a camp was set up at Guantánamo Bay, a U.S. naval base in Cuba, to house the refugees.

Fear of an even larger deluge of boat people was a major factor in the Clinton Administration's decision to send 20,000 American troops in September 1994 to restore Aristide to power. President Aristide returned to Haiti on October 15, 1994, and with United Nations peacekeepers maintaining a level of security, served out the little that remained of his term. Among his significant acts was disbanding the Haitian army. In February 1996 his elected successor, René Préval, took office.

Haitians in New York City protest the Clinton Administration's policies toward Haitian refugees in 1993.

Under Aristide and Préval, Haitians have enjoyed greater freedom from fear than at any time in the previous 30 years. Yet daunting problems remain. International peacekeepers failed to disarm many of the former soldiers and their paramilitary henchmen, who remain at large. The new civilian police force is composed of young, barely trained recruits, some of whom have already been accused of abuses against civilians. The judiciary remains deeply corrupt. Economic conditions have worsened as President Préval has imposed harsh austerity measures to satisfy the demands of foreign donors. In 1998, the vast majority of Haitians still face grinding poverty and an unemployment rate of some 70 percent.

A few Haitian-Americans have moved back to Haiti permanently. Many more have made short or long visits to pursue business ventures, offer humanitarian aid, or launch development projects. Political uncertainty and the stalled economic recovery have persuaded most to wait and see.

Where They Live

Estimates of people with Haitian ancestry in the United States range from 300,000 (the number counted by the 1990 census, and almost certainly too low) to 1.2 million. They are concentrated in the New York metropolitan area and in south Florida. Boston, Chicago, Philadelphia, Washington, Stamford and several other cities also have significant Haitian populations.

The early exiles settled mainly in New York City. From a small core settlement in upper Manhattan, the heart of the community later shifted to Brooklyn. Recent Haitian immigrants are concentrated in the Brooklyn neighborhoods of Flatbush and Crown Heights, which are also home to many English-speaking West Indians. Many of the more established Haitian-Americans have moved out to Queens and to suburban areas, especially Long Island and Rockland County, New York, and northern New Jersey.

While the New York-area community remains the largest, the Miami area has shown the fastest growth in recent years. Those boat people who manage to arrive and remain in the United States typically stay in south Florida. In the 1970s two-thirds of new Haitian immigrants settled in the New York area, but by the early 1990s only one-third did. In addition, a significant number of Haitians from New York, Chicago, Boston and even Canada have moved to Florida in recent years.

Life in the U.S.

In some ways, Haitian-Americans have followed the traditional path to upward mobility for immigrants. They have packed English, adult education and college classes. Many work two or even three jobs, saving for a home or for children's education. As a result, many U.S.-born offspring of Haitian immigrants are college-educated professionals. Together with educated Haitians who immigrated directly from Haiti, they are making contributions in every field, including health care, education, journalism and law.

Through petitioning for relatives, Haitians are gradually reuniting their extended families in the United States. These networks of kin and home-town acquaintances provide a support system for new immigrants. Haitian-Americans have started newspapers and radio programs, student organizations, professional groups, credit associations and social clubs. Many of these groups work to raise money for schools, clinics and development projects in Haiti.

Yet the experience of Haitian-Americans is unique in other respects, notably their "triple minority status" as black, foreign, and non-English-speaking. Haitians' position in the U.S. racial-ethnic spectrum is ambiguous and at times isolating. The white majority perceives them simply as "black." Yet within the larger black community, Haitians are separated from African-Americans and from other black immigrants by their language. This can be a lonely experience, as Haitian youngsters taunted with the label "Frenchie" can attest. At times, however, it can seem an advantage: knowledge of French, or at least Creole, enables Haitians to distance themselves from the African-American population and its perceived low status. At other times, a common racial identity has led to political alliances with African-Americans and also with West Indians.

A second distinguishing feature has been the community's intense preoccupation with events in Haiti. While many immigrants continue some involvement in home-country affairs, Haitian-

Martha Cooper, courtesy of Rockland County Historical Society

Mass is said in French and Haitian Creole for the Haitian congregation of St. Joseph's Church in Spring Valley, New York.

Americans tend to be passionately concerned with every twist and turn in the politics of their homeland.

Only sometimes, however, have they spoken with a single voice. Haitian-Americans are deeply divided by class, as well as by political differences. All efforts to mobilize for united action have had to contend with these basic schisms.

In the 1950s and early 1960s, the exile community was split by loyalties to rival politicians opposed to Duvalier. Small groups plotted against the dictator, but their self-serving schemes failed for lack of an organized base and the constant threat of reprisals against kin in Haiti.

As new waves of immigrants arrived, class differences intensified. Most of the early exiles were from the Haitian elite: well educated, speaking French as well as Creole, and largely although not entirely light-skinned. The newer immigrants, by contrast, were largely representative of the Haitian majority: darker-skinned, with less schooling, and speaking only Creole. The established Haitian-American community initially shunned the newcomers, above all the boat people, who were stereotyped in the U.S. media as impoverished and ignorant. This image persisted despite the fact that the boat people were not drawn from the poorest of the poor in Haiti, but rather were people able to raise $500 to $1,000 to purchase a place on a boat.

The influx of boat people nonetheless marked a turning point. The U.S. government's treatment of the boat people became a symbol of the racism all Haitians faced. U.S. rejection of the refugees was all the more stinging given that Washington supported Duvalier, and was therefore helping to maintain the conditions that forced people to flee. With support from African-American organizations and some legal and civil rights groups, broad sections of the Haitian-American community brought pressure for the release of the boat people from federal detention centers and their acceptance as refugees.

Newly arrived immigrants from Haiti in turn helped draw Haitian-Americans into the anti-Duvalier movement. In marches, meetings and church services, U.S. Haitians denounced the dicatatorship and demanded that Washington end its support for Duvalier. On February 8, 1986, thousands of Haitians danced through the streets of Brooklyn and Miami to celebrate the regime's fall.

The celebration was short-lived. But three subsequent events served as catalysts for a renewed push toward unity. The first came in 1990 when the federal government designated Haitians a "high-risk" group for the HIV virus and barred them from donating blood. The outrage that swept the Haitian-American community cut across class and political lines. Haitian-American physicians gathered data to refute the claim, and a protest march of 50,000 shook the Brooklyn Bridge. The government finally withdrew the policy, giving Haitian-Americans a taste of empowerment as a united force.

The victory provided a base for further activism. The following year, after the coup against Aristide, the exiled president appealed to Haitian-Americans for support. Thousands rallied and marched to denounce the coup and demand international action to reinstate the elected president.

The activism of the 1980s and early 1990s had focused on politics in Haiti and on the U.S. government's role. A shocking event in 1997 turned the attention of Haitians toward their experience in the United States. On August 9, 1997, Abner Louima, a Haitian immigrant, was tortured by police officers in the bathroom of a Brooklyn precinct station. The vicious sexual assault with a wooden pole left Louima critically injured. The case shook New York, prompting a federal investigation of allegations that New York City police routinely abused members of minority groups.

Other immigrants, notably Dominicans, have had their own problems with the city's police. But Haitians felt particularly betrayed, having risked their lives to flee a country where police and soldiers abused civilians with impunity. Tens of thousands of Haitian-Americans marched to City Hall to protest, drawing broad support from other minority and immigrant groups.

Like other Caribbean immigrants, Haitians are gradually turning their efforts toward improving their status and defending their rights in the United States. But for this community in particular, the quest for democracy and economic progress in the homeland will surely remain a focus for years to come. ❖

Dominicans

In Manhattan's narrow northern reaches, the neighborhood of Washington Heights/Inwood has been dubbed "Quisqueya Heights" after the indigenous name for the Dominican Republic. Around New York City, small groceries known as *bodegas* are passing from Cuban or Puerto Rican owners to Dominican entrepreneurs. An estimated 10 percent of the city's schoolchildren are Dominican, and at City College of New York, Dominicans now make up more than half of Latinos in the student body. Merengue, urban dance music of the Dominican Republic, is one of the hot sounds on the New York nightclub scene.

For three decades the Dominican Republic has been the leading source of legal immigrants to New York City. More than 20,000 Dominicans arrive in the city each year. Dominicans are the city's largest and fastest-growing immigrant group, accounting for 7 percent of the city's population in 1997.

Although most visible in New York, the Dominican influx is felt throughout the eastern seaboard states. The Dominican Republic sends almost 40,000 legal immigrants per year to the United States—more than all but five countries in the world, and more than any other Caribbean country. Although Puerto Ricans, who can enter freely, are the largest Caribbean-origin group in the 50 states, Dominicans are a growing presence.

Why They Come

Large-scale Dominican immigration is recent, but U.S. involvement in the Dominican Republic goes back more than a century. By 1907 Washington had gained extensive control over the Dominican Republic's financial affairs. U.S. gunboats invaded in 1916 to collect debts, and installed an American military government that ran the Caribbean country until 1924.

Before the Marines went home, they trained and equipped a National Guard and installed General Rafael Leonidas Trujillo at its head. The ruthless and murderous Trujillo made himself president in 1930. His dictatorship, supported by the United States, lasted three decades. Trujillo

Dominican Day parade in West New York and Union City, New Jersey. Marchers wave flags of an island-based political party, the PLD. The PLD candidate, Leonel Fernández, won the Dominican presidency in 1996 with support from many Dominicans living in the United States.

allowed few people to leave the country, so emigration was low during those years.

Following the assassination of Trujillo in 1961, a tumultuous series of events set in motion the mass migration that continues today. In 1962, in the country's first free elections ever, Dominicans gave a landslide victory to Juan Bosch. Bosch governed only seven months before being overthrown by a right-wing military coup. Plotting continued, and in April 1965 an armed popular revolt swept the capital. Nearly the entire population of Santo Domingo poured into the streets, demanding the return of the democratically elected Bosch government.

Officials in Washington, intent upon preventing "another Cuba," viewed this uprising in support of democracy as a threat. On April 28, 1965, President Johnson sent 22,000 U.S. Marines into Santo Domingo to crush the rebellion. Afterward, new elections held under U.S. supervision brought to power the U.S.-backed candidate: Joaquín

Balaguer, who had been the dictator Trujillo's right-hand man.

Before and after the election, the Dominican army continued to harass, jail and kill Bosch supporters. Thousands fled to exile in New York. Their departure was encouraged by U.S. officials, who wanted to remove potential opponents of the new Dominican government.

The exodus had begun. Two conditions caused it to continue and grow. One was the 1965 U.S. immigration law, under which legal immigrants could petition for their relatives. The other was a spiraling economic crisis in the Dominican Republic that left many people struggling just to survive.

With the Balaguer government, U.S. officials set out to remake the Dominican economy with U.S. private investment, aid and loans. Multinational corporations took over land in the Dominican countryside. Small farmers, uprooted, drifted to the cities or emigrated.

Since the 1980s the Dominican economy has been in steep decline. When world sugar prices tumbled, the United States drastically reduced its purchases of Dominican sugar. As an alternative to sugar, the Dominican government has promoted manufacturing for export, agribusiness, and tourism, all dependent on cheap labor. In the fenced industrial parks known as "free trade zones," workers assemble garments and other goods for the equivalent of 35 cents an hour.

Even at these wages, export manufacturing and tourism cannot provide jobs for all who have been displaced from the collapsing agricultural sector. Rural Dominicans have flocked to the slums of Santo Domingo and other cities. Meanwhile, loan agreements with the International Monetary Fund have forced the government to devalue the peso; with devaluation, the cost of food and other basic necessities has shot out of reach. Financial help from relatives in America is a lifeline for hundreds of thousands of families.

For three decades Balaguer held power through fraudulent elections, interrupted only by an eight-year period in which his political rivals governed. Balaguer reserved jobs and contracts for those loyal to him; others found their way blocked. Not only the poor but also many middle-class Dominicans saw no future for themselves if they remained in the country.

Elections in 1996 finally retired Balaguer and brought to power a younger politician, Leonel Fernández Reyna. Despite this new leadership, large-scale emigration will likely continue for the foreseeable future. The country's economic crisis has no quick solution, while the networks that bring Dominicans to the United States are firmly established. Many families are divided, creating an ongoing demand for U.S. visas for kin.

New York-based Dominicans, known on the island as "Dominican-Yorks," return to visit with cash and gifts, reinforcing the myth of easy opportunities up north. And remittances from U.S. Dominicans of as much as $1 billion a year are a source of national income that no Dominican government can ignore.

Where They Live

The 1990 census recorded slightly more than half a million Dominicans living in the United States. The real number is almost certainly much larger when undocumented immigrants and others uncounted by the census are included.

Of all Caribbean immigrants, Dominicans have shown the greatest tendency to settle in New York City. In 1996, the city was home to six of every ten Dominicans in the United States. New York attracted Dominicans in the 1960s and 1970s in part because a thriving manufacturing industry offered jobs. The presence of established Puerto Rican and Cuban communities also made the city seem hospitable to Spanish-speakers. As early arrivals were joined by relatives, the Dominican community grew.

Dominicans are most heavily concentrated in the Manhattan neighborhoods of Washington Heights and Inwood, north of 155th Street. The area is thought of as a Dominican enclave, although other ethnic groups also live there. Although blighted by poverty, Washington Heights offers Dominican newcomers an informal support system of family and friends. Businesses, social clubs and community services cater to Dominicans. Many Dominicans also live in the Bronx, Brooklyn and Queens.

The proportion of new Dominican immigrants who locate in New York City has diminished slightly in recent years. As established immigrants improve their economic situation, some have been able to move out of inner-city New York to areas such as Rockland County, New York, or northern New Jersey. When they send for their relatives, the new arrivals bypass New York and join their families wherever they are living. Dominican communities in other cities such as Boston, Miami, and Providence, Rhode Island are expanding in much the same way.

After New York state, New Jersey has the second-largest number of Dominicans. Significant Dominican populations also live in Florida and Massachusetts, followed by Rhode Island, Connecticut, Maryland, Texas, Pennsylvania, and Washington, D.C.

In addition, there are an estimated 80,000 Dominicans in Puerto Rico. Linked to U.S. cities by domestic flights, Puerto Rico has become a way station for people from various countries hoping to reach the United States. Each year thousands of Dominicans set out in small wooden boats to attempt the 90-mile crossing to Puerto Rico. Many have drowned in the rough, shark-infested waters. Of those who arrive safely, a substantial number are picked up and sent home. Those who manage to enter Puerto Rico undetected often stay and look for work before trying, sooner or later, to board a U.S.-bound plane.

Life in the U.S.

For most Dominicans, the reality of life in America is far more difficult than people on the island imagine. Dominicans in New York City are concentrated in poor neighborhoods with high levels of unemployment, crime and drug addiction. Rents are high for apartments in dingy tenement buildings, and children attend severely over-crowded schools. Having come with the dream of improving their lives, many have been bitterly disappointed.

Part of the reason is simply the relative newness of the Dominican migration. Compared to other Caribbean immigrants, a high proportion of Dominicans have arrived recently and are still struggling to establish themselves. Gaining an economic foothold will take time.

Over the last few years, however, the Dominican population of New York City has slipped further behind, suggesting that other factors are also at work. Per capita income for the city's Dominicans declined sharply in the 1990s, while unemployment and poverty rates rose.

Dominican sociologists who have tracked these changes point to a transformation of New York City's economy that has increasingly shut out unskilled workers. Two decades ago such workers could readily find jobs in New York City's thriving garment industry, but not today. Most factories have left the city, although some sweatshops remain. Dominicans are particularly vulnerable to these job losses. More than half of Dominican adults in the city have no high school diploma, and most are still learning English. Spanish-speaking and predominantly dark-skinned, Dominicans face negative stereotypes and discrimination in the workplace and the society.

The majority of Dominican workers today are in poorly paid service jobs such as office cleaners, home care attendants, parking attendants, waitresses and security guards. Unemployment is estimated at 18 percent, twice the city's average, and almost half of Dominicans in New York live below the poverty line.

This bleak inner-city reality, while a prominent part of the Dominican experience, is not the whole picture. A significant share of the Dominican population, especially those living outside the inner cities, has achieved economic stability if not affluence through education and hard work. Many Dominicans dream of someday opening their own business, and quite a few have succeeded. Groups of relatives and friends typically pool their money to purchase small storefronts. Dominicans now own an estimated 20,000 businesses in New York City, the most common being grocery stores, taxicabs, restaurants, travel agencies, and money-transfer offices known as *remesas*.

A professional middle class is small but growing. The 1980s saw increased immigration of Dominican professionals such as teachers and health workers. At the same time, Dominican immigrants and their U.S.-born children are attending community colleges and four-year colleges in growing numbers. The obstacles to academic success are enormous. Most Dominican college students, and even many in high school, must hold down jobs while they study to help support their households. Students whose parents have limited schooling and speak little English face the demands of higher education essentially on their own. The fact that some obtain college degrees is testimony to the great effort and sacrifice by students and their families.

Economic progress for the Dominican community will depend in large part on education: from more English classes to better urban schools to college opportunities for students of modest means. It will depend, as well, on the U.S. economy and the jobs and pay it offers blue-collar

Osvaldo Pérez, El Diario/La Prensa

Residents of Washington Heights protest the killing of a young Dominican immigrant by police in 1992.

As the years go by, however, there is a growing realization among U.S. Dominicans, especially those born in this country, that they are here to stay. Given this reality, they have no choice but to organize to improve their opportunities and defend their rights within U.S. society.

A turning point came in 1992, when an apparent incident of police brutality in Washington Heights caused long-simmering tensions to explode. The unrest started after a plainclothes New York City police-man shot and killed José García, a 23-year-old Dominican immigrant, in circumstances that were hotly contested. The killing ignited a week of angry street protests in Washington Heights. Police harassment, residents claimed, was a long-standing problem, fueled by police and media stereotypes of all Dominicans as drug dealers. Underlying the violence was seething frustration over problems such as joblessness, lack of affordable housing, and overcrowded schools.

The uprising symbolized the Dominican community's gradual turn from a preoccupation with island politics to more active engagement with problems of life in the United States. It gave new visibility to Dominican leaders in New York, who helped calm the violence. This emergent leadership includes heads of Dominican social service organizations as well as recently elected office-holders.

Dominican participation in U.S. elections, although still low, is slowly increasing as more immigrants naturalize and more U.S.-born Dominicans reach voting age. The community is already playing a role in New York City politics. First came the election of several Dominicans to local school boards. One of them, former schoolteacher Guillermo Linares, in 1991 became the first Dominican elected to the city council.

workers. And finally, it will reflect a decision by Dominican-Americans to channel their energies from island politics into a struggle for empowerment in this country.

Many U.S. Dominicans still believe they will eventually return. They remain emotionally tied to their homeland and actively involved in its politics. All the major political parties of the Dominican Republic have branches in New York and raise a large portion of their campaign funds from Dominican-Americans. In 1996 thousands of New York Dominicans flew home to vote in the Dominican Republic's presidential election or help run campaigns. U.S. Dominicans played a critical role in that election, which was won by Fernández, a Dominican raised in New York City.

At campaign headquarters for Guillermo Linares, a campaign worker handles the phone on primary day for the city council race in 1991. Linares was elected as the first Dominican member of the New York city council.

And in 1996 Manhattan voters sent Adriano Espaillat to serve in the State Assembly.

Although many obstacles remain, Dominicans clearly are on the way to greater participation in U.S. civic and political life. This need not mean breaking all ties to the homeland. President Fernández has publicly urged Dominicans who are eligible to become United States citizens, reminding them that they can keep their Dominican citizenship as well. "What follows now is the journey toward (Dominican-) Americanness ..." says Silvio Torres-Saillant, a Dominican scholar in New York. "There is no turning back." ❖

Immigration and the Law

ost foreigners who enter the United States come on temporary visas and return home after their stay. They include tourists, business visitors, students and diplomats. Obtaining permission to live permanently in the United States is much more difficult. All immigrants admitted legally must obtain a visa from one of the various "pools," or categories, defined by U.S. law. The number of visas available in each pool is limited by a yearly quota, and waits can be long.

How Legal Immigrants Are Admitted

Family-related visas
The Immigration and Nationality Act of 1965 gave priority to family reunification. Immigrants who are naturalized U.S. citizens or legal permanent residents of the United States can petition to obtain visas for their family members. At present, more than half the immigrants who enter the United States legally come in with family-related visas.

In allocating visas, highest priority is given to the immediate relatives of U.S. citizens: their spouses, unmarried minor children, and parents. No numerical limits are set on these visas. Other family members are given preference according to a complicated ranking system. A limited number of visas are available each year for the adult children and brothers and sisters of U.S. citizens, and for the spouses and children of legal permanent residents.

Changes in the law in 1996 made it more difficult to sponsor a relative. Legal immigrants wishing to petition for a family member must now have income that is at least 125 percent of the federal poverty level, and they must guarantee support for the relative. This income requirement effectively bars many people from reuniting with close family members, even spouses. Moreover, not every applicant with a willing and qualified sponsor can get in. When there are more people applying for visas in a particular category than there are visas available, applicants are wait-listed. Currently, waits can be ten years or more, depending on the preference category.

At the New York offices of the Immigration and Naturalization Service, volunteer attorneys from Medgar Evers College help West Indians apply to become legal U.S. residents. The INS is holding "Caribbean Day" as part of an amnesty program that targets immigrants from different groups on specific days.

Employment preferences

A certain number of visas are also available for people whose occupational skills are in demand. Highest preference is given to individuals with "extraordinary ability," as well as outstanding researchers and professionals and executives of multinational companies. Next preference is for professionals with advanced degrees, followed by skilled workers, professionals with bachelor's degrees, and unskilled workers who are especially needed. There are also visas for several special occupations such as clergy, and for investors.

Refugees

To be admitted to the United States as a refugee, a person must be able to prove that he or she has "a well-founded fear of persecution" in the home country. This persecution may be based on a person's race, religion, national origin, political opinion, or membership in a political or social group. In practice, the decision as to who gets refugee status is very often political and related to the U.S. government's foreign policy objectives. In general, people from communist countries have been readily admitted as refugees. People fleeing U.S.-allied regimes, however cruel and dictatorial, have had a much harder time gaining refugee status.

The President and Congress each year determine the number of refugees who will be permitted to enter. Refugees may receive resettlement assistance from private voluntary agencies or from the federal government. They are granted temporary visas and can apply to become permanent residents after one year.

Diversity immigration

The diversity program was created in 1990 to stimulate immigration from certain countries. A pool of visas is set aside for people without close relatives in the United States if they are nationals of certain under-represented countries.

Undocumented Immigrants

Most immigrants enter the United States legally and have status as either permanent resident aliens, naturalized U.S. citizens, or refugees. There is also a smaller, but still sizeable, population of undocumented or "illegal" immigrants. About half are people who enter legally and overstay their temporary visas; the other half enter without authorization. Many are seasonal farm workers.

Like legal immigrants, those without documents are attracted for the most part by the prospect of higher-wage work than what is available at home. Until the Immigration Reform and Control Act of 1986 was passed, there was no penalty for American employers who knowingly hired undocumented foreign workers. Such workers are easy to exploit through low wages and poor working conditions because their illegal status limits their rights in the United States.

The 1986 immigration law imposed, for the first time, penalties on employers who hire undocumented workers. As a result, some employers now discriminate against all "foreign-looking" job applicants, even those who are legal residents or U.S. citizens.

The 1986 law also allowed certain groups of undocumented immigrants to legalize their status under an amnesty provision. Those eligible were immigrants who had lived in the United States since January 1, 1982, as well as some seasonal farm workers. In addition, some undocumented immigrants have been able eventually to legalize their status by obtaining a family-sponsored or employer-sponsored visa.

Becoming a Citizen

Eligible legal immigrants can become U.S. citizens through a process called "naturalization." In most cases, an immigrant must have lived in the United States as a legal permanent resident for at least five years. An immigrant who has been married to a U.S. citizen for three years or who has been active in the U.S. armed forces can generally naturalize after just three years.

To be eligible for citizenship, a person must be able to speak, read and write basic English. This is an obstacle for many, because the demand for English classes far outstrips the number of classes available and those that exist have long waiting lists.

Once a person has applied for citizenship, months or even years of waiting often lie ahead. The problem became acute in 1997, when the backlog of unprocessed cases reached 1.4 million and applicants had to wait almost two years on average before being sworn in. Politics surrounding the immigration issue will largely decide whether the waiting time is reduced in the future, or whether it becomes longer still. ❖

Jack Kurtz, Impact Visuals

Cuban and Haitian immigrants attend English class at the Haitian Catholic Center in Miami, Florida.

Attitudes toward Immigration

It is often said that the United States is a nation of immigrants, and it is true: all Americans except for Native Americans trace their roots to somewhere else. But attitudes toward new immigrants have swung back and forth throughout this country's history. In general, the nation has welcomed and even recruited foreign-born workers in times of economic expansion. But when the economy is flat and jobs are scarce, recent immigrants have often been made scapegoats.

Hostility and even violence against the foreign-born have surged during these periods. The U.S. Congress and the states have passed laws that discriminate against immigrants or bar immigration by certain racial or ethnic groups. These surges of nativist sentiment have happened time and again in our nation's history.

In the early 1990s, another such cycle appeared to be under way. Both economic and cultural insecurities played a role. Although the nation's economy has been strong, many Americans, especially those in lower-skilled job categories, have not shared in the prosperity. At the same time, immigration since 1965 has brought large numbers of people from African, Asian and Latino backgrounds into the United States. Since U.S. society has not yet resolved its internal issues of racial inequality, attitudes toward the newcomers are influenced by both old and new prejudices.

In 1994 California voters passed Proposition 187, denying medical care and public schooling to undocumented immigrants. The measure led to copycat initiatives around the country. A closely linked movement sought to make English the "official" language of the United States and impose various restrictions on the use of other languages.

As the backlash gathered strength, the distinction between legal and illegal immigrants became blurred. Opponents of immigration, including some state and national politicians, were able to channel public resentment toward the undocumented into a demand for curbs on *legal* immigration. A new federal immigration law in 1996 tightened the requirements for obtaining legal immigrant status or political asylum. Also that year, Congress passed a welfare reform law denying food stamps and some other federal benefits to legal immigrants who are not U.S.

A young Haitian recently arrived in New York City.

Are immigrants good for the country?

To justify demands that immigration be reduced, opponents argue that the foreign-born are a burden on the nation's economy and taxpayers. The question is complex, but most research does not appear to support such claims.

A major study by the National Academy of Sciences in 1997 found that immigration produces economic benefits for the United States as a whole. The researchers estimated that immigration adds perhaps $10 billion a year to the nation's economic output. And the availability of low-wage immigrant labor helps keep down the prices of many goods and services.

Competition with immigrant workers does sometimes reduce the wages and job opportunities of low-skilled American workers, especially high school dropouts, the study found. But these effects are relatively small, and do not disadvantage any particular racial or ethnic group.

Immigrants at first add to public costs, mainly for education. But they later produce benefits as they finish school, start working and begin to pay taxes. This is potentially of great importance to the society. The country's population as a whole is hardly growing, but the proportion of the population that is elderly is increasing rapidly. The enormous population of "baby boomers" will begin reaching retirement age within two decades. This means that there could soon be a serious shortage of young adult workers to pay the taxes that help support the nation's elderly through Social Security and Medicare. In the long run, immigrants, many of whom arrive as young workers, will help pay the public costs of the aging baby-boom generation.

With an eye to their future labor pool, many U.S. businesses want to maintain reasonable levels of legal immigration. So do some mayors of the nation's big cities, especially in the Northeast and Midwest. At a time when the largest cities are losing population and watching their tax rolls dwindle, immigrants have brought new vitality to urban areas by working, paying taxes, starting small businesses and buying homes. Legal immigration is not a panacea for the nation's problems, but today, as in the past, it can be part of what makes the country grow and thrive. ❖

citizens. These lawful permanent residents of the United States can work and pay taxes just like anyone else. But if they should fall into need, the help that government provides to others will be denied them.

Social service providers and others concerned with human needs have reacted with alarm to the new measures. Pointing to the likely impact of denying benefits to children and the elderly, they have urged the government to reconsider.

Immigrant groups, meanwhile, have responded by urging their nationals to acquire U.S. citizenship and register to vote. Especially in the nation's cities, citizenship drives, voter registration and get-out-the-vote efforts among immigrants are steadily increasing their clout at the polls.

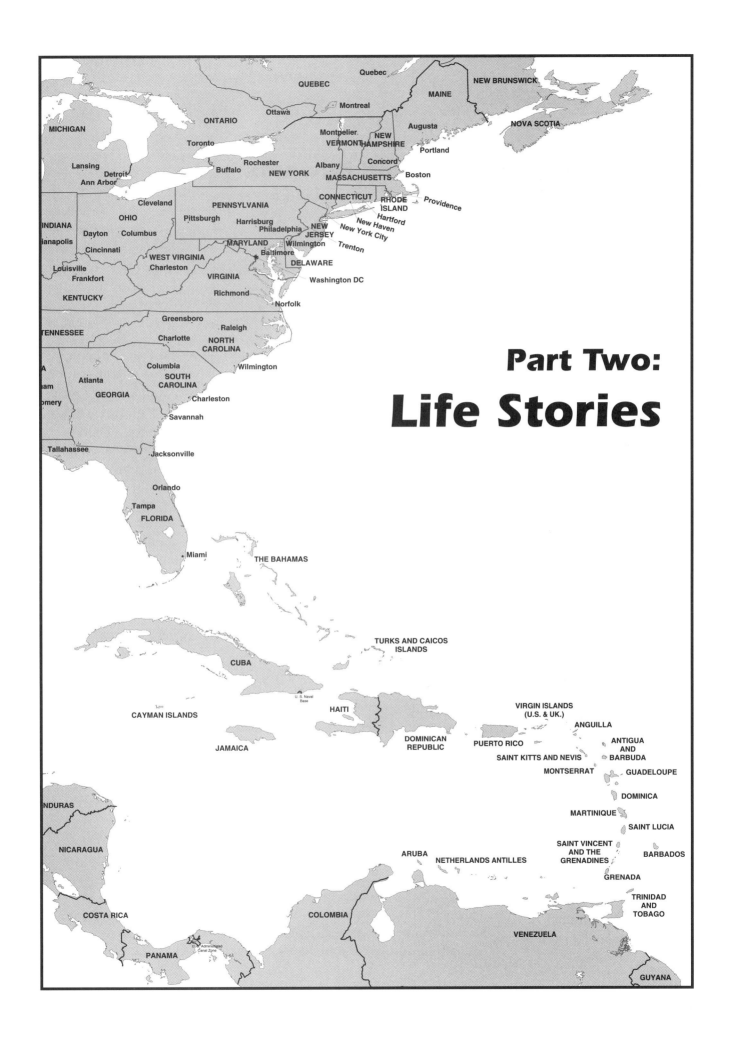

Part Two:
Life Stories

E. Leopold Edwards

E. Leopold Edwards was interviewed by Catherine Sunshine on December 18, 1996 in Washington, D.C. In 1997 he helped to found the National Coalition on Caribbean Affairs, which brings together organizations of Caribbean nationals in the United States to advance a Caribbean perspective on public policy issues of the day.

I grew up in Kingston, Jamaica in the 1930s and 1940s, when Jamaica was still a British colony. My father was a pharmacist, my mother was a nurse. From an early age it was assumed that I was going to study medicine, and in order to study I had to go away. There was no university in Jamaica or the English-speaking Caribbean at that time.

The British colonial authorities did not want most Jamaicans to become educated because that might give them the idea that they could rule themselves. If we were to have had a university, that would have been dangerous from the British point of view. Too many people would have become educated! Instead, the colonial government gave scholarships to a handful of Jamaican students to study at Oxford or another British university. You went away to England, you were embraced by Lord This and Lady That, and the Duke would have you to dinner, so by the time you came home to be a leader you were more British than West Indian.

For those of us who had no scholarship and still wanted to study, there was one other option. That was to go to America, where you could work your way through school. And so in 1948 I enrolled at Howard University in Washington, D.C.

People have been coming from the Caribbean to Howard since the 1800s. When I arrived there were more than 200 Caribbean students on campus. Many of them went on to become government officials all over the Caribbean. The head of the government department at Howard at that time was Eric Williams; he later became prime minister of Trinidad and Tobago and led his country to independence. I could take you through the Caribbean and name in every country at least 15 leaders who are Howard graduates.

My first experiences upon arriving here as a student were terribly unfortunate. Upon arriving at the airport in Miami, when I went to catch a cab, the ladies got in first, and then the men, and then the cabs stopped coming. And I was still standing there. After about ten minutes I said to someone, "This is very strange. Why have the cabs stopped?" He said, "Sir, you will need to take a colored cab." Well, in Jamaica the word "colored" means multicolored—like multicolored clothing. We don't use the word colored referring to people. So I said to him, "I don't care about the color of the cab! What difference does it make? I just want a cab." So he took me around the corner and there was a cab which, as it happened, was painted purple and white and something. This reinforced my idea that a colored cab was a cab that had many colors. And I got into the cab intending to go to the hotel where I had a reservation.

When I told the cab driver the name and address of the hotel, he told me firmly that someone had made an error. That was a "white hotel" at which I would not be welcome. I had to go to a "colored hotel." He said it was obvious that this was my first visit to America and he was therefore trying to be helpful and to save me from embarrassment. I told him I was tired and that he should do whatever he thought was best. So I went to the black hotel; not black in those days—"Negro hotel."

Imagine the shock ...

Growing up in Jamaica, I had never been exposed to that sort of thing. I'm not saying there were no racial problems, but I think it's true that class was more important than race. We were taught that it is culture and education that makes the person. If you were well educated and well brought up, you would have no problem in the world. That's what we were told, and we believed it, you see.

Imagine the shock for middle-class Caribbeans who came here and experienced stark racial discrimination for the first time. In America you're either white or you're black; there's no in-between. Within 24 hours America teaches you who you are. You get to understand that very quickly.

In Washington, D.C. in those days, they had signs saying "Jews, niggers and dogs not allowed." All the theaters, nightclubs and restaurants that would admit blacks were on U Street. If you went further downtown and tried to buy a Coke, they'd tell you to take it out. You couldn't drink it in the place.

When you left home in the morning you never knew whether you were going to return home alive. Because if it happened that a crime was committed, usually it came over the police radio that "A crime has been committed by a Negro. He is between 5' 6" and 6 feet, weighing between 140

and 185." That covers a lot of people! So if you happened to be walking in the neighborhood at that time, and you were anywhere between 5' 6" and 6 feet, weighing between 140 and 185, then you were the person! And when accosted by the police, if you showed any resentment, they would hit you in the head with a baton, put you in the car and take you to the police station. And if you continued to protest—as happened to friends of mine from Howard—they said to you, "Oh, you think you're one of these smart niggers because you're in school." And they'd beat you some more. I was president of the Caribbean Students Association for three years, and there never was a weekend that we didn't have to go get somebody out of jail for doing nothing more than acting like a human being.

We had no problems with school. We did very well academically. The problem was twofold: physical survival and work. In those days, we could drive a cab, work in a restaurant as a waiter or busboy, or work as a switchboard operator at night. Those were the categories of jobs available to us.

With a friend of mine who's now a minister of government, I went to what was then Hot Shoppes. A lady took us through an interview, asking who my grandparents and parents were, what they did, what schooling I had, everything in detail. When we were through she said to us, "You're the kind of people we want because of your backgrounds." We thought we'd hit the jackpot! Days later we got a call to report to the Hot Shoppes in Silver Spring, Maryland. We put on ties and jackets because we figured it must be some kind of big job for her to have gone through that kind of interview. We walked into the Hot Shoppes and everybody stopped eating. There was silence in the place. Everybody turned and looked at us. Eventually the hostess came over and said "What can I do for you?" very nervously. We said we'd been sent by the Hot Shoppes central employment office. She said "Oh!" and relaxed, took us downstairs, and gave us white uniforms and hats. I was told to wash dishes, and my friend was sent upstairs to bus dishes. All this after an interview lasting over an hour, inquiring into our parental, social and educational backgrounds!

It is not everlasting

Most Caribbean people here—they could be 90 years old—will tell you "I'm going home." The psychological escape is the knowledge that you can go home. You say to yourself, "I am here to achieve a certain objective. I can tolerate this for another week, another month, another year, because it is not everlasting." You'll meet Caribbean people who've been here for 50 years; they'll *never, ever* go home, but they still tell themselves that, in order to accept the nonsense they have to endure.

You supplement that by creating organizations where you can meet other Caribbean people and your common values can be sustained. These values are different in some cases from what we encounter here. For example, in the Caribbean our childrearing practices start by teaching cooperation. Then, later in life, through games and other mechanisms, we teach competition. But the core of our being is cooperation. In American society the core of your being is competition, and later on in life you're told that from time to time you may have to cooperate. It's a totally different approach.

Competitiveness permeates this society. Each one strives to make it on his own or her own, to compete with others at any cost. They tell me this is beginning now to develop in Jamaica, but it was not the norm when we were growing up there.

These are examples of the culture shock we experience. When you are coming into such a different society you have to create groupings of your own, so there is some little oasis into which you can withdraw from time to time. When I arrived, the social life of the Caribbean community in Washington revolved around two professors at the Howard medical school who used to give parties in their homes every weekend. Later on we began to give our own parties through the Caribbean Students Association.

On campus, we discovered that African and Caribbean students could not win elected office in the student government. And when we looked at it carefully we found it was because they were not joining fraternities and sororities. We discovered also that the student government had been dominated for a long time by one particular fraternity in alliance with one particular sorority.

And it happened that very few dark-complexioned students were in those two organizations. And so we formed an alliance between the Caribbean students, the African students, and the African-American students who did not wish to tolerate that kind of nonsense on campus, and ran a slate which won. And it broke the hold of that sorority and that fraternity over student government.

Thereafter, Caribbeans and Africans began to hold office in the Howard student government. We always put up a slate that included an African-American, an African and a Caribbean. It demonstrated in a concrete way what we could achieve through unity. We thought that kind of unified action should carry through beyond the university, into everyday life.

Out of the Caribbean Students Association we created the Caribbean-American Intercultural Organization (CAIO), which catered to Caribbean people off-campus. We wanted to disseminate Caribbean culture into the broader community, to let Americans know we have a culture of our own. We wanted them to know that Caribbeans have made outstanding contributions to the development of the United States, and that some Americans have contributed to the struggle for independence, freedom and justice in the Caribbean. And we wanted them to know that the linkage with Africa was profound.

CAIO also worked to meet the practical needs of Caribbean people in Washington. By the 1960s the demographics of the Caribbean community were changing. From a small cluster of students and professionals, it was expanding to include people from all walks of life. The reason was a new U.S. immigration law, which said that if workers for a certain type of employment were in short supply, people could come in from abroad and fill those jobs. The type of employment most often certified by the U.S. Labor Department as needing workers was "sleep-in domestic help"—that is, household servants. So women began coming up from the Caribbean to become domestics.

Living in the employer's home, they didn't have to pay room and board, so they could save money. At the end of three years they could send for their relatives. So very soon, the Caribbean community mushroomed tremendously.

Many of these new immigrants had nothing to do on their day off. They knew nobody, had nowhere to go and were totally lost. So we rented a place down on N Street Northwest where they could go and cook Caribbean food, meet each other and exchange telephone numbers. At night we would have music and dancing.

As the Caribbean population around Washington expanded, there came to be many more people in the area from each Caribbean country. Meanwhile, the territories of the Caribbean were gaining national independence one by one. As a result, each national group in Washington eventually wanted its own organization. So there came into being the Jamaica Nationals Association, the Trinidad and Tobago Association, the Guyana Nationals Association, and all the others. They were all doing the same thing, but instead of treating the Caribbean as a totality each was doing it for the nationals of one country.

We must speak with one voice

The problem then became how to get the community unified again. How to respect the need for national identity while at the same time helping the Caribbean community unify in order to promote its interests. Because when you go and speak as a Jamaican nobody pays any attention. You speak as a Trinidadian, nobody pays any attention. You say to a congressman, "I want you to do this for Dominica," and he'll say, "Where's that?" But the Caribbean—people have a picture of the Caribbean. We learned long ago that unless the Caribbean can speak with a unified voice, our influence on events both at home and abroad will be practically nonexistent.

Toward this end, we formed the Council of Caribbean Organizations to bring the different groups together under one umbrella. Today, COCO includes 32 Caribbean organizations in the Washington-Baltimore area.

People from the Caribbean have made outstanding contributions to community life in Washington. You'll find us at every level of government, academia, and the professions. At the federal level, to cite a well-known example, Colin Powell, former chairman of the joint chiefs of staff, is of Jamaican descent. In the D.C. mayor's office quite a few heads of departments are Caribbean. There are many Caribbean professors at Howard University and the University of the District of Columbia.

Caribbean people are prominent in all the professions: medicine, nursing, dentistry, law, business, engineering, architecture, computer science, astrophysics—everything. This is true not only in Washington but all over the United States and Canada, too. Any field you can name, I can name you a Caribbean person who is tops in that field. We are making contributions across the country. ❖

minister of government: government official equivalent to a cabinet-level secretary in the U.S.

Marguerite Lorent

Marguerite Lorent was interviewed by Ruth Glasser on July 16, 1996 in Stamford, Connecticut. Portions of this narrative are included in Lorent's forthcoming book KIMBE LA: JOURNEY OF A VODUN-ROOTS WOMAN.

When I was eight years old, my family had to get out of Haiti. My father owned a small travel and taxi business in Port-au-Prince, the capital. After 1957, when François Duvalier came to power, many entrepreneurs were forced to pay bribes to stay in business. The Duvalier regime's enforcers, the Tontons Macoutes, would extort from anyone who had money. If you had a job or a business, you had to buy protection or else be part of the police or the Macoute power structure.

Everything, including the taxi drivers' association, was controlled by Duvalier's mafia. The taxi drivers were required to drive around the city, honking their horns to show support for Duvalier. People were trucked in from the countryside to cheer in front of the palace. The Macoutes running the taxi association kept tabs on the cars that didn't show up. Drivers who refused to participate in the demonstrations or who did not pay bribes would be beaten or killed.

By 1967 my father was being harassed to the point where he couldn't run his business any more. A bomb exploded next to his car where all of us children were piled in. Then the house of a man my father did business with—an opponent of Duvalier—was burned to the ground and the man's family was killed. It was rumored that the Macoutes were looking for the man's friends to kill them, too. My father believed he would be next.

My father had friends in Connecticut, a wealthy Greenwich family who had visited Haiti many times over the years. When my father had to get out of Haiti, he called them. They brought him to Greenwich and he stayed for a year, working three jobs so he could earn enough money to send for his family. After a year he brought us up from Haiti to join him. We settled in Stamford, a few miles from Greenwich.

In Connecticut my mother worked as a domestic, cleaning houses. Although she came to join my father, many Haitian women came in the 1950s and 1960s in order to work as domestics. The civil rights movement had raised expectations among African-Americans coming up from the South, and most wanted to do other jobs. They may not have wanted to put on a little white outfit, little white shoes, and scrub floors. So employers recruited in the Caribbean. Today, if I were to introduce you to some of the mothers of the Haitian community here in Stamford, they're probably working for the same lady they worked for 35 years ago, doing "day work."

Immigrants who became legal permanent residents could petition to bring their family members here. My parents come from a village in Haiti called Fond des Blanc. Practically the whole village is in Stamford now, because people petitioned for their relatives one by one.

When a new Haitian family came to Stamford, often they would end up in our living room. We would fill out their card for Social Security and help them apply for a job and open a bank account. I was the person who would translate, fill out documents and make the calls. If a worker needed a sick day, for instance, he would call our house and eight-year-old Marguerite would call the employer. I learned to think on my feet for good explanations that would help them keep their jobs. That's probably one of the reasons I ended up being a lawyer. I was doing it then, and that's what I do now for my clients: show them where to sign and what to do, interpret the law for them, and speak on their behalf when necessary.

My father wanted us all to learn English right away, so he spoke to us only in English. I lost fluency in Kreyòl as a result, and had to relearn it later. I could understand it, of course, because my mother spoke Kreyòl to family members arriving from Haiti all the time.

My sister Chantal and I were the only Haitians in our fourth-grade class. I knew I was Haitian and was very proud of it, but there was really no one to talk to about it. While the white community regarded us as "black," the African-American kids saw the cultural differences immediately. They thought we were a bit strange because we wore pigtails tied with bright satin bows and little dresses handmade by my mother, even in winter. Before we lost our accents, the black kids used to call us "Frenchie." It wasn't until high school that there were two other Haitians in my graduating class.

Today, the Stamford public high schools are something like 60% black, and nearly half the black students are of Haitian descent. There was an influx of Haitians into the area from the late 1970s onward. The repression had grown worse in Haiti after Duvalier's son Jean-Claude came to power in 1971. Economic conditions were more desperate too, so many people were leaving Haiti.

The Haitians who came to Hartford and Stamford in the 1950s and 1960s were likely to be people who could take the plane, who had a higher economic status in Haiti. Those coming in after 1980 were a more diverse group. Many had fled Haiti in desperate and dangerous ways, typically in small boats. Refugees were intercepted by the U.S. Coast Guard on the high seas and "processed." If they had a relative in the United States, they might be allowed to go live with that person.

At the same time, quite a few of the earlier Haitian migrants were moving from New York to Connecticut, looking for a better standard of living with less crime. Before I went away to college in 1977 I could go to the Stamford Mall or anywhere and not encounter a single Haitian, or if I did, it was someone I knew well. But when I returned to the area ten years later, I would go to the grocery store, the mall or a restaurant, and there would be people I didn't know speaking Kreyòl.

Stamford was changing

While the Haitian community was growing in size, major changes were taking place in Stamford. Big corporations like Marriott, Champion, Xerox and General Electric came in during the 1980s and built their headquarters here.

Property values rose very high. Some Haitians, those who came early like my family, owned their homes. Some of them were able to sell their properties during the boom and retire to Florida.

But the ones who came in later had a really tough time. Working-class people—including African-Americans, Haitians, Latinos and whites—couldn't afford to live in Stamford any more. Most did not own their houses; they were renting. The landlords sold and they were out, or the houses were taken by eminent domain. Many could not afford to buy a house in the inflated property market, so they moved further north to Norwalk or Bridgeport, or went south to Georgia or Florida. They made way for the corporate headquarters, the skyscrapers, the trendy shops, the luxury condos for yuppies. For instance, the area around Atlantic Street and lower East Main, which now has the Stamford Mall, is where tenement houses used to be.

While real estate prices were rising, jobs were disappearing. Manufacturing jobs had been a mainstay for Haitian men, and Haitian women also had increasingly shifted from domestic work to better-paid factory work. My mother, for example, worked for 11 years at Carlan Products, assembling paper and plastic goods. But during the 1980s the factories here decided they didn't want to pay minimum wage any more. Some moved to the southern states while others went overseas to places like Taiwan, Malaysia or China. So there was a big increase in joblessness. The new corporations coming in employed highly skilled and educated people, mostly from outside the community.

That's why there are so many Haitians now in Stamford who cannot make it without Section 8 housing subsidies and Medicaid. When I was growing up that was unheard of. But with the changes in Stamford you can't feed a family, rent a $1,500-a-month apartment, and pay medical bills without some assistance.

By the late 1980s corporate America was downsizing and those in the middle class were feeling the pinch. Instead of blaming the corporations, they blamed the working class—especially the black community, of which Haitians are a subset. Haitians are particularly vulnerable to scapegoating. They're poor, black, non-English-speakers—the perfect "other" to blame. People with problems can tell themselves "It's because of the burden on our system by these Haitians."

In my work as a lawyer I see how Haitians here face discrimination. Like other blacks, Haitians are concentrated in the poorest schools in what is still a highly segregated school system. Black families in public housing get sent to high-rise towers as far as possible from the affluent parts of town, while white families get better subsidized housing, nice dwellings with lawns in less poverty-ridden areas.

Hard work and saving

In spite of it all, the dominant theme for the Haitian community has been hard work and saving. Haitians of my father's generation save a lot. My father, for example, worked three jobs. Some people, within five years of coming to this country, could put down their $30,000 deposit and closing costs and purchase a $150,000 house. And while it's harder now to do that,

it's still possible for the most industrious. For example, someone who works as a housekeeper at St. Joseph's Hospital may have started 30 years ago at $6 an hour. She may now be getting only $15 an hour, but she's been there for 30 years, saving. If you want to know where the Haitians are, go to the hotels, the hospitals, the corporate restaurants in Stamford. We hold up the city.

Haitians have pursued the American dream through education. My mother had two jobs and went to night school. All of us kids have attended college, and there are seven of us.

There are cultural differences between the older Haitian community and the recent arrivals. Those of us who came early assimilated quickly within the middle-class African-American community because there were so few of us. The Haitians coming later in larger numbers have maintained their culture better, but it has been harder for them to move out of poverty and into the middle class.

Haitian kids used to be ashamed to identify themselves as Haitians. They would call themselves Antilleans, Caribbeans, West Indians or African-Americans. I myself was always proud of being Ayisian. We use the term "Ayisian" to refer to the nation, the people, not the state called Haiti.

In the last few years a new cultural consciousness has emerged among Haitians. The successful overthrow of the Duvalier dictatorship, followed by the Lavalas movement in support of President Aristide, gave people the feeling of having accomplished something positive. It invigorated Haitians all over the world.

The church, which is the strongest organization in the Haitian community, has changed too. When I was growing up community life revolved around the Catholic church. Now, though, there are Protestant storefront churches as well as evangelical churches and vodun temples. Both the Catholic and Protestant churches have incorporated more of the Ti Legliz or "little church" model based on liberation theology, as Aristide was preaching.

Church services are in Kreyòl now, which is a big difference from the past. When I came here, every Haitian would say "I speak French," when in fact they only learned French in school. Now people are acknowledging that they speak Kreyòl. We have a Kreyòl Bible, and it's very beautiful.

Young people are doing roots music, singing about what it means to be Haitian. The hip-hop group called the Fugees—short for "refugees"—is working through music for Haitian self-determination. My generation is creating new ways of being Haitian so that the next generations don't go through the trials we went through.

Working for Haiti

I've always been an activist. As editor of my college newspaper I covered the anti-apartheid movement, and I coordinated a summer program to bring more black, Hispanic, Native American and Asian students to the college. In law school I was part of the Black Law Student Association and a delegate to its national convention where I proposed a resolution to stop U.S. aid to the Duvalier regime.

After finishing law school I worked in corporate finance. It was a large, prestigious law firm, and I was the only black lawyer they'd ever had. The firm's clients were mainly banks and corporations. Unless you paid the firm a large retainer you couldn't hire me, so I couldn't do much to help other Haitians.

After four years I started my own business, representing clients in areas like business, real estate, and entertainment law. I became more directly involved with the Haitian community. At this time, around 1987, Haiti was in turmoil because Duvalier had been overthrown and a neo-Duvalierist regime had taken over. I spoke to the press, and I went to Hartford to help refugees held in state detention centers. I also started speaking on behalf of the Haitian Community Center here in Stamford, doing fundraisers for college scholarships for Haitian students, and speaking about the plight of black students in our schools.

A turning point in my involvement came in 1989–1990 over the AIDS issue. The Food and Drug Administration came out with a policy that Haitians who had been to Haiti within the last seven years could not donate blood because Haitians were a "high-risk group" for AIDS. Working-class and professional Haitians alike were outraged. We knew that American tourists had brought AIDS to Haiti, not the other way around. The policy would have affected half my extended family, even those who had lived all their lives in

the United States but visited Haiti from time to time. Now they were all stigmatized. A coalition formed to protest the policy and we marched by the thousands across the Brooklyn Bridge. Some of us went to Washington and talked to the FDA.

The FDA finally rescinded the policy. That victory gave a big boost to grassroots activism among Haitian-Americans. Building on the momentum of that protest, the U.S. Haitian community mobilized to oppose the coup d'etat that overthrew President Aristide.

My advocacy work eventually came to Aristide's attention while he was in exile. We met when he came to give a speech at Yale University, and he asked me to help work on judicial reform for Haiti. I put together the Haitian Lawyers Leadership Network and began planning for a convention to reform the Haitian Constitution. A group of Haitian lawyers from New York got together to work on reforming laws, voting rights for Haitians outside Haiti, and a dual-citizenship amendment to the Haitian Constitution. One of the problems in Haiti is that once you leave the country, you can't vote in Haitian elections. If they allowed Haitians in the diaspora to vote, with their higher literacy levels and resources, it could strengthen participatory democracy and the electoral process.

After he went back to Haiti, President Aristide called and asked me to come down. I worked in Haiti as an advisor to the Ministry of Justice from March to June 1995, helping to reform Haiti's justice system.

This was the first time I had returned to Haiti since leaving as a child, 25 years before. I had never gone back with my parents: although my mother has visited Haiti, my father refuses to go. I was troubled by the long history of pain and suffering in Haiti and I didn't want to go back unless I could feel that I was bringing something. When Aristide called it was an opportunity to do that. I thought maybe I could help; I was used to solving problems; at least I had to try. So I went back with that hope. ❖

Kreyól: Haitian Creole
vodun: Haitian indigenous religion (sometimes spelled vodou or voodoo)

Eddie Pérez

Eddie Pérez was interviewed by Ruth Glasser on July 22, 1996 in Hartford, Connecticut.

I was born in Corozal, Puerto Rico, and came to the States with my family in 1966, when I was nine. My father had served in the U.S. Army, learned English and made some friends, and so we ended up in Brooklyn, New York.

My father worked in a factory, and he also owned a pool hall and a *bodega* and managed several others. We lived in a black neighborhood, in a big apartment building with maybe 60 to 80 families.

My father never was involved in running the household, so I was the one who went with my mom to the clinic, government offices, places like that. I was the second oldest and learned English sooner than my brothers. Although my father worked hard he was also a gambler and a ladies' man. So although we never went hungry, it was my mom who pretty much put it together for us.

She doesn't talk much about the breakup, but in 1969 my mom moved with us kids to Hartford. We had uncles and aunts living here who had come from Puerto Rico to Connecticut to do tobacco work and later moved into other occupations. So my mom's support system was here. We lived in a six-family building with a back yard, and our relatives lived nearby.

I was raised on welfare. The household was rather chaotic, and we basically grew up in the streets. We moved a lot. From sixth grade until high school I lived in maybe as many as 18 buildings in the neighborhoods of Clay Hill and Frog Hollow. In grade school and junior high I was continually changing schools because we had moved.

We rented in the most dilapidated buildings, and we were usually the last or next-to-last family to move before a building was condemned. We used space heaters to keep warm, and sometimes the pipes would freeze. When it got bad enough that would force us to go to the next apartment.

We had no car so my mom would walk down the street, looking for a vacancy. When she negotiated the rent I had to translate. One time she wanted two four-room apartments on the third floor. "A hole in the wall; make a doorway to connect the apartments!" she would insist. The landlord kept saying, "You're crazy! We just don't do this!" And then we would move. She would pack up some boxes and we would carry the refrigerator and the stove, with her at one end and me and my brothers at the other end.

Our housing situation finally stabilized when we had a fire that made us eligible for subsidized housing. It put us in a better apartment in a housing tract under the housing authority.

I went through the public schools. At that time most of my friends were black; I identified with black kids and hung out with them. I remember walking into my first class in a Hartford school after we arrived from New York City. My dress was black. My walk was black. All the black kids wanted to know, who was this cool little guy who's not a hick? Most of the Puerto Rican kids were considered hick; they got picked on. But I never got bullied.

Part of it was a survival skill, because I'm physically small. When my brothers and I got into fights, we knew you can't get stared down by anybody, you've got to stand up. We learned that in New York City. The other thing was, in New York schools I had been in advanced classes, so when I came here I was not only a cool kid, I was also way ahead of most of my peers.

I was also attracted to the excitement that seemed to surround the black kids. It was the height of the Black Power movement, and there was a small Black Panther school a couple of doors away from me. I got a sense of what was happening, and I began identifying with the Black Power movement and issues of blacks.

The year we arrived in Hartford, 1969, was the year of the riots and the National Guard was called in. The unrest continued for several summers, with people trying to create some action. I was out on the streets with the neighborhood kids by that point. When I was in seventh grade there was a teachers' strike in Hartford, and it was violent, with cars being turned over and substitute teachers being beat on by kids.

My life started to change when I was placed in a classroom at Barnard Brown School with the smartest kids. These were the movers and the shakers: we ran the school, everything from the clubs to the basketball team. That was the group that attracted me to Sacred Heart Church, because the basketball team at the school became the basketball team at Sacred Heart.

Introduced to activism

It was through Sacred Heart that I was reintroduced to the Puerto Rican community. In that era, everything that was happening in the Puerto Rican community seemed to begin at Sacred Heart. It was the hub of the Puerto Rican community in Hartford, politically, economically and socially, for maybe two decades.

The Catholic youth group at Sacred Heart, which I joined, was led by priests who guided us into activism on social justice issues. One time our group went down to North Carolina to join a protest in support of the Wilmington Ten and the Charlotte Three, civil rights activists who had been jailed unjustly. When we got on the bus we thought it was just another field trip, a day away from Clay Hill. But when we got down there our leaders started telling us what to do "when they start beating up on you." I could see the Ku Klux Klan up on the rooftops as we were marching. Although I didn't think the issues through clearly, I started to put things together.

The church was also working with the farm workers' union led by César Chavez to try to organize the tobacco workers. We went to celebrate a mass at the tobacco workers' camps. Although I didn't understand everything that was going on— my Spanish was real bad at that time—I did realize that this wasn't just another mass. So through the church I got a taste of social activism and organizing, and to a certain degree, Puerto Rican cultural pride.

I was always organizing something. Some years before we had a football team called the Quirk Crusaders. The black kids used to say, "Puerto Ricans can't play football." Before long, we got good at it. We could beat anybody in the city.

When I was in high school I helped organize a gang called the Ghetto Brothers. A friend of ours went to Brooklyn and encountered the Ghetto Brothers there, so we decided to start our own chapter. It was something new to do. At that time it was not a violent group. It was church-oriented, and Puerto Rican. It began with four of us, and the next day a hundred guys showed up because they heard there was a new gang in town. Pretty soon we were 500 strong.

The Ghetto Brothers was a clique. We bragged more than we actually did and therefore our reputation far exceeded the actual reality. We were the coolest Puerto Rican kids because most of us could relate to the black kids. And there was a mystique to being the group of kids who made up the leadership at Sacred Heart.

We co-existed with the two black gangs up in the North End, the Magnificent Twenties and the Blackstone Rangers. The Latin Locos were up there as well, but they were a smaller gang and our friends, since we went to school with them. Even so, there was tension all the time. We got into a couple of things which were minor, at least by gang standards. Eventually an outside gang from New York, the Savage Nomads, set up shop and that led to an escalation of violence.

Since the Ghetto Brothers and the Latin Locos were Puerto Rican, there was some sense of ethnic identity, although it wasn't really intentional. Most of us had come to the United States at an early age and grew up here. Most were raised in single-parent households and worked after school. Some of us didn't speak very much Spanish, and meetings were run bilingually. We were—I wouldn't say confused, but we were searching for our identity. Two black kids were part of the group, Gus and Tony, and they started speaking Spanish. So there was a cultural element, but I don't know that we were looking for that.

At one time there was a racial rift between the Puerto Ricans and the blacks in Clay Hill over drugs. Although drugs were all around me, I never got involved. Even the guys who played basketball at Sacred Heart Church, when they smoked a joint they would say, "Hey, go take a walk." Or they would take the walk. People would always make room for me, respect my space, and then look to me for advice, and I was never shy about providing advice or leading.

I graduated from Hartford High in 1976. Of the nine kids in my family, two graduated from high school; I think three have gone back and gotten their GED since then.

At that time college was not an option for me. So I sold furniture for a year, but I didn't want to do that all my life, and Father Tom Goeckler, one of the priests at Sacred Heart, suggested I join Vista.

As a Vista volunteer I ran a tenant organizing and welfare rights group based in the Puerto Rican community of Clay Hill.

After a year, I got a grant to start a community action group called CHANE—Clay Hill and North End, Inc. Clay Hill and the North End are two of the poorest neighborhoods in Hartford, full of rundown housing and vacant lots. We did tenant organizing and job training, and helped people become homeowners and fix up dilapidated houses.

There were 28 block clubs organized under our umbrella. At the beginning we worked out of a church basement; then we moved to the back of a car wash, and finally to an office on Main Street. CHANE was locally controlled. Most of the staff came from the neighborhood. Although corporations, foundations and federal agencies gave us grants, you couldn't be on the board that ran the organization unless you lived in the neighborhood.

Bridging communities

In my organizing, I've always believed in the democratic ideal, that people have certain rights. But they don't *get* those rights unless they empower themselves: I learned that early on. When it came to dealing with corporate folks and politicians, I found that my experience of moving between gangs and communities prepared me well. I could go to Chamber of Commerce meetings, or tenant meetings, or meetings in the black community, where they'd be talking about Puerto Ricans, and say, "Guys, that's not the way it really is!" I've been able to bridge communities.

I later worked for two years running a welfare-to-work program in a public housing project called Stowe Village, near where I used to live. I also began undergraduate work at Trinity College and graduated with a B.A. in economics in 1996.

In 1990, while I was working toward my college degree, I began my present job as director of neighborhood and government relations at Trinity. I work to bridge the gap between the college and the surrounding community of Frog Hollow.

Trinity College has launched an ambitious plan to help revitalize Frog Hollow through home ownership, new schools, and jobs. The plan is somewhat unusual. In these situations, where you have an elite institution in a very poor neighborhood, the usual tendency is not to consult the neighborhood. The tendency is to say, Well, what does the neighborhood want? We'll just do it! Our approach is different. We're trying to figure out how to help the neighborhood turn itself around, to let the people who live here build it up from within, with institutions like Trinity College assisting.

I'm in charge of organizing the participation of Frog Hollow residents, who are mostly Puerto Rican. At the same time I also deal with government agencies, with the college trustees, and with the superintendent of schools. I have a foothold in both worlds. It's what I love to do: break down the barriers, provide the resources, get people working together, and let it go. ❖

Along Park Street in Hartford's Frog Hollow section.

Carmen E. Boudier

Carmen E. Boudier was interviewed by Ruth Glasser on August 2, 1996 in Hartford, Connecticut. The New England Health Care Employees Union is a member union of the Service Employees International Union, AFL-CIO.

'm the secretary-treasurer of New England Health Care Employees Union, District 1199, which has its headquarters here in Hartford. I'm a trade unionist.

I came to the United States from Jamaica in 1968. In those days many of us came to work in homes, taking care of children or being a domestic "helper." The U.S. Department of Labor recruited women to come to the United States to do this work. You would apply and get a sponsor; or if you had relatives here who knew somebody who was looking for a helper, then that family would process your papers. In my case I had a cousin in Connecticut and he knew a family in West Hartford that needed a helper. That's how I came.

I grew up in a family of twelve. My parents were farmers. I had brothers and a sister who went off to England; several sisters who went off to America; and other siblings who went to Canada, all in search of jobs for a better life and to help support our family back home.

My contract with the West Hartford family was for one year. They were very nice to me, but still, it was awfully lonesome. My closest relative in the United States was a sister in Chicago. Many days I wanted to go back home. But then I would remind myself that I had a goal. Our culture emphasizes that family members have a responsibility to help each other, so you would be a failure if you didn't work toward that, knowing your sisters and brothers need help and that you are trying to make a better life for yourself.

I was married and had left my three children with my parents in Jamaica. Every Thursday I would buy children's clothes, pack them in a box and mail them. I would make sure to drop in $20 or $30 or whatever I had to help my parents with the additional responsibility. Later on, my husband and children came up from Jamaica to join me.

After my year as a domestic was up I decided that I needed to move forward: go to school or get another job. I began working as a nurse's aide at St. Mary's Home in West Hartford. It felt good to be caring for the elderly and other people who needed help.

But the work was poorly paid. At the beginning, in 1969, I was making $1.30 an hour. We had no health insurance, no sick leave, no holiday, no vacation. Our yearly raise was five cents or ten cents an hour. The bosses' attitude was you take it or you leave it. There was a huge turnover every year.

One of the things that drove me to be an organizer was the desire to help not only myself but also other women like me. Many of us who left Jamaica ended up in cities like Hartford, working in health care. St. Mary's Home had about 200 employees of whom maybe 125 were from the Caribbean—mostly Jamaicans, Barbadians, and Trinidadians. We also had some Hispanic workers and some Portuguese.

Almost all of them were women. In those days, hospital and nursing home work was one of the lowest-paid occupations. The vast majority of health care workers, maybe 90 or 95 percent, were women. It was only later, once wages started to rise, that men started to enter that type of work.

The union makes a difference

I got involved in the campaign to bring the union into St. Mary's Home. We had an election in the fall of 1969 and won our first contract in November of that year. I became an active committee member who went across the state of Connecticut, organizing other health care workers to join the union.

One campaign I worked on was the successful drive to organize Mt. Sinai Hospital in Hartford. Two years after that victory, I left St. Mary's and went to work at Mt. Sinai as a nurse's aide in the emergency room. While doing that, I also went back to school and became certified as an emergency room technician. I worked in the E.R. at Mt. Sinai for three years. Then I took a leave of absence to come on staff and work for the union.

By joining the union and fighting over the years we do make a difference. The same members I worked with in 1969, making $1.30 an hour, today are making $12 an hour or more. Plus they have a pension fund, and health insurance for themselves and their families. We negotiate these things in the contract.

I remember how we won the pension for nursing home workers in 1980. They told us it was impossible. But for us it was critical, because we

had members who had been in health care for 30 years, had become professional at their jobs and were nearing retirement age, and there was no pension. So we created a crisis. Our members in 15 nursing homes around the state went out on strike the same day, while we went and lobbied Governor Grasso. And we won. I'm very proud that today our members who retire from nursing homes and hospitals are able to have a pension. That was one of the great fights.

Today, New England Health Care District 1199 has 15,000 members in Connecticut and 3,000 in Rhode Island. Half of them are in the public sector and half in the private sector. We have every type of health care professional, including doctors, nurses, psychiatrists, nursing home workers, mental retardation specialists, laboratory technicians, and social workers.

We are a multicolored organization. Our members represent just about every background you can think of. Caribbean people work in health care throughout this state. In Hartford and New Haven most are English-speaking West Indians; in Bridgeport you'll find Haitians. There are also many African-American workers and in some parts of the state you have nursing homes with staffs that are all-white.

I can't think of another organization that is as effective as a trade union in forcing people to come together for a common cause. If a member proposes, when you're drawing up your contract proposal, that we should demand Dr. Martin Luther King's birthday as a holiday, or a member who is gay wants to fight for domestic partner rights—those issues are human issues. You can't say that one group should stay in the room and debate it and the other group should get out. People are forced to come together and discuss things. And I think it's a victory in itself to be able to do that, with all kinds of people from all kind of backgrounds.

When African-Americans and West Indians work side by side, they sometimes have conflicts. I remember I was in negotiation once at Mt. Sinai Hospital and we were getting ready to go on strike. And I noticed that quite a few workers were not in the room. It turned out there had been some conflict the day before. An African-American had said to a Jamaican, "You should go back home on the banana boat" or something to that effect, and that had caused friction. You have to stop what you're doing and deal with it. It's an uncomfortable dialogue and there is not always an answer for these conflicts, but you have to talk and let people work through their anger. You teach the members that we have to respect each other and not let this divide us.

The struggle against racism is something people often don't want to talk about. There is ugliness and bitterness. But one of the ways the union makes a contribution is that all workers—doesn't matter your birth place, your color, your background, your religion—all workers are in this with a common goal to unite and fight to make a difference in our lives. *That's* fighting racism.

I've been the secretary-treasurer of the union for the last six terms. Every two years the union officers run for election, and the members elect us. Often you get the sense that outsiders are uncomfortable or even shocked that a black person is secretary-treasurer of the union. People are more polite about it nowadays, but racism is still there, and you deal with it.

There's no question that being a black woman affects your dealings with bosses. Being a woman in this world is hard and difficult; it gets harder by your color, harder by your accent. You can see it when you walk into a room. You might set up an appointment over the phone. Then you walk in and see the look, like oh, these folks are very uncomfortable with you. You could almost become afraid to participate in things because of your color; that's something I still have to challenge.

Education and citizenship

One of the most important things our union has done is to create a training and upgrading fund. Many of our members are women who came to this country as I did, on the domestic program. They went on to become nurse's aides or dietary workers or laundry workers. Now they need the opportunity to upgrade their skills.

We offer some classes right here in our union headquarters. If you have no high school diploma,

you can get your GED. We also fought for a one percent gross increase per month in the contract to create a fund to help our members go back to school. Members have used this tuition assistance to attend community colleges and universities around the state, training in a wide range of health care occupations and in related fields such as accounting, business management and computer science. Quite a few of our members who were nurse's aides have become registered nurses or licensed practical nurses.

The union also offers classes to prepare our members to become U.S. citizens. Most of us who came from Jamaica believed we were going back home someday. "Oh, I'm not becoming a U.S. citizen, I'm going back home!" It's my job to show them that you can't be in a country for 10, 15, 20 years and simply say you're going back home. After I came here I took out U.S. citizenship as soon as I could because I believe that wherever you are, if you're going to speak out on issues, then you should have the right to vote and to fight for changes as a citizen of that country. And if you become a U.S. citizen you can still go home later if you want to, because Jamaica allows dual citizenship.

Many times when it gets rough—you're on strike for six months, you have workers out on the picket line in the heart of winter—you ask: Why am I doing this? And then you say to yourself, What other job would I want to do? Yes, you could be a millionaire. You could make money, and you still haven't touched anybody's life. And so each of us has to think about what we want to do while we're on this earth. Having ideas and talking is nice. But doing the hard, tough things, going against the bosses as we do in this union—that's something else. We may become unpopular. But it is something I believe in and I'm very proud of what we have accomplished.

You can't, as a human being, think only of making a difference in *your* life. You have to think about making a difference in *other* people's lives. And that drives me very, very, very much, and I stay committed to it until this day. ❖

Andrés Santana

Andrés Santana left Cuba in the Mariel boatlift of 1980, at the age of 21. He was interviewed by Lynn Geldof in 1989 in New York City. A longer version of this interview appears in CUBANS: VOICES OF CHANGE (New York: St. Martin's Press). © 1991 by Lynn Geldof. Used by permission of St. Martin's Press Inc.

I had put my name down to leave four days before, and a soldier came for me and said, "You've got to get over there right away." I put my name down because they were saying, "They're letting people who put their names down leave." And at the time so many people I knew were going, and I was dying to go, because I wanted to find something, I wanted to travel, I wanted to have things, so I said to myself I'm going to put my name down because this might be the opportunity. ...

After spending several tension-filled hours in the port of Mariel, Santana along with others was put on a shrimp boat headed for Miami.

The journey was appalling. Thanks be to God I didn't get sick or anything and I fell asleep. I don't know how I managed it. I don't know. I must have been so tired. We got to Miami, to Cayo Hueso, at 7:30 in the morning on May 1, 1980. What a date to arrive! As we were coming into Cayo Hueso, a Coast Guard [vessel] approached and escorted us to the bay. But before landing, the Cubans who were there—they were euphoric, blowing their horns—welcomed us like heroes ... I was moved, because these were my people, too. They were living here, and I was moved because I understood what I was leaving behind. At that point I felt well. I think it was the only time, perhaps it was the only time, since I've been in this country, that I honestly felt happy and contented; that I felt accepted by the people, even though it wasn't specifically directed toward me, it was directed toward everyone.

Upon their arrival, the Cubans faced the shouted questions of reporters amid tight security.

The soldiers, there were lots of soldiers, I do remember that. Especially the North American soldiers, you noticed that you weren't accepted by them, that there was a kind of rejection ... And from then on I began to suffer, not as a Cuban but as a human being. I see everyone as they are—human beings. I don't care where they are born, or about their race, and I owe a lot of that to my education in Cuba. So, I began to see that hatred they have of Hispanics, that lack of acceptance of Hispanics or blacks or poor people. I began to assimilate that. I picked up on it. And I said to myself, "Right, now you've got to live with it. Now you're here, you're stuck with it."

From Florida, Santana continued on to New York City, where his sister and her husband lived. He eventually found work as a cloakroom attendant at a prestigious art museum. Nine years after leaving Cuba, he reflected on his decision:

Everything I remember about my life in Cuba was, as Guillén says, "All time past was better," and I can't complain about my past life, and although I had tough times like everyone else, it was all beautiful.

I can't say the same for now. It's not so beautiful. Everything is so much more different: more difficult, more harsh, more spare, let's say. My life now is much more tense by comparison. In Cuba, although there were bad moments, it was much different, and more beautiful in the end. I used to write. I felt well. I had my family, no? My sister was already here since 1971, but ... it wasn't the desire to see my sister, it was the desire ... you know how it is when you're younger, you want to change the world and you dream of all sorts of things. You dream of having it all, and you think that this is a wonder, that this is the promised land, that everything will be fine.

So, as you're young you get caught up in all that talk, and when you get here you see the reality. I knew a bit about the reality of it before I came, but I didn't think it would be quite so hard. ...

My finances at the present ... I don't know what to think. I've gone over it so often I don't know what to think now, because I'm in a difficult situation. And despite the fact that I'm working here in the museum, which gives me a good wage looking at it in one way, I now have ... on top of my rent and the rest of it, I am paying what they call here "bankruptcy" so as not to lose my apartment. I was on the point of losing it in 1987. My life had become hopeless. Never, not even in the time of Batista, was anybody thrown onto the street. And I was terrified that would happen to me. And I had to file for bankruptcy, which cost me enormous sums ... vast sums, because I lost my job overnight. A job I had before, working in a restaurant, earning a lot of money. But fool that I was, I never saved a penny. They sold the restaurant and the new owner threw us all out. He wanted new people. I was in the street. No money. No work. And I said to myself, I have always had luck in that respect—I had always had luck since I'd arrived—I'll find something tomorrow.

I spent nearly six months without a job. I was starving, and I never wish what I went through on anyone. Then the landlord took me to court because I couldn't pay. I got a letter from a firm of lawyers saying, "Don't lose your apartment, come and see us." That they'd help me. The help was, I had to pay up a huge sum of money so as not to get thrown out. At that stage I was working here in the museum. I tried to come to some arrangement with the landlord but he wasn't having any of it. He wanted the money up front and I owed him a lot. I couldn't pay it all. I could, as I did, pay the lawyers, but I couldn't pay the landlord all I owed because it was a horrible figure. I finally made an arrangement to pay it over a time and I'm still paying it. You feel as if you are drowning.

You have to put up with a lot from people, especially people with money. ... On Christmas Eve last year I had a serious run-in with one of them, one of the millionaires who donates a great deal of money to the museum, because I said we could not accept responsibility for fur coats in the cloakroom. And he had a girl with a fur coat. I just said no. It was a regulation of the museum that we could not take fur coats. He slowly began to sort of insult me. Then in the end he was extremely rude. He said, "—— you." So then it transpired that I, who did nothing, didn't say a word, ended up with a final warning letter, and the boss himself said it was because he was a trustee, a millionaire who donated money. He didn't want to tell me the whole story, but they used me as a scapegoat. Because [the millionaire] had said, "I'm going to do everything in my power to get you fired." And I didn't say a word, because I have witnesses. And then, in order to accuse me of something or have some grounds, the boss said that I had responded by saying the same to him, "—— you." Which is not true, because everyone you just saw here was around me. They heard everything. They saw everything and they said I never said anything. Then our boss said to me, "Right. If you get me a letter from each of them saying that you said nothing insulting, that you said nothing to him, everything will be sorted out." I got three letters from the girls who were around. "No, he never said a word at any time. We were present." And about four days later I get the final warning letter. And when you get a final warning it means if you get one more, or there's another incident, they fire you.

I'm still in that situation. I'm in the process of fighting it through the union, since we pay for it. So I'm working at trying to get the notice rescinded through the union. It's not that you just have the final warning, but if at some future date I try to get another job, that will go against me.

Santana was asked: Would you like to go back to Cuba for good?

I don't know. I say that not for me, but I don't know how people would accept me if I went back for good. I feel as if I have committed a crime, having gone and left my family, my friends, the places I love so much. My country. I think I would always feel as if I had committed a crime, as if I had been in jail, and although I would have repaid my crime there'd always be the feeling that I had committed it.

As I was saying, I've been a writer for a long time. One of the things I'd like to do is write about all this. About the part in Cuba before I left, the journey, what's happened since I've been here. Because the Americans always talk about the American Dream, and I want to do a kind of story or article called My Not So American Dream. Because it's just really arrive, work, live, let live, but at the same time it's got nothing to do with that dream about the house and the car, which all seems so strange to me, so hard to swallow. It's like a pill that, I don't know ... It all seems so absurd—the house, then the couple with the two children, the boy and the girl. The children always seem to be a boy and a girl, the dog, the car in the garage and the big house and the big job. I don't know. I think life is something bigger, something more beautiful. ❖

Guillén: Cuban poet Nicolás Guillén
Batista: Fulgencio Batista, the Cuban dictator overthrown by the Cuban Revolution in 1959

Miguelina Sosa

Miguelina Sosa was interviewed by Ruth Glasser on February 23, 1996, in New York City. Translation from the Spanish by Catherine Sunshine.

I was born in 1955 in the Dominican Republic, in a small village called Esperanza—that means "hope." I was the oldest of eight, so I had to spend much of my time taking care of my brothers and sisters.

My father and mother were farmers. They grew a bit of everything—tobacco, cassava, plantains, pigeon peas—and also raised livestock. That kind of life was better back then than it is now. Nowadays it's not easy to make a living working the land. So people prefer to move to the city, or to emigrate.

My mother's oldest son by her first marriage had moved to New York, and he bought a house for her in Santo Domingo. He sent back money regularly, too. We moved to the capital and I finished eleventh grade.

When I was 20 we emigrated to New York—my mother, one brother, one sister and me. The older brother who was already here petitioned to bring us in. We lived in his house in the Bronx. Since I was too old to attend high school, I studied and got my GED degree. We all had to work—my brother was supporting us, plus there were five more brothers and sisters back in the Dominican Republic who needed assistance. My other brother and I got jobs in an electronics factory in Queens and worked there for five years. But then the factory closed. The company went out of business or maybe moved to Japan, I don't know precisely.

By that time I had married a Dominican man who worked as a carpenter for a company in New Jersey. We had two small children. While I was out on leave after the second birth, my husband became critically ill with kidney disease.

When he came home from the hospital I had three people to take care of: my sick husband, a newborn, and a three-year-old. There was no way I could leave the house to go out to work. My husband eventually received disability benefits, and we got food stamps, welfare and Medicaid for the children. He had to have dialysis three times a week. I learned to give his medicines and prepare a special diet.

Eventually he had a kidney transplant, and after that he went back to work. Soon, though, he lost the kidney through rejection and had other serious complications. Luckily, he was able to receive another transplant

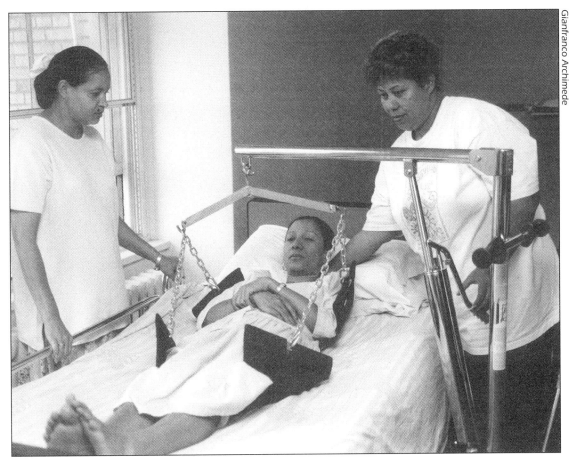

Miguelina Sosa (left) observing two trainees during a session at Cooperative Home Care Associates. The trainees are being evaluated on their ability to use a Hoyer lift, a device to move patients from bed to wheelchair.

which was successful. But the doctor said he couldn't work any longer. He wants to but he can't, so he's retired.

I stayed home until my younger child was in kindergarten. Then I got to thinking, and I said to my husband: "Suppose I were to look for a job; you could pick up the children from school." And we came to an agreement. We were concerned about what kind of example we were setting for our children. They needed to see their parents working, at least one of us, to learn the importance of work.

I began looking for a job, but without success. I went to offices, factories and stores. I even went back to school and completed courses in English and business, but my English still wasn't good enough for a business-related job.

Since I had so much experience taking care of others, I began applying for positions as a home attendant. By chance I wound up at Cooperative

Home Care, a worker-owned firm in the Bronx that employs home health aides. A home health aide is different from a home attendant. An attendant cleans the house, while a home health aide cares for the sick person directly.

I didn't think I was going to pass the training course. I've always been somewhat shy, and most of the other students had much better English than mine. My self-esteem was low. But when I took the examination, I passed with an 89! Another student who was born here got only 70-something. When I realized that, it encouraged me tremendously. Now I realize that differences in education between the trainees had something to do with it. I had completed high school, and even though most of my schooling was in Spanish, what I had learned about the structure of language helped me organize my words in English.

My first patient was a woman who had asthma and used a portable pump. The situation wasn't quite what I expected. The woman's apartment was a mess—she had two dogs—and I spent most of the time helping her cook for her grandchildren. My next assignment was a woman with emphysema who used an oxygen tank. I had to give her sponge baths, cook for her, do the laundry. I went with her to the hospital many times.

Little by little I became experienced. One of the most delicate aspects of the job is that you can't get involved in family disputes in the client's household. One difficult case was a 92-year-old Puerto Rican woman. She had two sons and a married granddaughter who were always arguing with her. Whenever she became angry with them, she took it out on me, and she could be quite nasty. Then one day, as I was on my knees scrubbing the tub, I saw her staring at me. "You do everything for me," she said. "Without you I wouldn't be here. And I treat you so badly." We sat down and talked for a long time, and things were much easier after that. I stayed with her until she died, a year later.

Becoming an instructor

After three and a half years working as a home health aide, I was asked to train to become an assistant instructor. At first I said no because of my shyness, my problems with English. But my husband encouraged me and the staff encouraged me, and finally I gave in and took the training course.

As an instructor, I give demonstrations and check to see whether the trainees are doing the procedures correctly. Teaching adults requires special skill. If a trainee is doing something incorrectly, you have to tell her in a way that isn't a put-down, but helps her to improve. You can't treat the person like a child. She is an adult like you, only she is learning something new to her.

Some of the trainees lack confidence. Sometimes they need to hear someone say, "You can do it." They relax when I tell them that I'm a home health aide, that I did the same training and took care of patients, and I probably will again.

When I came to Cooperative Home Care, my life changed for the better, and not only because I began working and earning money. Also because I've learned so much from the people I've cared for ... You learn how to care for different illnesses and about people of all backgrounds. Almost all of the clients are older and have had many experiences, and they can teach you about life.

Now that I'm a trainer, I'm earning more money and learning things I never imagined I would learn, such as computer skills. I prepare my own lectures and demonstrations, with help from the training staff. I believe in myself much more than before.

Sometimes when I have to work late, my children don't understand; they want me to be home at five o'clock. But they've gotten used to it. Sometimes I cook the family's dinner in the morning before work and set it aside for them, or I might cook enough for two days in a row. Or my husband cooks; we share like that. He understands the situation because we have good communication between us, always have had.

To succeed in this work you have to have two things: patience and a desire to help. You have to have something inside to give. If you don't have plenty of patience and a little love, you won't get anywhere. ❖

Shukdeo Sankar

Shukdeo Sankar was interviewed by Catherine Sunshine on August 9, 1996 in Washington, D.C. In 1997 Dr. Sankar became a hospital-based internist in infectious disease at Washington Hospital Center.

In 1963, my birth year, most people in Guyana were born at home. I was born in my grandmother's house in a village called Clonbrook, about six miles from my family's home. It's said that if your navel string, that's your umbilical cord, is buried somewhere, you always have to go back to that place. So my navel string is buried in Clonbrook, Guyana.

My great-grandparents on my mother's side came to Guyana from India. They came in the 1870s or 1880s, along with thousands of others, to work in the sugar-cane fields. My father's father also came from India. His mother was born in Guyana.

My father worked for the government in "sea defense." Most people in Guyana live along the coast, where the land is six or seven feet below sea level. The Dutch colonized Guyana first, and they built a series of dykes to keep the water back, much as they did in the Netherlands. My father helped maintain the dykes, fighting a constant battle against the high tide.

Unlike most people of his time, my father had had the opportunity to study. His parents raised cattle and were not rich, but they valued education. They had put aside a fund for my father to go to college. But he didn't fulfill his parents' dreams: although he's a very intelligent person, he doesn't have any paper certificates. And since he didn't do it, we, his children, *had* to do it. He took extreme pains to ensure that we would go to school and do well.

The government of Guyana at that time mainly gave scholarships to supporters of the ruling party. That did not include my family. However, if you were clearly outstanding you had a chance anyway. When I was 16, I won a scholarship from the government to study medicine.

As a teenager I had grand ideas. I remember thinking "I have outgrown this small village and I'm ready to see the world." Although my hometown is ten or twelve miles from the capital, it's considered rural. It's the kind of place where nobody ever went to university, or even went very far from home.

I went to medical school at the University of the West Indies in Jamaica. At first, when I got the scholarship to go to Jamaica, in my mind it was an A-minus. It wasn't an A, because if you had an A you would go to England. Jamaica was just short of the greatest, I thought. However, within six months I realized that it *was* the greatest. The University of the West Indies is sometimes misperceived as "one of those offshore medical schools." But it's far from it. It started as a college of the University of London, and today it's a highly regarded independent university serving the whole Caribbean.

I graduated from medical school in 1986 at age 22 and chose Trinidad to do my internship. Since the University of the West Indies is a regional institution, you can do your internship in Barbados, Trinidad, Jamaica, or the Bahamas.

After completing my internship I wanted advanced training in a specialty. I came to Howard University in Washington, D.C., and did three years of residency in internal medicine.

Stereotypes of immigrants

I think people who choose to come to America are a special group. If you're an immigrant, there's a stereotype that you jumped over the border and turned up here without a shirt on your back. And that's a very big injustice, because many immigrants have left good lives. I was actually better off financially before I came to the United States. My internship and medical officer post in Trinidad were well paid. But after I came here I was suddenly counting every dollar, because my resident's salary of $1,500 a month didn't go far in the expensive Washington area.

When I came to the States, I didn't realize how foreign medical graduates are thought of here. You can't really blame people for holding stereotypes, yet it's unfair. Foreign medical graduates are a very diverse group. There are some who are excellent and some who are not. There is no single standard.

There's a myth that a U.S. medical education is automatically the best. But I think our training at University of the West Indies was superior in a number of ways. We spend five years in medical school as opposed to four. Furthermore, it's harder to get into medical school in the Caribbean than here: there are just 100 slots for a population of five million. So it's extremely competitive.

Howard had had medical residents from the University of the West Indies before, and they had done exceptionally well. In my year, nine of the 26 medical residents were from the Caribbean. When we took our board examinations in internal medicine, the scores of the West Indian students were far above the national average.

After I finished at Howard, I spent two years at Georgetown University specializing in infectious diseases. I became board-certified in internal medicine and infectious diseases, and started looking for a job.

Like many foreign physicians, I was on a "J" visa. It's like an agreement that you're coming here to train, but when you're done you'll go back to your country. You have to spend at least two years in your home country, and then you can reapply to work in the United States.

My fiancee from Trinidad had come up to join me, and we got married in 1991. She's a nurse, and because that profession was in demand she was able to become a legal permanent resident of the United States. Normally, if you are the spouse of a permanent resident you can get permission to stay in the United States, but that does not apply if you are on a J visa.

There is one way to get a waiver, however. The U.S. government keeps a list of "under-served areas," neglected areas of the United States that really need doctors. If you agree to work in one of these places for two or three years, the immigration service will let you stay.

Serving the inner city

Big metropolitan areas have plenty of doctors. Rural areas don't. And within the cities, there are specific areas that don't have enough doctors—usually the poorest parts of the inner city. Many doctors don't want to go into these neighborhoods, and the patients don't usually have much money. So that's where you often find foreign medical graduates.

When you work in a neglected rural or inner-city area, you are doing some good. At the same time, it provides you a way to remain in this country. So there are benefits on both sides.

My life was getting serious. We had a daughter in 1994 and we had to make a decision about where to settle as a family. We decided that we wanted to stay in the United States, preferably in the Washington area. That's how I ended up at Whitman Walker Clinic taking care of AIDS patients.

When I applied for this job I was not an AIDS doctor, I was an infectious disease doctor. The field of infectious disease is vast; AIDS is a small part of the spectrum. But nowadays if you are an infectious disease doctor, working in a big city hospital in this country, 70 percent of what you do is AIDS. I had experience working with AIDS patients at Georgetown and I was comfortable with it.

Not many people want to work with AIDS patients anymore. Once upon a time, people wanted to work with HIV infection because HIV was a gay white disease. It isn't any more; increasingly, it's the destitute who suffer from AIDS. So volunteers and physicians interested in the disease are becoming scarce. What's more, the salaries offered by a nonprofit organization like this one are low. Most doctors can make twice as much elsewhere.

The main Whitman Walker clinic is in northwest Washington, but it has a satellite clinic in a very rundown area of southeast D.C. In 1994, when I started, this clinic was a room in a church basement. It had previously had a part-time nurse practitioner, who had since resigned; there was no doctor. I began treating patients there and we later built it into an active clinic, with a full-time nurse and secretary and more than 150 patients, in a building that has now been renovated.

I enjoy working there. I know all the patients by their first names. But the neighborhood is rough. There's drug and alcohol abuse. Violence is close by. We have problems in terms of compliance—people not keeping appointments, not having 50 cents for the Medicaid co-pay on a prescription, that kind of thing. I know what treatments to give, but many patients can't get the medications. You have to beg drug samples from here and there. It's frustrating.

This is a very uneven society. It's the land of dreams for immigrants, but it's the land of nightmares for many people who grew up here.

It's always satisfying to help people. But AIDS is difficult to work with. The long and short of it is that many people die. And if you care about the patients ... you try not to take it to heart, but it can bother you. And their cases are complicated; they have all kinds of problems. For each person you're a doctor, a psychologist, a counselor and a helper. At the end of the day, you're drained.

I will always be West Indian

I think you can make a difference wherever you are. It would give me greater joy, if that's possible, to help people back home in the Caribbean. But there are obstacles. In Guyana, for instance, the only medications they have are basic antibiotics like tetracycline and ampicillin; there isn't much else. I couldn't be effective in an environment like that. And even in a small place it can be hard to break in. Five guys run the hospital, they've been there for the last 40 years. You're an American-trained outsider, and you're not necessarily welcome.

I think deep down I will always be West Indian. Most of my dreams and fantasies are there. During my residency and fellowship I had little time for outside interests, but recently I've been doing more to connect with the West Indian community here in Washington. I found the Guyana Web site on the Internet so I can get news from Guyana.

One of my passions is cricket. It's more than a sport for us. This year I rejoined the Metro Cricket Club, which is one of maybe 18 clubs in the Washington Cricket League. I don't play extremely well, but I guess it's in my blood. My wife dislikes the game—the players are all men, and one match lasts all day!

I'm Hindu, and recently I took my daughter to a little temple in someone's garage in Maryland. I don't know what she's going to become, but I want her to have a frame of reference. It's family, culture, religion, all put together that forms the person.

I do go back to the Caribbean every now and then; my parents and some of my sisters still live there. I would like to become more actively involved with Caribbean concerns. But I'm also in a phase of life where I'm building a career and setting down roots. I have a wife and a daughter, and another baby coming in November. It's fine to want to do all the ideal things, but you also have to take one day at a time. And you have responsibilities and you have commitments. ❖

Lina and Efraín De Jesús

Lina and Efraín De Jesús were interviewed by Ruth Glasser on November 1, 1995 in Wallingford, Connecticut. Translation from the Spanish by Catherine Sunshine. Portions of this interview appear in Glasser, AQUÍ ME QUEDO: PUERTO RICANS IN CONNECTICUT (Connecticut Humanities Council, 1997).

Efraín: I was born in Utuado, a mountain town in central Puerto Rico. My wife, Lina, was born in New York, but she was taken to Puerto Rico when she was two years old and grew up there. We got married in Utuado in 1941.

I never had any intention of coming to the United States. I was a carpenter, and for almost five years I worked at Roosevelt Roads, the huge U.S. naval base located at Ceiba, Puerto Rico. One of my brothers had been in the U.S. Army, and when he got out of the army he came to Ceiba. He persuaded me to move to New York, along with my sister and mother.

When I arrived in New York for the first time in 1946, I wanted to turn around and go back to Puerto Rico. It was a tremendous shock. But little by little I got used to it, and eventually I came to love New York. I worked in factories that made furniture. At that time there were plenty of jobs.

Lina: When we came from Puerto Rico I was 18, with two small children. I began working in a clothing factory on 38th Street. My mother-in-law lived with us and took care of the children while we worked. At first I was cutting threads from garments. After a while they gave me other tasks, so little by little I learned to sew. It didn't pay much. Later I found better jobs in other garment firms, and I learned how to make a complete suit.

Efraín: Our street in the Bronx was nice at first, but after a while it started to go downhill. We had visited Wallingford, Connecticut, in 1951 because I had a nephew working here. My wife really liked the town. So when things began to deteriorate in the Bronx, we decided to move to Wallingford.

Again, it was a difficult change for me. I love sports, especially baseball and boxing. In New York there are so many rings I could go to a boxing match two or three times a week. Movie theaters too, are plentiful there. Moving to a town with one little theater was an adjustment. But again I adapted.

We came to Wallingford on September 7, 1953, and on September 9 I began working for the American Cyanamid Company, which made plastics. At that time Wallingford had many big factories: International Silver, Revere, and others. There were plenty of jobs to be had. The language wasn't a problem; if you didn't know English it didn't matter.

Lina and Efraín De Jesús

Lina: We suffered when we couldn't find an apartment. Because we seemed different, racially and culturally, it was difficult to get housing. Plus, no one wanted to rent to a family with children. We couldn't buy a house because we had no credit yet. To rent an apartment we had to accept the very worst that was available, what nobody else wanted.

Efraín: They wouldn't rent to Puerto Ricans. We went to see an apartment that had been advertised in the newspaper. I was just parking the car when the owner of the house rushed out and said "It's already rented!" That wasn't true, as we found out later. Our daughter had a similar experience many years later when she tried to rent an apartment. However, once we moved into an apartment and people got to know us, they accepted us. Then they didn't want us to leave because they saw we were good tenants and neighbors.

Lina: After about a year I was able to establish credit, and we bought a two-family house on Orchard Street. We lived in that house for six years

and then sold it and bought another. We lived there 19 years, then sold that one and bought this house where we live now.

When I came to Wallingford I already knew how to sew, and I belonged to the International Ladies Garment Workers Union. But the factories weren't unionized in Wallingford, and garment work here paid next to nothing.

So I went to work for Eyelet Specialty, making containers for cosmetics. They used chemicals to change plastic and glass into a material that was shiny like metal. As the years went by, I developed breathing problems. The chemicals and paints we used gave me asthma. On Saturdays and Sundays I'd feel well, but on Monday when I went back to work the pains in my chest would start again. They moved me to another department that didn't use paints, where I did assembly work.

I started out at Eyelet earning $1.65 an hour. We had no union. But we worked long hours and they gave us an incentive—the more you worked the more you earned. So unless something happened to slow down production, we earned more than the flat rate of $1.65.

After I'd been there about a year, the steelworkers' union came in. We all joined, because we were sure that we were very underpaid. There was an election, and the union won. After that our pay nearly doubled. The incentive was increased, everything increased, so we could earn up to $30 a day.

Eventually the company began to downsize. The union was demanding more benefits and higher pay, and meanwhile cheap products were coming in from Taiwan. The company claimed it was losing money. Soon it was lay off, lay off and lay off.

I had worked there 19 years, and they let me go just like that. They sold all their machinery to another company, but that company didn't take on the workers. We got severance pay and the factory closed.

Efraín: When we came in 1953, Wallingford was a very small town. There were only a few Hispanics. A group of Spaniards had lived here for years, but they were quite elderly. The Spaniards had their Spanish-American Club, but as the Puerto Ricans began coming in and the Spaniards passed away, the club became more Puerto Rican.

Among the Americans there were many Poles, Hungarians and Italians. They had their own churches and clubs. We socialized mainly with other Spanish-speakers.

In those days we went out often, visiting or doing *parranda,* which is a Puerto Rican Christmas tradition of house-to-house serenading. One summer when we lived in the countryside we had a picnic with *lechón asado,* a roasted whole pig on a spit, and we partied until dawn. We could do that because the houses nearest us were quite far away. We were careful not to disturb the neighbors.

We used to go to church in Meriden because they had a Spanish mass there. In 1972 or 1973 we began a Spanish mass here in Wallingford at Holy Trinity Church. It was a small group at first, and we worked hard to maintain it. It's grown tremendously since then.

Lina: Back then all the stores were along Center Street; there were no shopping centers like the ones you have today. On Friday, which was pay day, you'd see everyone out shopping. I knew everyone who worked with me—most of them were Americans. We'd meet, stop and chat. It was like a big family.

There are many Hispanics here now

Efraín: Today the town of Wallingford has grown immensely. There are many, many Hispanics here now, and we Puerto Ricans have become a minority. The biggest group are the Mexicans. There's a factory here called Connecticut Steel that used to be in Texas and employed only Mexicans. When the company moved the factory to Wallingford they brought along all the workers who wanted to come. So the Mexicans kept coming in, mainly to this factory. There are also Colombians and people from Peru, El Salvador, Guatemala and Panama.

Very few of these people own their homes. It's much harder to buy nowadays. Our first house cost $10,500; they practically gave it away. I know carpentry and plumbing, a little about electricity, and we renovated it completely. When we sold the first house we reinvested the proceeds in the second, and the second into the third. But people who buy houses today, I ask myself how they can possibly pay for it! Thousand-dollar mortgage payments—how can they?

Most of the big factories have closed now. For example, the Stanley Drapery Company, a huge factory that employed over 1,000 workers, closed down. Many people have left Wallingford because all those factories that closed laid off thousands of workers. Some went south, to Florida or Texas, looking for jobs.

I worked at American Cyanamid for 31 years and four days. I retired on September 13, 1984.

Lina: Today most of our social life is through the church. We've made friends in many different parishes through our work with the *cursillos,* which are weekend religious workshops. We're in contact with people in Hartford, New London, Guilford, Willimantic, Waterbury, even as far away as Springfield.

Efraín: We also have friends through the Hispanic community organization here in Wallingford. I'm president of the board of directors and I volunteer there, doing whatever needs to be done. We help people who don't speak much English—help them find a lawyer, a doctor, or a visiting nurse, or go with them to the hospital, to court, to school. We translate documents and answer questions about immigration or Social Security.

Family is also important to us. My family in Puerto Rico is very close-knit, and those of us who came here have kept up that unity. Even our grandchildren, who were born here and hardly speak any Spanish, invite us to their parties and everything.

Lina: Our daughter lives in Meriden with her three younger children; the older two are married. Our oldest granddaughter is the one who has our great-grandchild, and she lives in Maine. We have a son who lives in Maryland. The two younger grandchildren are in college.

Moving from New York to Connecticut was difficult, but I believe it was a change for the better. It allowed us to improve our lives and our children's lives.

Efraín: My dream has always been to go back to Puerto Rico. But I have four grandchildren and she has a great-grandchild. I say *she* has, because I'm too young to have a great-grandchild! If you took her away from them, that would be the end of her. We're content here, we live peacefully, we get along with everybody. Even the cold and snow doesn't bother me, not to say that I like it. Here we are and here we'll stay. ❖

Jean Desir

Jean Desir (a pseudonym) fled Haiti in 1991 after a military coup overthrew the elected government of President Jean-Bertrand Aristide. The military killed hundreds, perhaps thousands of people who had supported Aristide's Lavalas movement. It targeted grassroots groups such as the Peasant Movement of Papaye, of which Jean Desir was a member.

The first time Desir tried to reach the United States, U.S. immigration officials forcibly returned him to Haiti. There he was attacked and beaten by soldiers who threatened his life.

He fled Haiti again. After being picked up and detained at the Guantánamo refugee camp, he was granted provisional asylum in the United States. He has since become a legal permanent resident.

Jean Desir gave this sworn statement to an immigration lawyer on March 23, 1992, while Haiti was still under military rule.

I have fled Haiti twice. I fled in November 1991 after the coup because the military had attacked many of those who belonged to the same peasant organization that I belonged to. I was returned to Haiti by the U.S. Coast Guard on November 20, 1991. After being returned, I was attacked and beaten by the military as an example to others who may want to flee. After being released I hid in the countryside and fled Haiti again on December 2, 1991. I was brought to the United States in mid-January from Guantánamo.

I was born in Bazin, Acul du Nord, Haiti. I attended school but have very little formal education. After school I worked as a fisherman and farmer in Bazin. When Jean-Bertrand Aristide was elected president of Haiti I joined the Mouvement Peyizan Papaye [Peasant Movement of Papaye, or MPP].

Through MPP we worked together to keep the community clean, build restrooms, provide literacy programs for children, and we formed a treasury for those who fell ill. During the months President Aristide was in power, we told the Tontons Macoutes we would welcome them if they would change.

I wasn't involved in politics before Aristide. Only during Aristide's time I saw what benefit people could have with government, then I got involved.

Immediately after the coup, I was involved in a large demonstration in Bazin. We were in the streets screaming "Give us our president back!" and "We won't let this happen again!" and "Macoutes give us a chance!" There were so many in the streets I would have been unable to count them all. While we were in the streets we heard on the radio that people were being shot in the streets. The radio station told us to stay off the streets. We all fled.

After we fled, I know that the military came and arrested some of the MPP members. These people disappeared. Because of this treatment we couldn't bring the sick and injured to the hospital because we would have been caught. The military was working to track us down, so I went into hiding in the bush.

While I was hiding from the military, who were running after us, I broke my leg. This was on the day after the coup, I believe. I could hear the soldiers shooting at us. Because no one could take me to the hospital for fear of being caught, I could not get medical attention. And my family was too scared that I could be killed if they took me to a hospital for my broken leg.

After some time in the bush, a group of us decided to leave. There were about 115 of us on our boat. Some friends carried me to the boat and we sailed away from Haiti.

Picked up by the Coast Guard

After a short time we were picked up by the U.S. Coast Guard. I was held on the Coast Guard boat and asked questions about why I left Haiti. They didn't spend much time questioning me. They didn't ask me the important questions I wanted to address. The people questioning me didn't identify themselves. There was a white person doing the interviewing and a Haitian doing the interpreting. I was afraid during the interview because they didn't ask me those important questions and I was afraid they were going to return me to Haiti.

They asked me about my house, where I lived, my mother's name, where she lived, where I was born, that kind of thing, and then why I left Haiti. To the question of why did I leave Haiti, I said I left Haiti because of political problems. I told them how dangerous it was for people like me there in Haiti and how my leg got broken fleeing from the military. I wanted to tell them more details, for example about what political groups I was a member of and why politics caused me to leave Haiti and why I was not able to go back now. I was cut off by this man interviewing me or by the Haitian interpreter, I don't recall which, from telling these things. Before the interview I had not had much to eat and I was weak and not feeling well. I was also tired and my leg was hurting. I was only taken off the Coast Guard boat to have a cast put on my broken leg. I was then returned to Haiti.

At Port-au-Prince upon my return I was asked questions by the Red Cross and given $10 for bus fare. The Red Cross also made me sign something but they didn't tell me what I was signing so I don't know. Because I had a broken leg, a Red Cross van drove me from the boat terminal in Port-au-Prince to a bus station.

When I was in the Red Cross van, before the van started moving from the dock area, a group of soldiers was lined up outside the van. They sent one of the soldiers to the van and he asked me a number of questions: my mother's name, my father's name, where I lived, my age, and how I broke my leg. I lied about how I broke my leg, told the soldier that it happened before the coup, but I told him the truth about the other questions because I didn't know whether they returned me to Haiti with my file—which had my real name, address, etc.

I was afraid and felt the situation didn't make sense because I was photographed many times when I got off the Coast Guard boat in Haiti at the port. And I didn't know who the photographers were, whether they were the Tontons Macoutes or the government. I think maybe some journalists took pictures of us too, when we got off the boat, but I was afraid of the Macoutes taking my picture, not of the journalists. I was afraid the Macoutes were taking my picture because once they knew I was in the struggle they would come to my house to kill me.

The Red Cross then dropped me off at the bus station. Because I would have needed $18 to travel to my family's house in Cap Haitien and the Red Cross only gave me $10, I could only travel to my cousin's house in Cité Soleil. He gave me food and money. After I ate at my cousin's house, I left on foot to get transportation to my mother's home in Bazin which is in Cap Haitien.

Seized by soldiers

Shortly after I left my cousin's house, I was stopped by a group of soldiers. This was still in Cité Soleil. I hadn't walked very far because my leg was in a cast and I was limping. These soldiers were in blue uniforms and they were carrying guns: small pistols were attached to their belts and some had long guns too. I think maybe they belonged to a section of the military called the Cafeteria.

These soldiers asked me who I supported in the election. I lied and told them that I had supported Marc Bazin. Then they asked me why I left Haiti. I lied again and told them that Lavalas members had broken my leg. They did not believe me. They made me walk on my broken leg to a house where they detained me.

Once I was in this house, the soldiers ordered me to lie flat on the floor, on my stomach. Then they hit me with a stick on my behind on my left side, the same side as my broken leg. They hit me I'm sure at least 15 times. But I never changed my story.

I was out of myself with pain from the beating. The soldiers were saying to me "You're going to have to tell us the truth." I knew if I told them the truth about my political involvement I would be killed. I pretended I didn't know anything about Lavalas, that I hated that group. The soldiers kept me in that house for a while, long enough to beat me.

After they beat me, before the soldiers let me go, they told me that they could hurt me more but would not because they wanted people to see me and for me to tell others what can happen to Haitians who take boats and leave Haiti. They told me that they wanted me to be an example to others so they do not try to escape Haiti. One soldier told me, "Those of you who are leaving, you are causing trouble to Haiti."

The soldiers told me that the military was willing to counter these people with measures, that people who left the country like me could be arrested, beaten, killed and their bodies disposed of outside of anybody's awareness. The soldiers also said about the Haitians who left by boat, "You people have weapons and you're part of a group of Macoutes that Aristide hired, the same way Duvalier had." But we don't have weapons and all we want is fairness and justice and no more terrorizing of the people.

These soldiers may have followed me from the dock to my cousin's house, I don't know. I wouldn't be able to recognize the soldiers because you don't look soldiers straight in the face in Haiti.

After I was released from the house, I used some of the money my cousin gave me to go to Gonaives and then on to Cap Haitien. When I arrived in Cap Haitien, my mother and the people in my neighborhood told me that I could not go home because the military had been by my home regularly to try to find me.

So my friends hid me in the countryside and would come to check on me. I stayed in hiding and my mother would sometimes visit me at night to sneak me food. She told me on one of her visits that the military had searched my house and told me to leave Haiti and never to return while these military people were there. My mother was very upset.

At this point my friends found me another boat and I fled again on December 2, 1991. On December 3, I was picked up by the U.S. Coast Guard.

At the Guantánamo refugee camp

This time I was taken to Guantánamo where I explained that this was the second time I had fled Haiti. I was very scared and shaken up; I was afraid that I would be sent back automatically, since immigration officials did not believe me the first time I left Haiti.

But the second time I was interviewed I was asked many more questions and I had the opportunity to say much more about why I left Haiti again. I didn't get interviewed the same day the Coast Guard picked us up. I know I had slept and showered before they questioned me. Also I was questioned not on the boat, but on land.

But I was still very worried because I knew what had happened the first time and they still sent me back to Haiti and I was afraid they would do that again. I knew that my photographs had been seen in Haiti and that I would die if they sent me back. But this time it was a much, much, much longer interview. I told the persons questioning me what happened when I was returned to Haiti and how they were angry with people like me who had left the country.

A friend that I met at the hospital on Guantánamo, Pierre, gave me a newspaper article in which I was pictured being carried by two individuals back to the Haitian authorities. This was when I was first sent back to Haiti after the coup [the photo appeared in *The New York Times* on November 21, 1991—ed.]. But some in the military at Guantánamo didn't seem to want the information I was giving. For example, when I received the newspaper with my picture I wanted to give it to the Immigration. But there was a military officer, a major I think, in charge of the camp who grabbed the newspaper photo away from me and placed me in a small uncovered detention pen behind barbed wire. The major told me my signature was on this paper and I couldn't have it. I was out in the sun for about three hours until the major came back and touched my head to see how hot I was. When he realized how hot I was he released me.

I had family members who were also in Guantánamo but I wasn't allowed to go see them. I thought I wasn't allowed visiting rights by the military because they had the photograph of me in the newspaper and they knew I wanted to send the photo and letter to Immigration. I had written a letter in French to give to Immigration and handed it to a reporter so he would take it to Immigration. I made sure no soldiers saw me when I did that. I was afraid of the soldiers for two reasons: first, I was obsessed with seeing soldiers in Haiti and that brings you fear and terror because you feel you are about to live through the same thing again; and second, I thought they would turn me back to Haiti again.

Right now, I have three cousins who were in the MPP with me, hiding in the countryside in Haiti because they are afraid they will be killed by the military. I am certain that if I am returned to Haiti again, I will be recognized and killed. I would rather take my own life than be returned to a certain death.

There is no safe area in Haiti for me to return to. I was photographed several times after my return in Port-au-Prince and I'm sure I'd be killed.

It wasn't my idea to come back here, to leave Haiti. But because I was sent back to Haiti the first time, I had to leave again. As long as we have the kind of regime we have in Haiti now I can't go back. The army would have to be under control and the constitutional rights of the people respected. ❖

Guantánamo: The U.S. naval base at Guantánamo Bay, Cuba, where Haitian and Cuban refugees were sheltered.

María Elena and Claire Alonso

María Elena and Claire Alonso were interviewed by Ruth Glasser on April 6, 1997, in Stamford, Connecticut. Portions of the interview were translated from the Spanish by Catherine Sunshine.

María Elena: I came from Cuba in 1970, when I was 22. I came with *los vuelos de la libertad,* the freedom flights, which went directly from Havana to Miami. I left Cuba because of Fidel and the government there. But I always wanted to come to the United States anyway, even before Fidel. When I was little, an aunt of mine lived here. She sent me photos, showing that life was better here than in Cuba.

When Fidel came I was in seventh grade. After ninth grade, I had to leave school because I had problems with the Young Communists. They wanted you to say something was one color, and you knew it was another color. No one could persuade me to embrace communism, so I decided to leave school.

I got married and had a son, Gerardo. Before I could leave Cuba, I had to spend three or four months in the countryside doing voluntary work. Afterward they gave me permission to go. I left my mother and father and sister behind, and came here with my son of eight months. I was supposed to wait for my husband, who would be able to emigrate a few years later. But I eventually divorced him because he never came and meanwhile he had another woman over there, you know how it is.

I arrived in Miami at the Casa de la Libertad. The next day they put me on a plane for New York. I went to live with my aunt in Manhattan.

I had never worked in Cuba. And when I came to the United States I didn't work either, because I had a young child. I never wanted to leave any of my children with a babysitter, never! Instead, I went on welfare. But within a couple of years I met my present husband, José Manuel Alonso. He had immigrated from Spain the same year I came from Cuba.

After we married, I left welfare. My husband worked as a handyman in the building on 93rd Street where we lived. We had an apartment that we furnished beautifully. We got into debt doing it, because when you get married you have to buy everything new, living room set, dining room set, everything.

The year or so that I lived in that building, I didn't like the way the Hispanics there behaved. My husband is the type of person who always says "Hi! How are you?" and so forth. But I'm not like that. The women would see my husband and shout "Hey José, *¡galleguito! ¡Estas gordito!*" or whatever. That kind of thing got to me because I was always very jealous.

Luckily he received a job offer here in Connecticut, to be the building superintendent at Knot Hill Condominiums in Bridgeport. We moved in 1975, the year my first daughter Claribel was born. Four years later, after my second daughter María del Carmen was born, we moved from Bridgeport to Stamford. We've been here 18 years.

Compared to New York, I love Connecticut. I don't deny that New York is pretty at night, when you can see the Hudson River and all the tall buildings and everything. It's impressive. But there were other things I didn't like about New York.

Claire: My name is Claribel Alonso, but I prefer Claire because it's shorter. Although my mother is Cuban and my father is from Spain, I basically grew up like a white person, like an Anglo, I don't know the proper term. My parents didn't emphasize my roots. They put me in a private school that was primarily white. There were almost no minorities, no Spanish—that is, Hispanics.

María Elena: I can't really explain to you our thinking. But my son had an experience at the public school here, when he started seventh grade. The first day of school he was wearing his gold neck chain, and this boy of 11 or so ripped off his chain. When my husband heard about this he said forget it. Our kids are not going to this school, nor to any public school. We sent them to the most expensive private school in Stamford, on a partial scholarship.

Claire: I could have gone to Stamford High or any public school, and still gotten into college. But my parents thought if you go to Stamford High, you'll cut class and get in with the bad kids. Little did they know: a lot of bad things went on at that private school, but you didn't see it because the kids were all rich. I could have gotten mixed up with the bad kids there. It's just a choice that you make.

When I was in high school, one of my best friends was black and one was Spanish. My parents didn't like that. But I didn't like the fact that I could count the minorities on the fingers of both hands. It was disgusting! I wasn't white; the white guys liked the white girls; so what was left? Ten guys in the whole school. Dating was just

ridiculous. I'd like a white guy, but oh, I'm not white and ... like I'm over here.

At the University of Connecticut, I started making more Hispanic and black friends. So many of my friends were *so* into their roots. They'd ask me something and I'd be like, huh? Salsa, merengue? Oh I can't dance that to save my life! And I felt ashamed that my parents raised me with no roots, with no background.

María Elena: Just a minute. Since my girls were born, I have *always* spoken to them in Spanish. I wanted them to learn to speak it. But they refuse to answer me in Spanish! They always answer in English. Nothing can convince them to speak Spanish, although they understand it perfectly.

Claire: I've been taking Spanish since I was in seventh grade. I *can* speak it. I just don't speak it at home. It's easier for me to speak English, so I speak English. But she thinks I don't know a word of Spanish.

María Elena: Yesterday I was telling her, speak Spanish! But she doesn't want to!

Claire: I don't know, I don't feel comfortable speaking it. I have a fine Spanish accent, but I feel like people realize I don't speak it often, you know? I can't speak fast. So I'd just rather speak English.

My second cousin lives in New York. Her mom raised her listening to salsa and merengue, and she talks Spanish 24-7, to her parents at least. She's more in tune with her Spanish.

María Elena: That's because she lives in New York. Where we live it's more Italian, more Jewish; you see a few Hispanics.

Claire: Since my parents are in America, they kind of left their Spanish behind. I don't know much about Cuba and Spain because they never taught me. My mother hasn't been back to Cuba since 1970, and I've never been. Granted, they had their reasons.

María Elena: When Fidel is finished in Cuba, then we'll go to Cuba and you will see Cuba. But for the moment, forget Cuba!

Claire: My mom does cook Spanish food. She seasons it in a certain style.

María Elena: Oh yes, I cook white rice, black beans, roast pork, steak, fried bananas. *Arroz con pollo, arroz congris*—rice with red beans or black beans. But on Thanksgiving I stuff a turkey, the same as all Americans. We live here like we are American, absolutely.

Apart from the food, I don't preserve many traditions from Cuba. If I lived in Florida, it would be a different story. There it's easier to get Cuban things.

I don't have many Hispanic friends. When my youngest daughter began kindergarten I took my first job, working part-time at Caldor. I later worked at J.C.Penney for seven years, and I was one of their best saleswomen. I met Cubans and other Hispanics who came into the store, and we would chat, but not for me to visit them or them to visit me.

Now I'm here at home. I sometimes work as a babysitter, and I help my husband when he has to get a vacant apartment ready for the next tenant.

My children will know Spanish

Claire: If I have children, I'd definitely like to pass on more Spanishness to them. They're going to know Spanish. I'm going to tell them more about Cuba and Spain, slowly put them in salsa and merengue and all those wonderful kinds of music, so that when they meet Spanish friends, they'll be on the same level.

I really wouldn't want to change anything in terms of how my parents raised me. I love my parents, they're good. I liked how my mom taught us certain morals and values. It's just that when I have my kids, things are going to be different from a cultural point of view.

María Elena: I love my life here. I love this country, and I've already become an American citizen. I also hope in the future we can go to my country with my daughters and they will like it.

In Cuba you can't speak freely. That's why I've never gone back to Cuba, because they follow you to hear if you say anything bad about the government. I left school because I refused to go along with that. But my sister stayed in school and became a doctor. She knew how to say yes, even though she didn't really agree, you know. She graduated, went to university and became a doctor, all in Cuba.

I wanted to be a meteorologist. Oh, I love the weather! Do you know what I used to do in Cuba when a hurricane was coming? On a sheet of paper I would put down all the parallels, the meridians, the degrees, and I could draw you a map of the Antilles and tell you everything about the

hurricane. If I had stayed in Cuba I would have been a meteorologist.

I stay in touch with my family. We talk on the telephone, and write. My mother has come to visit three times, and my sister has also come. They left here with four suitcases of clothes as well as big packages. I've also sent goods and money to my family there.

As far as going back to Cuba, I'll never go until Fidel falls. I would go back after that, but only to visit. And only if things are fixed up afterwards. Because Cuba has been totally ruined. When Fidel goes, right away the Americans, or rather, Cuban-Americans, will go start up businesses there. They have everything ready, they're just waiting for Fidel to fall. Then yes, I want to go with my girls and with José Manuel so they can see Cuba, how beautiful it is.

Claire: I'm a senior now, and a Latin American Studies major. I switched to that last year. I started out in sports medicine, then I wanted to do international business, and in my junior year I wanted to do business Spanish. I was doing fine with that, but I felt I could do better if it was something I enjoyed more. I ended up taking a class in Latin American Studies that had to do with the Caribbean, and I did well in it and I liked it.

So that's my major now, and I love it. It's history and political science, about Guatemala and Nicaragua and other Latin American countries, and I'm fascinated by it.

María Elena: I don't know if I've brought up my children wrongly, given that I haven't passed on much Hispanic culture to them. But I think that's something they have to decide for themselves, rather than having me impose it. They know what is American and what is Hispanic. They're the ones who have to decide which they really want to be. ❖

Casa de la Libertad: "Freedom House," a reception center for Cuban refugees
galleguito: nickname for an immigrant from Spain
salsa: music developed in New York by musicians of various Latin American and Caribbean backgrounds
merengue: popular dance music of the Dominican Republic

George Hudson

During World War II, there was a great demand for tobacco products to supply the American soldiers fighting overseas. The health hazards of smoking were not yet widely known, and "keeping the boys in smokes" was deemed essential to winning the war.

Almost all able-bodied American men had been drafted to serve in the armed forces or work in defense plants. The tobacco industry faced a desperate shortage of workers. In a special project, the U.S. government arranged with the government of Jamaica to recruit Jamaican men to work on farms in the United States.

Thousands signed up, eager to earn money and contribute to the war effort. One was George Hudson, age 24. With many others, he was sent to work on the rich tobacco farms along the Connecticut River, an area known as "Tobacco Valley."

After the war most of the workers returned to

(continued on next page)

Born in 1919, he was the first of nine children. He grew up on his family's farm in the parish of Saint Catherine, Jamaica.

We never had to work for anyone. The farm was self-supporting. I went to Jubilee Elementary School and finished the eighth grade. My father could not afford for me to go on further, so he sent me to trade school instead. I learned tailoring.

At the time I decided to come to America, we had a big storm in Jamaica. Just about all the plantation was destroyed. Banana, pimento, chocolate, and coffee were all gone. We were able to replant, but that year the war broke out. In May 1943, the Farm Association started recruiting workers for the U.S., and that is when I signed up.

The Jamaican recruits were transported to the United States by the thousands in overcrowded ships that frequently lacked adequate food and drinking water.

After we left Jamaica and were on the ocean, we started taking in water. The boat was almost flooded. They did not have enough food for all the men on the boat, and three days before we landed in Louisiana they said there was no food. There was no food and no water. In the morning you would get a sandwich, and you had to eat half of that sandwich and put the other half in your pocket for the afternoon. In the afternoon you would get a bowl of what they called soup, but we called it hot water. We survived on that for three days. There was no fresh water. Many got sick on that boat.

Some of the men had traveled before to Panama and Cuba, but it was the first voyage for me. When we were up on deck, the boat would be listing so much that water would come in on deck and we could see big sharks in the water. I was not scared. We were all young men and so it was like an adventure.

Florida and Louisiana were the main ports of entry. Holding camps, mostly soldiers' barracks, were used to house the men until they could be sent to their assignments in various parts of the country.

We landed in New Orleans, where it was hotter than fire. We waited for transportation in an army barrack. The ration of food was scarce as usual, but it did not bother us that much. I can remember one thing that happened to me while we were there. One day, I started to walk down the road to look at the place. A policeman came up to me and said, "Boy, where are you going?" I looked at him and said, "I am just walking." He said, "Get back where you belong." So I looked at him very sarcastically and he looked at me nasty, too. I don't know which one of our "looks" was better than the other. Anyway, I turned around and went back, because I did not know the customs and I did not want to cause any trouble.

We boarded the train to the next destination. Some went to Illinois, others to New Jersey or Connecticut. My batch came to Connecticut. I was sent to Broad Brook, Somers.

Arriving in Connecticut in the summer of 1943, the men were sent to their assigned camps. They received $4.50 a day for nine hours' work. One dollar a day was deducted for food and another $1 was deducted by order of the Jamaican government to be sent to the men's families. With $2.50 left, the men were still able to send additional money home to their families.

George Hudson

When we arrived the tobacco seeds were already sown into hotbeds indoors. Some of us were given the job between April and May of transplanting the seedlings to the fields. We would walk behind the plows and as the machines went through we would sow the seedlings. I did not have to do much of that, as I used to sew the nets and run the wires. I was very fast with my hands because I was a trained tailor in Jamaica. The men would also ride behind the three-wheeled tractors, which had seats in the middle. As they went along you would stick the seedlings in the ground.

The dorms were equipped with regular bunk beds and the lifestyle was primitive, but we tried to adapt ourselves to the conditions. We were up from 5:00 A.M. and worked till about 5:00 P.M. We worked mostly six days per week with Sundays off; however, if they were behind in planting and reaping we would work on Sundays. The tobacco crops went through several stages before they were ready for the market—first picking, second picking, third picking, and stripping. Some men fired up the sheds at night for the drying of tobacco.

Connecticut was unfamiliar territory to the men, yet they sometimes ventured out of the camps to attend church, go to a movie, or eat in a restaurant.

Prejudice was there, so we did not go out of our way to experience it. Most of the people [in the area] did not know anything about black people. There were a few American blacks around before we came, but they did not mix in the suburbs too much. There was no television and communication was limited, so many whites never saw a black person before us.

Many of the discrimination barriers were broken down by us. For example, there was a theater called the Strand. They did not want to admit us, but we showed up in force, sometimes 10 to 15 of us, and

Jamaica. But some, like Hudson, remained and became legal permanent residents of the United States. Hudson settled his family in the Hartford area. In 1993, 50 years after coming to Connecticut, he told his story to Jamaican-born author Fay Clarke Johnson, herself a resident of the Tobacco Valley.

This interview is reprinted from Johnson's history of the farmworker program in Connecticut, SOLDIERS OF THE SOIL (Vantage Press). © 1995 by Fay Clarke Johnson. Used by permission of Fay Clarke Johnson and George Hudson.

demanded they let us in. After a while there was no more problem in us going to any theater. ... The people were also aware that we were here working for the government and our behavior was also commendable.

The restaurants were the same thing. I did not experience this, but I heard that in the bars, when you went in to have a drink, the bartenders would break the glass when you left. The men found out about this and they would go in a restaurant in a busload. They would all order drinks. Each person would order drinks for the group. When the owners found out that they were breaking 40 to 50 glasses a night, they then stopped the practice.

By the close of the tobacco growing season, Connecticut farmers and state officials were full of praise for the Jamaicans' work. The men were credited with saving Connecticut's multimillion-dollar tobacco crop. At farewell ceremonies, it was announced that the Jamaican guest workers would be invited back the next year. The U.S. government also expanded the farmworker program to include workers from other Caribbean islands such as Barbados.

At the end of the season some of the men went back to Jamaica, some went to the South [Florida], and some stayed here during the winter to work in the tobacco warehouse. I stayed and worked.

After the war ended, the official farmworker program came to a close. However, some of the Jamaicans stayed to work for the Connecticut tobacco growers under private contracts. Some, like George Hudson, were able to adjust their status to become permanent residents and later citizens of the United States. They found jobs in factories or on farms, or returned to school. Married and starting families, they faced the challenge of making new lives on their own in Connecticut.

My wife and I lived in a room because back then [in 1951] we could not even get an apartment to rent. The Saint Monica's Episcopal Church family was very good to us. We then moved into Charter Oak Terrace. Each year we

had to fill out forms to stay there and I did not like the kinds of discriminatory questions that were being asked. At that time I was going to school, but I decided that I had to get out of that housing project. I got a part-time job to go along with my full-time job at Pratt and Whitney. I learned to drive, as the family started to expand, and decided that we needed to buy a house.

The first agent I called came to pick me up and when he saw who I was he was so frightened he lit about ten cigarettes in five seconds. He did not even say, "Come." I went in the car and he drove me by the house. He would not even point to the house. I knew what was going on, but I did not say anything. I wanted my family to be safe and not suffer any abuse. I looked for about two years and then I found this house, in this area. I just about made the down payment and the mortgage was passed. When I picked up the check the bank manager said to me, "I will let you hold this because this will be the biggest you will hold in your life." Imagine that. I just smiled within myself.

The former farmworkers longed for the camaraderie they had shared in the camps. Some of them worked on forming a club that would be a home away from home for West Indians in the Hartford area. Incorporated in 1950, the West Indian Social Club is still going strong almost half a century later.

Old age and retirement now shape the lives of these former "soldiers of the soil." Some have returned to Jamaica. Others, like George Hudson, have retired to Florida for its warmer weather. Leaving Connecticut in 1993, in frail health, Hudson was honored with a reception at the West Indian Social Club.

I was always the type of person that was independent. The family background was always that you try to have the first shilling, then you can go and ask for the next shilling. My wife has been very supportive to me and has been the most influential person in my life. Our firm belief in God has helped us all the way. Retirement is beautiful; my only drawback is my physical weakness. ❖

Josefina Báez

Josefina Báez was interviewed by Catherine Sunshine on July 28, 1996 in New York City.

I'm a founding member of the theater group Latinarte. We promote Latino artists, and Dominicans in particular. We write our work and perform it in neighborhoods in and around New York City, and on tour.

I was born and raised in the Dominican Republic in the town of La Romana. My father owned a *bodega*, a little grocery store. After my father died in 1961 my mother was left with ten kids to support, so her decision to migrate was an economic one.

Migration was not something that I chose. My mother came here first and then some of my brothers and sisters, leaving the rest of us behind with one of my older sisters. They brought me to New York when I was 11 years old.

We lived on the Upper West Side, on 107th Street. I graduated from Brandeis High School on West 84th Street. While I was in high school I took classical dance and started doing theater. After high school I began working with community theater groups in *El Barrio*, that is East Harlem. I traveled overseas for international theater festivals and workshops.

Theater became for me much more than a passion or a hobby. I knew this was the work I wanted to do. But it was not very convincing to my family. They didn't see theater as a profession.

At Latinarte we have three core members. We do theater—we produce it, we write it, we perform it, we tour it. We lose the money, we make the money, we do everything. We create visual art exhibits, and we give workshops, seminars and classes all over New York City.

When Dominicans see us perform, they're seeing people who look like them, who talk like them, because we are them. One piece we did was called *Negritude Dominicana*. It was based on work of Pedro Mir and several other Dominican writers. We looked at the theme of Dominican black consciousness, of being black and Dominican.

There's a stereotype of how you should look if you're an immigrant. "What is that accent you have? It sounds English when you say this, it sounds Latino when you say the other!" Even some Dominicans will say, "You don't look Dominican." And I don't even know how Dominicans look.

Migration is an ongoing theme in our work. We show how we Dominicans live and feel in New York. How we dance a very sad merengue every day. Because I think the so-called dream is a nightmare in many respects. We see families disintegrating. Kids have problems with drugs, with education. It's getting worse and worse, I don't see it getting better and that scares me. And the only remedy is educating yourself. Education has to start with the individual, with that inner drive to better yourself: that sense of responsibility that we all must have to ourselves first. Then you broaden that process to the community, to share and grow with the collective.

My art mirrors the community

I write what I see, what I feel. A major source of ideas for me is oral history—the lives of people who are not in the history books. My art is a mirror of the community of which I am a part.

In our performances we don't give answers to problems. We present a proposal and begin a dialogue aimed at solving a problem. You might see yourself in the work, and hopefully then we will click. At the end we always have a dialogue with the audience. The audience suggests different endings, that we should change this or that. For instance I did a play about how we women give in to powerful relationships. At the end, how it was addressed by the audience was the most important thing, not the performance itself.

Inspiration also comes from my students. I teach creative writing and theater in the New York City public schools as an artist in residence, from kindergarten to grade 12. I tell my students, we have to create and write from the heart. Most of the students in the schools where I teach are Dominicans, and for them it's unusual to have a Dominican teacher. I read my work to them and assure them that I'm not inventing anything, that I write what I live. As soon as I do that, they open themselves. They know I'm not pretending, that I'm being truthful, and they respect that.

I know the pains and the blessings of migrating. On the positive side, you have so many people from so many places here in New York that you don't have any choice but to learn to respect difference. I might say, "Oh no no, *pero mi comida es mejor,*" because mine is the only food that I have

known. But then I go to my friend's house and she cooks another way, I see how she cooks the *chócolo,* the *maíz,* how different it is, and it's great! I don't have the right to say that mine is better. For me that's wonderful. And that opportunity doesn't happen if you just stay in one place.

I do a lot of "non-Dominican" things. I meditate, I dance Indian dance. In recent years, my personal training for my theater work has been based on Oriental and Russian theater techniques. I do Chinese painting. I like the contrast between the two cultures, the Dominican and the Oriental, and how you have universal signals that go beyond being Dominican, beyond being Asian, beyond being North American. They belong to everyone, and I have appropriated them, and I like that.

I feel that I'm *una dominicana muy dominicana.* I think that by going out and looking for elements of other cultures, you tend to go back richer to your own culture and appreciate it more.

The negatives of migration ... I doubt that we will ever be accepted here as who we are. Accepted not just as the person with the red passport, or the Dominican citizenship, or that accent, or that way of dancing, but as a human being. And it's painful, because while we are not accepted here, at the same time we are no longer completely accepted there. So we have created a creole culture: we're not here, we're not there. And that does not give us a sense of grounding, of belonging.

I think about the Dominican Republic every day. In 30, 40 years I'll be doing the same. I'll be saying that next year I will leave, that I'm going back home to work there. But that may never happen.

I love what I do. I always have energy, and that energy comes from knowing what I want to do in life. That's what I tell myself, and that's what I tell the young people: try to decide what you want to do, what you *need* to do as urgently as you need air to breathe. That will show you the path you should follow. ❖

merengue: popular dance music of the Dominican Republic
pero mi comida es mejor: my food is better
chócolo, maíz: corn
una dominicana muy dominicana: a Dominican who is very Dominican

Virgilio Cruz

Virgilio Cruz was interviewed by Ruth Glasser on July 22, 1996, in Hartford, Connecticut. Translation from the Spanish by Catherine Sunshine.

My childhood in the 1950s was spent in a rural, isolated community in southern Puerto Rico without roads, electricity, television or radio. Transportation was by horses and mules. Nearly everyone in the community lived by farming, a simple life. I remember people would gather in their yards in the evenings and talk about all kinds of things. They would tell jokes, stories and legends, and sometimes sing.

My father was a person who could do many things well. Like everyone in the community, he was a farmer. During part of the year he did wage work cutting sugar cane, and when the cane was finished, he and my mother tended our family's own crops. We ate what we grew, and if the harvest was good we would sell the surplus in the market and use the money to buy what we needed—dried codfish, canned meat, and sometimes fresh meat, but usually not, because there was no refrigeration. We didn't have to buy juice because there were fruit trees all around, like orange, mango and soursop.

My father was also the neighborhood musician. He played the Puerto Rican *cuatro* and the guitar, and he could sing; people would pay him to play at dances. He was a songwriter and composed *aguinaldos* and *seises*. And he was also a craftsman who made cuatros and guitars.

Of the six kids in the family, I had the most interest in my father's music. When he played I would sit beside him, listening. He began teaching me some chords and simple melodies on the guitar, and later I was able to play some songs with him. This was rustic country music, nothing fancy, but I learned the rudiments from him.

I had to walk several miles to school every day barefoot, but I loved school and was determined to go. Beginning in the seventh grade I went to a school in the nearest large town, Juana Díaz. Because my grades were good, I received a government scholarship that I used to buy shoes and clothes. After graduating from high school I went to the University of Puerto Rico in Río Piedras.

At that time I was playing the guitar, and the cuatro a little bit, and writing some songs that weren't very good. But at the university I met students who were experimenting with different musical styles, who were involved with a new song movement based on Puerto Rico's folk tradition.

After graduating from university in 1973 I joined the U.S. Army and spent two years working as a communications specialist in the United States. When I returned to Puerto Rico I used my veterans' benefits to take some additional university courses, and I also began working as a supervisor in a Puerto Rican government agency.

I became a cuatro player

During that time I began seriously learning to play the cuatro. Our house had always been filled with cuatros when I was growing up, since my father made them. But I didn't want to learn it the way I had learned the guitar, by ear. I wanted more formal instruction. So I took private lessons for a few months, then enrolled in the Institute of Puerto Rican Culture in San Juan in 1977.

In the past, the art of cuatro playing was simply handed down in families or shared among friends. Musicians who composed for the cuatro played by ear and never wrote down their material. So when the Institute of Puerto Rican Culture began teaching the cuatro formally, like the violin or the piano, this marked a big change. A number of other music schools in Puerto Rico are now doing the same.

As a result of this change, instructors have had to take the songs by cuatro musicians like Maso Rivera, Ladí, and others, and write them down as sheet music. That means these songs will be preserved and taught; they will not be forgotten.

I was not a cultural activist in Puerto Rico. I simply studied music for my own satisfaction. I played at parties and events, singing and accompanying myself on the guitar.

That changed when, in 1986, I moved to the United States. I chose Hartford, Connecticut because I had a brother here. When I got to Hartford and saw the Puerto Rican festivals and parades being held here, I realized that this city was culturally behind the times. There was no movement to promote the cuatro, for instance; no school teaching cuatro and no written music for the cuatro. Puerto Ricans in Connecticut listened to music that's considered out of date in Puerto Rico. On the island people were developing new types of Puerto Rican song, new styles of seises and aguinaldos. But there was none of this in Hartford.

In fact, at Puerto Rican parades in Connecticut you'd mainly hear merengue and salsa. Of course merengue isn't Puerto Rican—it's Dominican. And salsa is an incredible mix, with contributions from various Latin American musical styles and even some that aren't Latin American. Although Puerto Ricans have made a big contribution to the development of salsa and are fine salsa musicians, we didn't originate it and we can't claim it as ours. I myself like to dance to merengue and salsa, but I'm very clear that when we talk about Puerto Rican culture, we can't include them.

It's true, of course, that other musical traditions have influenced our music. No music is totally new. But some styles are more original, more authentically Puerto Rican. If you ask where one hears salsa, you can say Venezuela, Colombia, Panama and Cuba, among others. But a *seis mapeye*—you won't hear that anywhere but Puerto Rico. The same with *plena:* there are similar styles elsewhere, but true plena—only Puerto Rico. And these musical traditions that are most genuinely ours are the ones we need to conserve and develop.

This is especially true for those of us who live outside Puerto Rico. Even though Puerto Rico has a political relationship with the United States, we're really living in a foreign country. The culture here is very different from our own. For the benefit of the other communities here—African-American, Anglo, and so on—and for our own benefit and our children's, we need to make sure that "Puerto Rican" activities feature true Puerto Rican cultural expression.

When I saw this wasn't happening, I felt I had to do something. Soon after arriving in Hartford, I formed a musical group called Canto Isleño with several people I met whose views on Puerto Rican culture coincided with my own. They included a lawyer, a teacher in the Hartford public schools, and several others. The group chose carefully the music it would perform, distinguishing between what is genuinely Puerto Rican and what isn't.

We use traditional Puerto Rican instruments: the cuatro, the guitar, the *bongó,* the *güiro,* and *congas.* Our performances feature various types of traditional Puerto Rican music, not only seises and aguinaldos but also *guarachas, plenas, bombas, danzas,* and *mazurcas.*

Virgilio Cruz (left) teaching a music class.

Through this group I began to be known as a cuatro player. A guy I'd met wanted to learn to play, and I began giving him lessons in my apartment. He was pleased, and he told one of his co-workers, and she too decided to take lessons. And they told others and before I knew it, quite a few people were asking to take cuatro lessons from me.

Since my apartment was small, a friend lent me his basement for the classes. When that became too small, we moved classes to the Hartford YMCA, and later we got a space of our own. By then we had formed a school called "La Primera Orquesta de Cuatros de Connecticut," that was incorporated and registered with the state. We provided lessons in guitar, cuatro and folk song to about 150 students a year. It was hard for me because I was doing all this as a volunteer in my spare time, and every night we were there until 10:30 or 11 o'clock. Our courses were very popular.

The school closed in 1995, but I still give private lessons in folk singing, in song writing, and in cuatro and guitar.

Puerto Rico has two excellent folk song competitions, one sponsored by the Institute of Puerto Rican Culture and the other by the Bacardi rum company. In Hartford, by contrast, folk song competitions tended to be very informal. The judges came from the audience and knew little about improvisation or musical technique; they judged by audience applause and gave the winner $25 and a bottle of whiskey. I could see that Hartford needed something fresh and new.

With my friend Camille, who had been president of the school, I decided to start a new folk song competition. We called it the Concurso de Trovadores de Nueva Inglaterra—the New England Troubadours Contest. We raised some money, wrote regulations, and found a panel of judges. We asked the musicians to dress well and be serious about the music.

The contest requires the singers to improvise. The song has to be a *décima*, which is a type of traditional poetry in which each stanza has ten lines. Each singer, as he comes on stage, picks from a box a piece of paper containing a line of verse, called a *pie forzado*. The singer then has to improvise a décima in which the last verse ends with that line.

Singers come to compete from all over Connecticut and from New York, Pennsylvania, Massachusetts and New Jersey. By the sixth contest we awarded more than $2,500 in prizes.

Our folk tradition is our soul

I am proud of these successes in promoting Puerto Rican culture in Connecticut. That's not to say there aren't difficulties; there are. One is the climate. Puerto Rico has cultural events in the open air all year round, but you can't hold outdoor festivals here in December.

Another obstacle is what I would call a kind of resistance to change in the Puerto Rican community here. Migrants naturally tend to hold on to the culture they knew before migrating. In the struggle to maintain their identity, they remain fixed, even fossilized, in a certain cultural era.

In Connecticut many people have continued playing and listening to the music they brought with them, mainly Puerto Rican music from the 1950s and '60s. The result is both positive and negative: Puerto Rican identity is maintained, but on the other hand, it keeps people from being open to new things. For example, people have told me that the cuatro is never taught formally, that it's learned only by ear and that the great cuatro players never read a note of music. That was true at one time; but since the 1980s the cuatro has been taught in schools like any other instrument.

What defines a people, the soul of a people, is their folk tradition. It's what distinguishes us from every other people in the Americas. Our folk music is not only the seis and aguinaldo, but also the danza, the mazurca, the *vals criollo*, the plena, the bomba. The music of Rafael Hernández, of Pedro Flores, of Silvia Resach, of Roberto Cole, of Noel Estrada—this is what we should offer.

If a people want to be something and someone, they first have to discover their spirit, their soul, their identity. Puerto Ricans need to be Puerto Ricans. We'll never be African-Americans, Jamaicans, or Anglo-Americans. In particular we'll never be Anglo-Americans, because even if a Puerto Rican feels Anglo, speaks English without an accent and rises high in the corporate world, that person will not stop being Puerto Rican. And if he forgets it someone will surely remind him. Even if you're born in the United States, if your name is Cruz you're still Puerto Rican in the eyes of the world.

Our community has many problems, many needs. It's up to all of us—politicians, community leaders, teachers, social workers, factory workers, shopkeepers, journalists—to work together to solve these problems. Artists too, because you can accomplish a social purpose through art. My songs send a message that oftentimes deals with social realities. As an artist you can't separate your art from social and political problems.

Each of us has a part to play, and we need to do our work with deep commitment. It's not just a matter of earning $30,000, $40,000, or $45,000 a year. You have to look back as you walk and see what kind of footprints you are leaving. ❖

cuatro: instrument with five sets of double strings, considered the national instrument of Puerto Rico

aguinaldos, seises: traditional melodies

merengue: popular dance music of the Dominican Republic

salsa: hybrid music developed in New York City by musicians of various Latin American and Caribbean backgrounds

seis mapeye: a particular kind of seis

plena: songs of social commentary

bongó, conga: percussion instruments from the Afro-Puerto Rican tradition

güiro: rattle made from a dried gourd

guaracha: music of Spanish and Cuban origin, widely played in Puerto Rico

bomba: drum dance rooted in the Afro-Puerto Rican tradition

danza, mazurca: music of European origin, mainly instrumental

décima: A form of poetry widely used for Puerto Rican folk songs. It has ten lines of either eight or six syllables each. Eight-syllable décimas are sung to aguinaldos and those with six syllables are sung to seises.

vals criollo: type of waltz played with Puerto Rican musical instruments

Part Three:
Fiction, Memoirs and Poetry

Nabel String

Merle Collins

Merle Collins was born and raised in Grenada. She was educated in Jamaica, England and the United States, and currently teaches creative writing and Caribbean literature at the University of Maryland at College Park. She has published poetry, short stories and two novels about contemporary life in the English-speaking Caribbean.

Traditionally, in Grenada and other West Indian societies, after a child is born the umbilical cord or "navel string" is buried near the birth place. It is said that a person must always return to the place where his or her navel string is buried.

Reprinted from ROTTEN POMERACK (London: Virago Press). © 1992 by Merle Collins. Used by permission of the author.

That part of me
that is there, not here
home, not wandering
not hey, how you doing?
but doodoo darling, you awright?

Not going up to this enclosed home
in the elevator, on stairs, in silent
unconcerned, instinctive hostility
with the neighbor I do not know
not turning the key for the umpteenth time
in the door of number 204 and suddenly
pausing, intent, attention on 203
I wonder who livin there? Not that
absence of you, of me, of warmth, of life.

but running outside with the piece of bread
Ay! Teacher Clearie! Shout the bus for me, nuh!
Ay! James! Wait! Take the kerosene pan!
I not taking no damn kerosene pan!
Eh! But he ignorant, eh!
Awright! Awright! Bring it! Ka dammit!

There, where the neighbor is friend and enemy
to be cussed and caressed
so damn annoying you could scream sometimes
so blasted fast in you business
you could hate, most times
but when you're far away
hate is a memory of feeling
loving and cussing and laughing and needing
is living. The blank stare from the unknown
next door neighbor kills something inside

and the sound that pulls
is of the heartbeat, of the drum
voice. Is River Sallee, is a drummer
soaring, is Victoria, is Belmont,
those places that you, I, we left
left to search, as always, for a better life.
Left sometimes, just because of a need to search
for the reason, the beginning, the end, the all.
So left, and will always be leaving
Left, too, to escape the lime
by the place they call the kwese, by the L'anse,
by the market. Left to find jobs, to chase education.

Go on child, take what I didn't get, you hear
I have no money to leave. All I have
is in your head. Left, too, because every year
more out of school, less work to get
because chemistry in fifth form this year
and standing on Market Hill straight
for the whole of next year
just didn't kind of make no sense.

Left, too, because love turned hate
is bitter, not sweet
Because the landless somehow becoming
more landless yet but still loving
some leader because of a memory
Left sometimes because things not so good
and something better is always somewhere else
Left because even if things going all right
the world big, and home is a feeling you're seeking

but in this new speaking, in the elevator, the lift
from over the sea there's the pull of the heartbeat
of the drum voice. Ay! Bury the child nabel
string under the coconut tree, you know
by where I bury she father own!
So the nabel string there
and as the palm branch swaying

It pulling, it pulling, it pulling
❖

    doodoo: an endearment
    fast: nosy
    River Sallee, Victoria, Belmont, L'Anse, Market Hill: places in Grenada
    lime: hanging out on the street corner—associated with joblessness
    kwese: place in Grenada's capital known as a gathering spot for idlers

Welcome to New York

Edwidge Danticat

Edwidge Danticat was born in Haiti. Her parents emigrated to the United States when she was a young child, and she was raised in Haiti by an aunt. In 1981, when she was twelve, her parents sent for her to join them in New York City. She graduated from Barnard College and Brown University and has published a novel and a collection of short stories.

The novel BREATH, EYES, MEMORY tells of Sophie Caco, a fatherless girl whose mother emigrated from Haiti when Sophie was very young. Sophie's childhood is spent in rural Haiti amid the beauty of daffodils, in the loving care of her aunt, Tante Atie. When Sophie is twelve, her mother abruptly sends for her. Everyone tells Sophie how lucky she is to be going to New York, but her world has collapsed. She must leave Tante Atie and join a mother she does not remember in a country she has never seen.

(continued on next page)

I only knew my mother from the picture on the night table by Tante Atie's pillow. She waved from inside the frame with a wide grin on her face and a large flower in her hair. She witnessed everything that went on in the bougainvillea, each step, each stumble, each hug and kiss. She saw us when we got up, when we went to sleep, when we laughed, when we got upset at each other. Her expression never changed. Her grin never went away.

I sometimes saw my mother in my dreams. She would chase me through a field of wildflowers as tall as the sky. When she caught me, she would try to squeeze me into the small frame so I could be in the picture with her. I would scream and scream until my voice gave out, then Tante Atie would come and save me from her grasp.

After her mother sends a plane ticket for her, Sophie is put on a flight to New York in the care of a stranger. Her mother is waiting at the airport to meet the flight.

My mother came forward. I knew it was my mother because she came up to me and grabbed me and began to spin me like a top, so she could look at me.

The woman who had been with me looked on without saying anything.

"Stay here," my mother said to me in Creole.

She walked over to a corner with the woman, whispered a few things to her, and handed her what seemed like money.

"I cannot thank you enough," my mother said.

"There is no need," the woman said. She bowed slightly and walked away.

I raised my hand to wave goodbye. The woman had already turned her back and was heading inside. It was as though I had disappeared. She did not even see me anymore.

As the woman went through the gate, my mother kissed me on the lips.

"I cannot believe that I am looking at you," she said. "You are my little girl. You are here."

She pinched my cheeks and patted my head.

"Say something," she urged. "Say something. Just speak to me. Let me hear your voice."

She pressed my face against hers and held fast.

"How are you feeling?" she asked. "Did you have a nice plane flight?"

I nodded.

"You must be very tired," she said. "Let us go home."

She grabbed my suitcase with one hand and my arm with the other.

Outside it was overcast and cool.

"My goodness." Her scrawny body shivered. "I didn't even bring you something to put over your dress."

She dropped the suitcase on the sidewalk, took off the denim jacket she had on and guided my arms through the sleeves.

A line of cars stopped as we crossed the street to the parking lot. She was wobbling under the weight of my suitcase.

She stopped in front of a pale yellow car with a long crack across the windshield glass. The paint was peeling off the side door that she opened for me. I peered inside and hesitated to climb onto the tattered cushions on the seats.

She dropped the suitcase in the trunk and walked back to me.

"Don't be afraid. Go right in."

She tried to lift my body into the front seat but she stumbled under my weight and quickly put me back down.

I climbed in and tried not to squirm. The sharp edge of a loose spring was sticking into my thigh.

She sat in the driver's seat and turned on the engine. It made a loud grating noise as though it were about to explode.

"We will soon be on our way," she said.

She rubbed her hands together and pressed her head back against the seat. She did not look like the picture Tante Atie had on her night table. Her face was long and hollow. Her hair had a blunt cut and she had long spindly legs. She had dark circles under her eyes and, as she smiled, lines of wrinkles tightened her expression. Her fingers were scarred and sunburned. It was as though she had never stopped working in the cane fields after all.

"It is ready now," she said.

She strapped the seatbelt across her flat chest, pressing herself even further into the torn cushions. She leaned over and attached my seatbelt as the car finally drove off.

Night had just fallen. Lights glowed everywhere. A long string of cars sped along the highway, each like a single diamond on a very long bracelet.

"We will be in the city soon," she said.

I still had not said anything to her.

"How is your Tante Atie?" she asked. "Does she still go to night school?"

Excerpted from BREATH, EYES, MEMORY (New York: Soho Press). © 1994 by Edwidge Danticat. Used by permission of Soho Press and Edwidge Danticat.

"Night school?"

"She told me once in a cassette that she was going to start night school. Did she ever start it?"

"*Non.*"

"The old girl lost her nerve. She lost her fight. You should have seen us when we were young. We always dreamt of becoming important women. We were going to be the first women doctors from my mother's village. We would not stop at being doctors either. We were going to be engineers too. Imagine our surprise when we found out we had limits."

All the street lights were suddenly gone. The streets we drove down now were dim and hazy. The windows were draped with bars; black trash bags blew out into the night air.

There were young men standing on street corners, throwing empty cans at passing cars. My mother swerved the car to avoid a bottle that almost came crashing through the windshield.

"How is Lotus?" she asked. "Donald's wife, Madame Augustin."

"She is fine," I said.

"Atie has sent me cassettes about that. You know Lotus was not meant to marry Donald. Your aunt Atie was supposed to. But the heart is fickle, what can you say? When Lotus came along, he did not want my sister anymore."

There was writing all over the building. As we walked towards it, my mother nearly tripped over a man sleeping under a blanket of newspapers.

"Your schooling is the only thing that will make people respect you," my mother said as she put a key in the front door.

The thick dirty glass was covered with names written in graffiti bubbles.

"You are going to work hard here," she said, "and no one is going to break your heart because you cannot read or write. You have a chance to become the kind of woman Atie and I have always wanted to be. If you make something of yourself in life, we will all succeed. You can *raise our heads.*"

A smell of old musty walls met us at the entrance to her apartment. She closed the door behind her and dragged the suitcase inside.

"You wait for me here," she said, once we got inside. I stood on the other side of a heavy door in the dark hall, waiting for her.

She disappeared behind a bedroom door. I wandered in and slid my fingers across the table and chairs neatly lined up in the kitchen. The tablecloth was shielded with a red plastic cover, the same blush red as the sofa in the living room.

There were books scattered all over the counter. I flipped through the pages quickly. The books had pictures of sick old people in them and women dressed in white helping them.

I was startled to hear my name when she called it.

"Sophie, where are you?"

I ran back to the spot where she had left me. She was standing there with a tall well-dressed doll at her side. The doll was caramel-colored with a fine pointy nose.

"Come," she said. "We will show you to your room."

I followed her through a dark doorway. She turned on the light and laid the doll down on a small day-bed by the window.

I kept my eyes on the blue wallpaper and the water stains that crept from the ceiling down to the floor.

She kept staring at my face for a reaction.

"Don't you like it?" she asked.

"Yes. I like it. Thank you."

Sitting on the edge of the bed, she unbraided the doll's hair, taking out the ribbons and barrettes that matched the yellow dress. She put them on a night table near the bed. There was a picture of her and Tante Atie there. Tante Atie was holding a baby and my mother had her hand around Tante Atie's shoulder.

I moved closer to get a better look at the baby in Tante Atie's arms. I had never seen an infant picture of myself, but somehow I knew that it was me. Who else could it have been? I looked for traces in the child, a feature that was my mother's but still mine too. It was the first time in my life that I noticed that I looked like no one in my family. Not my mother. Not my Tante Atie. I did not look like them when I was a baby and I did not look like them now.

"If you don't like the room," my mother said, "we can always change it."

She glanced at the picture as she picked up a small brush and combed the doll's hair into a ponytail.

"I like the room fine," I stuttered.

She tied a rubber band around the doll's ponytail, then reached under the bed for a small trunk.

Edwidge Danticat

She unbuttoned the back of the doll's dress and changed her into a pajama set.

"You won't resent sharing your room, will you?" She stroked the doll's back. "She is like a friend to me. She kept me company while we were apart. It seems crazy, I know. A grown woman like me with a doll. I am giving her to you now. You take good care of her."

She motioned for me to walk over and sit on her lap. I was not sure that her thin legs would hold me without snapping. I walked over and sat on her lap anyway.

"You're not going to be alone," she said. "I'm never going to be farther than a few feet away. Do you understand that?"

She gently helped me down from her lap. Her knees seemed to be weakening under my weight.

"Do you want to eat something? We can sit and talk. Or do you want to go to bed?"

"Bed."

She reached over to unbutton the back of my dress.

"I can do that," I said.

"Do you want me to show you where I sleep, in case you need me during the night?"

We went back to the living room. She unfolded the sofa and turned it into a bed.

"This is where I'll be. You see, I'm not far away at all."

When we went back to the bedroom, I turned my back to her as I undressed. She took the dress from me, opened the closet door, and squeezed it in between some of her own.

The rumpled Mother's Day card was sticking out from my dress pocket.

"What is that?" she asked, pulling it out.

She unfolded the card and began to read it. I lay down on the bed and tried to slip under the yellow sheets. There was not enough room for both me and the doll on the bed. I picked her up and laid her down sideways. She still left little room for me.

My mother looked up from the card, walked over, and took the doll out of the bed. She put her down carefully in a corner.

"Was that for me?" she asked looking down at the card.

"Tante Atie said I should give it to you."

"Did you know how much I loved daffodils when I was a girl?"

"Tante Atie told me."

She ran her fingers along the cardboard, over the empty space where the daffodil had been.

"I haven't gone out and looked for daffodils since I've been here. For all I know, they might not even have them here."

She ran the card along her cheek, then pressed it against her chest.

"Are there still lots of daffodils?"

"Oui," I said. "There are a lot of them."

Her face beamed even more than when she first saw me at the airport. She bent down and kissed my forehead.

"Thank God for that," she said.

I couldn't fall asleep. At home, when I couldn't sleep, Tante Atie would stay up with me. The two of us would sit by the window and Tante Atie would tell me stories about our lives, about the way things had been in the family, even before I was born. One time I asked her how it was that I was born with a mother and no father. She told me the story of a little girl who was born out of the petals of roses, water from the stream, and a chunk of the sky. That little girl, she said was me.

As I lay in the dark, I heard my mother talking on the phone.

"Yes," she said in Creole. "She is very much here. In bone and flesh. I cannot believe it myself."

Later that night, I heard that same voice screaming as though someone was trying to kill her. I rushed over, but my mother was alone thrashing against the sheets. I shook her and finally woke her up. When she saw me, she quickly covered her face with her hands and turned away.

"*Ou byen?* Are you all right?" I asked her.

She shook her head yes.

"It is the night," she said. "Sometimes, I see horrible visions in my sleep."

"Do you have any tea you can boil?" I asked.

Tante Atie would have known all the right herbs.

"Don't worry, it will pass," she said, avoiding my eyes. "I will be fine. I always am. The nightmares, they come and go."

There were sirens and loud radios blaring outside the building.

I climbed on the bed and tried to soothe her. She grabbed my face and squeezed it between her palms.

"What is it? Are you scared too?" she asked. "Don't worry." She pulled me down into the bed with her. "You can sleep here tonight if you want. It's okay. I'm here."

She pulled the sheet over both our bodies. Her voice began to fade as she drifted back to sleep.

I leaned back in the bed, listening to her snoring.

Soon, the morning light came creeping through the living room window. I kept staring at the ceiling as I listened to her heart beating along with the ticking clock.

"Sophie," she whispered. Her eyes were still closed. "Sophie, I will never let you go again."

Tears burst out of her eyes when she opened them.

"Sophie, I am glad you are with me. We can get along, you and me. I know we can."

She clung to my hand as she drifted off to sleep.

The sun stung my eyes as it came through the curtains. I slid my hand out of hers to go to the bathroom. The grey linoleum felt surprisingly warm under my feet. I looked at my red eyes in the mirror while splashing cold water over my face. New eyes seemed to be looking back at me. A new face all together. Someone who had aged in one day, as though she had been through a time machine, rather than an airplane. Welcome to New York, this face seemed to be saying. Accept your new life. I greeted the challenge, like one greets a new day. As my mother's daughter and Tante Atie's child. ❖

Celebrating Puerto Rican Style

Victor Hernández Cruz

For my children

Taking an airplane from one age to another was the highlight of my childhood. You must get the picture of what it felt like to move, at five years old, from a small tropical village in Puerto Rico to New York City, the largest, most developed urban center on the planet. It was as if we penetrated another dimension. I remember my town, Aguas Buenas: small wooden homes with the touch of Spanish colonial, which in turn contained the Arabic influence of the Moorish occupation of Spain. The town's steep streets were surrounded by a green, lush flora from which descended the singing of the coquí, a unique Puerto Rican toad that permeates the island nights with its mating call.

The Puerto Rican migration of the late forties and early fifties was one of the great exoduses of recent times, emptying out much of the campesino population amid a collapse of the agricultural system, mainly sugar cane. The bulk of those immigrants arrived in the large northern cities of the U.S. mainland.

We are a people descended in part from the indigenous population that Columbus described as copper-skinned with straight jet black hair, living in oval-shaped villages of wooden homes that had palm-leaf rooftops. They had their own linguistic, religious and governmental systems until, the anthropologists tell us, this society was exterminated by the cruel policies of the Spaniards. In their quest for cheap labor, the Spaniards introduced Puerto Rico's African element, mostly Yorubas from that continent's west coast. And so the Indian, the Spaniard and the African are the ancestors of the Puerto Rican people—imparting a lasting flavor in language, music, food and spirituality which we describe as criollo.

On the island of Puerto Rico we never dream of a white Christmas or of a Santa Claus being guided through the clouds by Rudolph the Reindeer. On Christmas Day on our island it might be 87 degrees with the gentle East Trade Winds blowing. Islanders begin their festive spirit some three weeks before Christmas Day and go on for another two weeks after. It is as if Christ's radiance were descending upon the earth.

I remember Christmases as joyful and full of music. Aguinaldo, a form of Puerto Rican carol, jumps with the vitality of life, using drums, guitars and maracas. The songs speak of Jesus as if he were being born again that very moment when the voice and the heart administer the lyric. The songs glorify the Virgen María and her divine conception. They venerate the divine, and—as if on the same note—the joys of drinking rum and dancing, of flirting and falling in love, of piercing a hog with a spear and roasting it in the open air.

Jesus wants us to have a beautiful time, to dance the traditional mapayes, plenas and bombas as well as any boogaloo of invention on the day of his birth.

A most important feature of Christmas in the traditional towns of Puerto Rico is the asaltos or musical assaults. Each town has its own groups of singing bards who go on a musical rampage, stopping at the entrances of homes or directly below balconies, singing the famous Christmas jingles or improvising their own on the spot. At the end of their rendition it is the custom for members of the household to bestow gifts of food or drink as a sign of appreciation.

Coquito, a blend of coconut milk and rum, is a traditional Christmas drink that should be sipped sparingly, for it gives you the illusion that you can gulp it down like milk—a great way to end up falling down a mountain and finding yourself in a bushel of guayabas. The Puerto Rican pastel is another must around the holidays—grated plantain, pork meat, olives, garbanzos and hot peppers placed within a banana leaf and boiled. The aromas of this and other traditional dishes rise from Puerto Rico's towns on Christmas, waking the palates of the living and the dead.

In North America's cities, Christmas trees are purchased in lots set up under freeways. In Puerto Rico the tradition is different. The holiday of Los Tres Reyes Magos, the three wise kings, is celebrated on January 6th, and it is on that date that Puerto Rican children receive their gifts. But first they must prepare for them. Each must go out

The Three Kings Day parade in East Harlem, New York City. Every year in January, El Barrio (East Harlem) celebrates El Día de los Reyes Magos with a joyous procession dramatizing the three wise Kings' biblical journey to the Christ child. Led by three kings in jeweled costumes and a burro, hundreds of children march through the neighborhood and hundreds more line the streets. A live band provides music, and the kings' camels, donkeys and sheep are interspersed with large rolling puppets. For weeks before the parade, children prepare floats, costumes and puppets, their enthusiasm fueled by anticipation of the Puerto Rican community's major gift-giving holiday. — City Lore, Volume 5, 1995–96.

into the countryside with a box and gather grass. They then place the boxes under their beds, and it is there that they discover their gifts on the morning of January 6th. This grass under the bed is Puerto Rico's Christmas tree.

My island home is fighting for its cultural values and economic survival under the pressure of North American control. But at Christmastime Puerto Rico may have the upper hand. All airlines going into San Juan around the holidays are booked down to every seat. If you fly standby, rumor has it that sometimes you can get in but you can't get out.

Well, if that happens to you, take to the mountains of the interior, for those are the pictures sent by Christ from the heavens.

Feliz Navidad. ❖

campesino: farmer
Virgen María: the Virgin Mary
guayabas: guavas
grass under the bed: Puerto Rican children put a bit of grass under their beds for the three kings' camels to eat

To Da-duh, in Memoriam

Paule Marshall

Paule Marshall was born in Brooklyn, New York, to parents who emigrated from Barbados during World War I. She grew up in Brooklyn's emergent West Indian community during the Depression years and graduated from Brooklyn College. She later spent periods of time living in the Caribbean. The author of four novels and two collections of short stories, Marshall teaches modern literature at Virginia Commonwealth University.

"To Da-duh, in Memoriam" is among the most autobiographical of Marshall's stories. It draws on the author's memories of a visit to her grandmother (whose nickname was Da-duh) in Barbados when she was nine.

Reprinted from REENA AND OTHER STORIES (Old Westbury, N.Y.: The Feminist Press, 1983). © 1983 by Paule Marshall. Used by permission of The Feminist Press at The City University of New York.

"... Oh Nana! all of you is not involved in this evil business
Death, Nor all of us in life."
— From "At My Grandmother's Grave," by Lebert Bethune

I did not see her at first I remember. For not only was it dark inside the crowded disembarkation shed in spite of the daylight flooding in from outside, but standing there waiting for her with my mother and sister I was still somewhat blinded from the sheen of tropical sunlight on the water of the bay which we had just crossed in the landing boat, leaving behind us the ship that had brought us from New York lying in the offing. Besides, being only nine years of age at the time and knowing nothing of islands I was busy attending to the alien sights and sounds of Barbados, the unfamiliar smells.

I did not see her, but I was alerted to her approach by my mother's hand which suddenly tightened around mine, and looking up I traced her gaze through the gloom in the shed until I finally made out the small, purposeful, painfully erect figure of the old woman headed our way.

Her face was drowned in the shadow of an ugly rolled-brim brown felt hat, but the details of her slight body and of the struggle taking place within it were clear enough—an intense, unrelenting struggle between her back which was beginning to bend ever so slightly under the weight of her eighty-odd years and the rest of her which sought to deny those years and hold that back straight, keep it in line. Moving swiftly toward us (so swiftly it seemed she did not intend stopping when she reached us but would sweep past us out the doorway which opened onto the sea and like Christ walk upon the water!), she was caught between the sunlight at her end of the building and the darkness inside—and for a moment she appeared to contain them both: the light in the long severe old-fashioned white dress she wore which brought the sense of a past that was still alive into our bustling present and in the snatch of white at her eye; the darkness in her black high-top shoes and in her face which was visible now that she was closer.

It was as stark and fleshless as a death mask, that face. The maggots might have already done their work, leaving only the framework of bone beneath the ruined skin and deep wells at the temple and jaw. But her eyes were alive, unnervingly so for one so old, with a sharp light that flicked out of the dim clouded depths like a lizard's tongue to snap up all in her view. Those eyes betrayed a child's curiosity about the world, and I wondered vaguely seeing them, and seeing the way the bodice of her ancient dress had collapsed in on her flat chest (what had happened to her breasts?), whether she might not be some kind of child at the same time that she was a woman, with fourteen children, my mother included, to prove it. Perhaps she was both, both child and woman, darkness and light, past and present, life and death—all the opposites contained and reconciled in her.

"My Da-duh," my mother said formally and stepped forward. The name sounded like thunder fading softly in the distance.

"Child," Da-duh said, and her tone, her quick scrutiny of my mother, the brief embrace in which they appeared to shy from each other rather than touch, wiped out the fifteen years my mother had been away and restored the old relationship. My mother, who was such a formidable figure in my eyes, had suddenly with a word been reduced to my status.

"Yes, God is good," Da-duh said with a nod that was like a tic. "He has spared me to see my child again."

We were led forward then, apologetically because not only did Da-duh prefer boys but she also liked her grandchildren to be "white," that is, fair-skinned; and we had, I was to discover, a number of cousins, the outside children of white estate managers and the like, who qualified. We, though, were as black as she.

My sister being the oldest was presented first. "This one takes after the father," my mother said and waited to be reproved.

Frowning, Da-duh tilted my sister's face toward the light. But her frown soon gave way to a grudging smile, for my sister with her large mild eyes and little broad winged nose, with our father's high-cheeked Barbadian cast to her face, was pretty.

"She's goin' be lucky," Da-duh said and patted her once on the cheek. "Any girl child that takes after the father does be lucky."

She turned then to me. But oddly enough she did not touch me. Instead leaning close, she peered hard at me, and then quickly drew back. I thought I saw her hand start up as though to shield her eyes. It was almost as if she saw not only me, a thin truculent child who it was said took after no one but myself, but something in me which for some reason she found disturbing, even threatening. We looked silently at each other for a long time there in the noisy shed, our gaze locked. She was the first to look away.

"But Adry," she said to my mother and her laugh was cracked, thin, apprehensive. "Where did you get this one here with this fierce look?"

"We don't know where she came out of, my Da-duh," my mother said, laughing also. Even I smiled to myself. After all I had won the encounter. Da-duh had recognized my small strength—and this was all I ever asked of the adults in my life then.

"Come, soul," Da-duh said and took my hand. "You must be one of those New York terrors you hear so much about."

She led us, me at her side and my sister and mother behind, out of the shed into the sunlight that was like a bright driving summer rain and over to a group of people clustered beside a decrepit lorry. They were our relatives, most of them from St. Andrews although Da-duh herself lived in St. Thomas, the women wearing bright print dresses, the colors vivid against their darkness, the men rusty black suits that encased them like straitjackets. Da-duh, holding fast to my hand, became my anchor as they circled round us like a nervous sea, exclaiming, touching us with their calloused hands, embracing us shyly. They laughed in awed bursts "But look Adry got big-big children!"/ "And see the nice things they wearing, wrist watch and all!"/ "I tell you, Adry has done all right for sheself in New York. ..."

Da-duh, ashamed at their wonder, embarrassed for them, admonished them the while. "But oh Christ," she said, "why you all got to get on like you never saw people from 'Away' before? You would think New York is the only place in the world to hear wunna. That's why I don't like to go anyplace with you St. Andrews people, you know. You all ain't been colonized."

We were in the back of the lorry finally, packed in among the barrels of ham, flour, cornmeal and rice and the trunks of clothes that my mother had brought as gifts. We made our way slowly through Bridgetown's clogged streets, part of a funereal procession of cars and open-sided buses, bicycles and donkey carts. The dim little limestone shops and offices along the way marched with us, at the same mournful pace, toward the same grave ceremony—as did the people, the women balancing huge baskets on top their heads as if they were no more than hats they wore to shade them from the sun. Looking over the edge of the lorry I watched as their feet slurred the dust. I listened, and their voices, raw and loud and dissonant in the heat, seemed to be grappling with each other high overhead.

Da-duh sat on a trunk in our midst, a monarch amid her court. She still held my hand, but it was different now. I had suddenly become her anchor, for I felt her fear of the lorry with its asthmatic motor (a fear and distrust, I later learned, she held of all machines) beating like a pulse in her rough palm.

As soon as we left Bridgetown behind though, she relaxed, and while the others around us talked she gazed at the canes standing tall on either side of the winding marl road. "C'dear," she said softly to herself after a time. "The canes this side are pretty enough."

They were too much for me. I thought of them as giant weeds that had overrun the island, leaving scarcely any room for the small tottering houses of sunbleached pine we passed or the people, dark streaks as our lorry hurtled by. I suddenly feared that we were journeying, unaware that we were, toward some dangerous place where the canes, grown as high and thick as a forest, would close in on us and run us through with their stiletto blades. I longed then for the familiar: for the street in Brooklyn where I lived, for my father who had refused to accompany us ("Blowing out good money on foolishness," he had said of the trip), for a game of tag with my friends under the chestnut tree outside our aging brownstone house.

"Yes, but wait till you see St. Thomas canes," Da-duh was saying to me. "They's canes father, bo,"

Paule Marshall

she gave a proud arrogant nod. "Tomorrow, God willing, I goin' take you out in the ground and show them to you."

True to her word Da-duh took me with her the following day out into the ground. It was a fairly large plot adjoining her weathered board and shingle house and consisting of a small orchard, a good-sized canepiece and behind the canes, where the land sloped abruptly down, a gully. She had purchased it with Panama money sent her by her eldest son, my uncle Joseph, who had died working on the canal. We entered the ground along a trail no wider than her body and as devious and complex as her reasons for showing me her land. Da-duh strode briskly ahead, her slight form filled out this morning by the layers of sacking petticoats she wore under her working dress to protect her against the damp. A fresh white cloth, elaborately arranged around her head, added to her height, and lent her a vain, almost roguish air.

Her pace slowed once we reached the orchard, and glancing back at me occasionally over her shoulder, she pointed out the various trees.

"This here is a breadfruit," she said. "That one yonder is a papaw. Here's a guava. This is a mango. I know you don't have anything like these in New York. Here's a sugar apple." (The fruit looked more like artichokes than apples to me.) "This one bears limes. ..." She went on for some time, intoning the names of the trees as though they were those of her gods. Finally, turning to me, she said, "I know you don't have anything this nice where you come from." Then, as I hesitated: "I said I know you don't have anything this nice where you come from. ..."

"No," I said and my world did seem suddenly lacking.

Da-duh nodded and passed on. The orchard ended and we were on the narrow cart road that led through the canepiece, the canes clashing like swords above my cowering head. Again she turned and her thin muscular arms spread wide, her dim gaze embracing the small field of canes, she said—and her voice almost broke under the weight of her pride, "Tell me, have you got anything like these in that place where you were born?"

"No."

"I din' think so. I bet you don't even know that these canes here and the sugar you eat is one and the same thing. That they does throw the canes into some damn machine at the factory and squeeze out all the little life in them to make sugar for you all so in New York to eat. I bet you don't know that."

"I've got two cavities and I'm not allowed to eat a lot of sugar."

But Da-duh didn't hear me. She had turned with an inexplicably angry motion and was making her way rapidly out of the canes and down the slope at the edge of the field which led to the gully below. Following her apprehensively down the incline amid a stand of banana plants whose leaves flapped like elephants' ears in the wind, I found myself in the middle of a small tropical wood—a place dense and damp and gloomy and tremulous with the fitful play of light and shadow as the leaves high above moved against the sun that was almost hidden from view. It was a violent place, the tangled foliage fighting each other for a chance at the sunlight, the branches of the trees locked in what seemed an immemorial struggle, one both necessary and inevitable. But despite the violence, it was pleasant, almost peaceful in the gully, and beneath the thick undergrowth the earth smelled like spring.

This time Da-duh didn't even bother to ask her usual question, but simply turned and waited for me to speak.

"No," I said, my head bowed. "We don't have anything like this in New York."

"Ah," she cried, her triumph complete. "I din' think so. Why, I've heard that's a place where you can walk till you near drop and never see a tree."

"We've got a chestnut tree in front of our house," I said.

"Does it bear?" She waited. "I ask you, does it bear?"

"Not anymore," I muttered. "It used to, but not anymore."

She gave the nod that was like a nervous twitch. "You see," she said. "Nothing can bear there." Then, secure behind her scorn, she added, "But tell me, what's this snow like that you hear so much about?"

Looking up, I studied her closely, sensing my chance, and then I told her, describing at length and with as much drama as I could summon not only what snow in the city was like, but what it would be like here, in her perennial summer kingdom.

"... And you see all these trees you got here," I said. "Well, they'd be bare. No leaves, no fruit, nothing. They'd be covered in snow. You see your canes. They'd be buried under tons of snow. The snow would be higher than your head, higher than your house, and you wouldn't be able to come down into this here gully because it would be snowed under. ..."

She searched my face for the lie, still scornful but intrigued. "What a thing, huh?" she said finally, whispering it softly to herself.

"And when it snows you couldn't dress like you are now," I said. "Oh no, you'd freeze to death. You'd have to wear a hat and gloves and galoshes and ear muffs so your ears wouldn't freeze and drop off, and a heavy coat. I've got a Shirley Temple coat with fur on the collar. I can dance. You wanna see?"

Before she could answer I began, with a dance called the Truck which was popular back then in the 1930's. My right forefinger waving, I trucked around the nearby trees and around Da-duh's awed and rigid form. After the Truck I did the Suzy-Q, my lean hips swishing, my sneakers sidling zigzag over the ground. "I can sing," I said and did so, starting with "I'm Gonna Sit Right Down and Write Myself a Letter," then without pausing, "Tea For Two," and ending with "I Found a Million Dollar Baby in a Five and Ten Cent Store."

For long moments afterwards Da-duh stared at me as if I were a creature from Mars, an emissary from some world she did not know but which intrigued her and whose power she both felt and feared. Yet something about my performance must have pleased her, because bending down she slowly lifted her long skirt and then, one by one, the layers of petticoats until she came to a drawstring purse dangling at the end of a long strip of cloth tied round her waist. Opening the purse she handed me a penny. "Here," she said half-smiling against her will. "Take this to buy yourself a sweet at the shop up the road. There's nothing to be done with you, soul."

From then on, whenever I wasn't taken to visit relatives, I accompanied Da-duh out into the ground, and alone with her amid the canes or down in the gully I told her about New York. It always began with some slighting remark on her part: "I know they don't have anything this nice where you come from," or "Tell me, I hear those foolish people in New York does do such and such. ..." But as I answered, recreating my towering world of steel and concrete and machines for her, building the city out of words, I would feel her give way. I came to know the signs of her surrender: the total stillness that would come over her little hard dry form, the probing gaze that like a surgeon's knife sought to cut through my skull to get at the images there, to see if I were lying; above all, her fear, a fear nameless and profound, the same one I had felt beating in the palm of her hand that day in the lorry.

Over the weeks I told her about refrigerators, radios, gas stoves, elevators, trolley cars, wringer washing machines, movies, airplanes, the cyclone at Coney Island, subways, toasters, electric lights: "At night, see, all you have to do is flip this little switch on the wall and all the lights in the house go on. Just like that. Like magic. It's like turning on the sun at night."

"But tell me," she said to me once with a faint mocking smile, "do the white people have all these things too or it's only the people looking like us?"

I laughed. "What d'ya mean," I said. "The white people have even better." Then: "I beat up a white girl in my class last term."

"Beating up white people!" Her tone was incredulous.

"How you mean!" I said, using an expression of hers. "She called me a name."

For some reason Da-duh could not quite get over this and repeated in the same hushed, shocked voice, "Beating up white people now! Oh, the lord, the world's changing up so I can scarce recognize it anymore."

One morning toward the end of our stay, Da-duh led me into a part of the gully that we had never visited before, an area darker and more thickly overgrown than the rest, almost impenetrable. There in a small clearing amid the dense bush, she stopped before an incredibly tall royal palm which rose cleanly out of the ground, and drawing the eye up with it, soared high above the trees around it into the sky. It appeared to be touching the blue dome of sky, to be flaunting its dark crown of fronds right in the blinding white face of the late morning sun.

Da-duh watched me a long time before she spoke, and then she said, very quietly, "All right, now, tell me if you've got anything this tall in that place you're from."

I almost wished, seeing her face, that I could have said no. "Yes," I said. "We've got buildings hundreds of times this tall in New York. There's one called the Empire State Building that's the tallest in the world. My class visited it last year and I went all the way to the top. It's got over a hundred floors. I can't describe how tall it is. Wait a minute. What's the name of that hill I went to visit the other day, where they have the police station?"

"You mean Bissex?"

"Yes, Bissex. Well, the Empire State Building is way taller than that."

You're lying now!" she shouted, trembling with rage. Her hand lifted to strike me.

"No, I'm not," I said. "It really is, if you don't believe me I'll send you a picture postcard of it soon as I get back home so you can see for yourself. But it's way taller than Bissex."

All the fight went out of her at that. The hand poised to strike me fell limp to her side, and as she stared at me, seeing not me but the building that was taller than the highest hill she knew, the small stubborn light in her eyes (it was the same amber as the flame in the kerosene lamp she lit at dusk) began to fail. Finally, with a vague gesture that even in the midst of her defeat still tried to dismiss me and my world, she turned and started back through the gully, walking slowly, her steps groping and uncertain, as if she were suddenly no longer sure of the way, while I followed triumphant yet strangely saddened behind.

The next morning I found her dressed for our morning walk but stretched out on the Berbice chair in the tiny drawing room where she sometimes napped during the afternoon heat, her face turned to the window beside her. She appeared thinner and suddenly indescribably old.

"My Da-duh," I said.

"Yes, nuh," she said. Her voice was listless and the face she slowly turned my way was, now that I think back on it, like a Benin mask, the features drawn and almost distorted by an ancient abstract sorrow.

"Don't you feel well?" I asked.

"Girl, I don't know."

"My Da-duh, I goin' boil you some bush tea," my aunt, Da-duh's youngest child, who lived with her, called from the shed roof kitchen.

"Who tell you I need bush tea?" she cried, her voice assuming for a moment its old authority. "You can't even rest nowadays without some malicious person looking for you to be dead. Come girl," she motioned me to a place beside her on the old-fashioned lounge chair, "give us a tune."

I sang for her until breakfast at eleven, all my brash irreverent Tin Pan Alley songs, and then just before noon we went out into the ground. But it was a short, dispirited walk. Da-duh didn't even notice that the mangoes were beginning to ripen and would have to be picked before the village boys got to them. And when she paused occasionally and looked out across the canes or up at her trees it wasn't as if she were seeing them but something else. Some huge, monolithic shape had imposed itself, it seemed, between her and the land, obstructing her vision. Returning to the house she slept the entire afternoon on the Berbice chair.

She remained like this until we left, languishing away the mornings on the chair at the window gazing out at the land as if it were already doomed; then, at noon, taking the brief stroll with me through the ground during which she seldom spoke, and afterwards returning home to sleep till almost dusk sometimes.

On the day of our departure she put on the austere, ankle length white dress, the black shoes and brown felt hat (her town clothes she called them), but she did not go with us to town. She saw us off on the road outside her house and in the midst of my mother's tearful protracted farewell, she leaned down and whispered in my ear, "Girl, you're not to forget now to send me the picture of that building, you hear."

By the time I mailed her the large colored picture postcard of the Empire State Building she was dead. She died during the famous '37 strike which began shortly after we left. On the day of her death England sent planes flying low over the island in a show of force—so low, according to my aunt's letter, that the downdraft from them shook the ripened mangoes from the trees in Da-duh's orchard. Frightened, everyone in the village fled into the canes. Except Da-duh. She remained in the house at the window so my aunt said, watching as the planes came swooping and screaming like monstrous birds down over the village, over her house, rattling her trees and flattening the young canes in her field. It must have seemed to her lying there that they did not intend pulling out of their dive, but like the hardback beetles which hurled themselves with suicidal force against the walls of the house at night, those menacing silver shapes would hurl themselves in an ecstasy of self-immolation onto the land, destroying it utterly.

When the planes finally left and the villagers returned they found her dead on the Berbice chair at the window.

She died and I lived, but always, to this day even, within the shadow of her death. For a brief period after I was grown I went to live alone, like one doing penance, in a loft above a noisy factory in downtown New York and there painted seas of sugar-cane and huge swirling Van Gogh suns and palm trees striding like brightly-plumed Tutsi warriors across a tropical landscape, while the thunderous tread of the machines downstairs jarred the floor beneath my easel, mocking my efforts. ❖

Bridgetown: capital of Barbados
canepiece: area planted with sugar cane
St. Andrews, St. Thomas: parishes (like counties) in Barbados

By the Fireside

Denizé Lauture

For the Haitian migrant workers of upstate New York

Denizé Lauture was born in Haiti, the oldest of 13 children in a rural farming family. He migrated to the United States in 1968 at age 22. While working as a welder in Harlem, he attended evening classes at City College of New York and earned degrees in sociology and bilingual education.

Lauture writes and performs poetry in Haitian Creole, English and French. He is the author of two volumes of poetry and two children's books. He is on the faculty of Saint Thomas Aquinas College in Sparkill, New York.

In 1983, Denizé Lauture was invited to give a poetry reading to a group of Haitian farm workers. The Haitians worked alongside Puerto Ricans and Dominicans as apple-pickers in orchards near Geneseo, in upstate New York. "By the Fireside" was written and performed for the workers in Haitian Creole at the request of Sylvia Kelly of the Geneseo Migrant Center.

Come, come close to me
all of you
come close to me
still closer to me
form a circle around me
I am made of good firewood, not green
no smoke will fill your eyes ...

Please don't be afraid
my left hand won't burn you
with a smoldering twig
Don't be afraid
My right hand won't gather hot ash
to throw into your eyes
Don't be afraid
my feet
won't roll the hot rocks
to burn your legs ...

The same fingers
fashioned us
with the same clay
in the same mold
We were plunged
into the same wooden tub
bathed with the same herbal water
and our umbilical cords
were buried under the same *mapou* tree ...

My beard is not yet grey
I bring no advice
I am not a prophet
I can't say what tomorrow holds

My star, just like yours,
leans to the wrong side ...

I don't come singing
I know well
our hearts are too troubled
I know well
we have bled too much
My star, just like yours,
leans to the wrong side ...

I don't intend to instruct you
You have already mastered
life's most difficult feat
I bring no medicine
for your illnesses
I cannot cure mine
My star, just like yours,
leans to the wrong side ...

Dark clouds have gathered
they stole our sun
it has disappeared completely
Dark clouds have gathered
they stole our moon
Oh, how shall we ask our children
to raise their heads
to gaze at the sun
to gaze at the moon
or to count the stars
in our sky?
Our children's stars,
just like ours,
lean to the wrong side ...

I dreamed and dreamed
dreamed and dreamed
Grandfather came and went
came and went
riding his ailing pony
confronting darkness
and the invisible pathways
with his *Lanj Kondiktè*
and candles
he made himself
with his beeswax
Grandfather was a farmer
he planted coffee trees

A 9-year-old Haitian child working in a vegetable field near Salisbury, Maryland.

and raised bees for their honey
He was also a *pè savann*
He buried the dead
prayed for the departed souls
comforted the grieving relatives
and drew the marks of death
around gardens
on the trunks of grapefruit and orange trees
avocado and mango trees
plantain and coconut trees ...

We find no life anywhere
we die badly everywhere
by the roadside
on the street
in the snow
at sea
in prisons
in factories
in sugar cane fields
under tractors
in fields that grow sweet vegetables

We are like stray and blind dogs
running head down
in a land hostile to canines
We turn left
a shower of rocks
batters our skulls
We turn right
and face an army of sticks
that shatter our ribs
We limp on one foot ...

But I remember
I used to see us
pounding our chests three times to say:
We have pride
We have willpower in our minds
We have veins in our wrists
We have courage in our loins
like all people
but—damn it—
I am dreaming when I see that!

Behind us there is
a muddy pigs' wallow
Yes, we have come far
so very far
Ahead there are
many detours
many dangerous crossroads
many jagged peaks to climb
many seas to cross
We have no Moses
to turn rocks into clear water
to make manna fall from the sky
to turn sticks into snakes
that will poison our enemies ...
We have no God
who can open the seas
to let us pass
and close them again
on the deadly armies pursuing us ...

A country midwife
assisted my mother
and my birth took place
on a piece of plantain mat
A red-hot knife
cut my umbilical cord

Like you
I grew up barefoot
and bare-bottomed
I never went to a doctor
A compress of medicinal herbs
calmed my headaches
Pepper tea
cured my bellyaches

Years went by
I never heard "Happy Birthday"
I never knew about Santa Claus
I heard about "Tonton Joudlan"
but I don't remember what he brought me

I was a wanted child
first-born son
nephew of *sanbas!*
I sang happily
carrying three full calabashes of water
one on my head and one in each hand
from the distant spring
I sang happily
carrying on my shoulder
great bundles of firewood
I sang happily
uprooting thorny weeds
to feed our few pigs
our only donkey
and our one cow
I danced when clearing the land
and digging the furrows
to plant sweet potatoes
I danced as I sowed
corn kernels and beans
into mother earth's womb

My uncles, good sanbas
taught me to sing
to beat the drum
to sign my name
and to make love
under the green leafy covers
of our coffee bushes
They taught me
how to look for fallen avocados at night
using flaming torches
made from dried leaves of the coconut palm

My grandfather, the pè savann,
taught me to read his Lanj Kondiktè
He made me understand
that broomsticks cannot turn into airplanes
that werewolves only fly
in the minds of foolish people

But how many real werewolves
have we met
on the hellish road
we travel in our lives!
They drink our salty sweat
they turn into leeches
they splatter our blood
they take our women
they rape our girls and even our boys
they force us to flee across the ocean ...

My friends, let me go back to my story
Where there is no light
we can still catch lightning bugs
capture all wandering lightning bugs
bring their heads together
so there will be light
so that we do not fall into the abyss

One day, how could I ever forget?
My father placed me in front of him
and we began to walk
barefoot I walked
barefoot he walked
and he showed me the way to school

My father uses an old measuring tape
to measure the people
who wear the clothes he makes
He writes his customers' names
in broken French
because he was never taught
how to write his beautiful mother tongue
His son turned into
a fiery bird
chattering clearly
in many languages ...

Yes, cornmeal today
millet tomorrow
millet today
cornmeal tomorrow
hunger in the belly
head on fire
son and father
father and son
Once there was a crazy bird
that began all its songs
with its father's name
            up and down
            every day
            I leave with the moon
            return with the stars
            leave with the stars
            and return with the moon
            learning a
            learning b
            counting 1
            counting 2
            hunger today
            hunger tomorrow
            won't turn me from my path

On the school bench
the master's whip
devoured my back
On a mat at home
in the evening
my father's guava switch
beat my backside
            learning a
            learning b
            counting 1
            counting 2
            hunger today
            hunger tomorrow
            won't turn me from my path

Rocks and stones
cut my toes
they sliced
the soles of my feet
the blow of the ruler
twisted my fingers
        learning a
        learning b
        counting 1
        counting 2
        hunger today
        hunger tomorrow
        won't turn me from my path

One day I leaped
I grabbed the limb
of a sacred tree
I held it firmly
I didn't let go
I leaped again
I grabbed a higher limb
I held it firmly
I didn't let go
Still a higher leap
and I became a bird
I flew right into the sun's eye
I grabbed the waist of the rainbow
I held it and kissed it
I caressed it
I took it
I stole all its colors
and I will never let them go

I saw
in a universe of light
my grandfather's book
my uncles' shakers
my father's measuring tape
his old notebook
I heard
the sweetest songs the fiery bird can sing ...

But when sleep overcomes me
I always see
the shadow of the wings
of the accursed *malfini*
Oh, evil bird!
When will you give us back our skies?
When will our chicks grow up
without seeing
your dark shadow?

It is not our destiny
to come to a bad end
There are people who suffer
more than we do
We do not have volcanoes
to burn us
We are not too heavy for the sea
It would have swallowed us long ago
We do not have twelve tribes
In our country
there are mountains behind mountains
but we have no deadly deserts
The day we manage to lasso
the horns of the bull
named progress
we shall tie it
to our *poto mitan*
to mate with all future
generations of cows

The sun does not hate us
It bathes us with its light
every day
The moon does not hate us
It is the glowing torch
that guides our steps
upon the dark hills at night
The sea does not hate us
It caresses our shores
ceaselessly

The wind might be angry today
but tomorrow it is gentle
Ever since the flood
no one speaks ill of the rain
But our fires
we fuel them with wood

We know well
that burning wood
becomes ash
and too much ash
can become another sea of whiteness
to blind us
The primeval fires of life
dance the *kalinda*
when lightning rends the sky
when volcanoes erupt
or when the great genius of the universe
with the force of a powerful magnet
strikes all heads together
like rolling thunder
to recreate the earth
then
hands strike foreheads
hands pound chests
throats cry out in rage
accusing
all of us who have not done what we should
all of us who recite the colonizer's prayer
and our ears hear the answering rhythm
from the dead and the living
the young and the old
the incantatory words
"Mea culpa! Mea culpa! Mea culpa!"
Then there will be a rainbow's cap
to fit each person's head
The flames of the fire of life
will engulf our valleys and our mountains

LOVE AND LIFE
BOUND UP IN THE SEVEN COLORS OF THE
RAINBOW
COME CASCADING DOWN
ONTO OUR LAND!

❖

mapou: tree in Haiti to which many Haitians attribute some kind of magic function

Lanj Kondikte: literally "guiding angel": book of ancient French and Latin prayers used in Haiti for religious functions

pè savann: literally "bush priest": layperson who performs Catholic rites such as baptisms, marriages and funerals in rural communities

Tonton Joudlan: in Haitian folklore, a generous figure who brings gifts to children on New Year's Day

sanba: singer/storyteller

calabash: container made from a hollowed-out gourd

werewolf: terrifying magic figure in Haitian folklore that supposedly flies through the air and feeds on human blood

shaker: rattle made from a dried gourd, used as a musical instrument

malfini: literally "bad ending": local hawk in Haiti which preys upon chickens and is believed to be a bad omen

mountains behind mountains: evokes a Haitian proverb, *Dèyè mòn, gen mòn* ("Behind the mountains, more mountains")

poto mitan: sacred center post in a vodou sanctuary

rainbow's cap: In rural Haitian lore, something like the pot of gold at the end of the rainbow. When a rainbow appears it is said to be drinking water from a stream or spring; if you follow the rainbow you will arrive at the water, and if you steal the "cap" while the rainbow is drinking, you will become wealthy.

La Ciguapa

Josefina Báez

Josefina Báez, born in the Dominican Republic, came to New York City at age 11. An actress, dancer and writer, she heads the theater group Latinarte and teaches creative writing and theater in the New York City public schools.

La Ciguapa is a character in Dominican folklore. The figure is drawn from the mythology of the Taíno Indians who lived on the island of Hispaniola before the Europeans arrived. La Ciguapa is usually pictured as a woman with long flowing hair and the feet fixed on backwards.

Our deity La Ciguapa arrived in New York too.
The subway steps changed her nature.
In the ups and downs, to and from the train,
her feet became like everybody else's in the rush hour crowd.
She did not notice the drastic change.
This was the first sign of assimilation
—a concept not to be understood, but experienced.

And Ciguapa cut her hair.
Maybe to be fashionable or just to simplify her rituals.

Her lover was not a hunter, as the legend goes.
He was a medical doctor by profession
turned taxi driver by necessity.
He, the gypsy taxi driver, worked for an uptown car service.
In that context, our deity was codified to a mere 10-13.
It meant companion or wife;
we never knew and she never cared.
Their love was filled with few words, passionate actions,
fast merengues, tasty sancochos,
and predictable as well as strictly scheduled trips
to la remesa "El Sol Sale Para Todos."
These trips, energized by green dollars, reforested the island.

Ciguapa works in a factory making pinkish dolls.
Dolls she never had.
Dolls dulled by the unique smell of new things.
Earning less than the minimum wage,
she managed to pay an immigration lawyer she never met.
She got her green card. It was not green.

By heart she knows 33 English words. Enough tools for today's
communication exchange by heart.

What a triumph!
She is going to visit the Dominican Republic,
first time in seven years.
She made it!
Huge suitcases that she bought
at BBB (Bueno Bonito Barato) on 14th Street
are filled with unthinkable, unnecessary items.
To be sold at laughable prices.
Prices calculated in dollars, paid in pesos.
Laughable reality.

Her laugh is based on a constant and bitter cry.
Constant nostalgia,
bitter reality,
unheard cry.

Here in no man's land
Here in no woman's stand
You can become what you are not
by lotto, circumstance, opportunity, luck/unluck,
karma.
You might forget your divinity or from your
worldly corner
become a saint

❖

    10-13: code for wife or female companion,
used in radio communications between taxi
drivers and dispatchers in parts of New York
City
merengue: popular dance music of the
Dominican Republic
sancocho: savory stew of meat and root
vegetables
remesa: money transfer office, used by
immigrants to send support to family
members in the home country
green card: identifies a legal permanent
resident of the United States

My School Years

Nicholasa Mohr

Nicholasa Mohr was born in New York City to parents from Puerto Rico. She grew up in East Harlem and the Bronx during the 1940s. In this excerpt from Mohr's memoir, she remembers her school experiences and her struggle to realize her dream of becoming an artist.

While Mohr was in junior high, her mother became ill. After her mother's death, 14-year-old Nicholasa returned to her art work. She had promised her mother that she would achieve her goals, no matter what.

She studied fashion illustration in high school, and after graduation studied art at the New School for Social Research, the Brooklyn Museum Art School, and the Pratt Graphics Center. Mohr achieved success first as a painter and printmaker and later as a writer of fiction. Her novels and short stories have won many awards.

Excerpted from IN MY OWN WORDS: GROWING UP INSIDE THE SANCTUARY OF MY IMAGINATION (New York: Simon & Schuster). © 1994 by Nicholasa Mohr. Used by permission of the author.

Kindergarten

I had waited with anticipation for school and practiced all my letters and all my numbers. My brother Vincent had tutored me carefully so that now I could count to one hundred. I felt very proud and set out to show the teacher all I knew.

I was told to obey and listen to my teacher because I had been instructed that a teacher "is a very important individual." I was cautioned not to misbehave or speak out of turn.

"You must be a good girl and do exactly as you're told," my mother warned me. Otherwise, she promised, I'd have to answer to her and my father.

In class I sat at my desk like all the other children and looked with awe at my teacher. I don't remember her name, but I can still see her. She was a slender woman; now I can only guess her age to be her late forties. She had short gray hair, wore rimless glasses and a loose-fitting brown dress decorated with a white-and-green flower print.

Her manner was reserved and she seldom smiled. Occasionally she brought her index finger to her mouth and said, "Shhh ... no talking. We must be quiet."

From time to time I checked out my classmates. Everyone had their hair neatly combed and sported new school clothes, just like me. My mother had brushed my hair till it shone. We sat with our hands clasped on our desks as instructed by our teacher.

Many details of that first day are a blur in my memory. However, the feeling of excitement that filled my being as I prepared to show the teacher that I could read lots of words and count way up to one hundred is still quite clear in my mind. I wanted to make her proud of me so that I could please her and please my family.

My reward would be teacher's praise.

The right moment arrived when I heard her ask the question, "How many of you here know how to count your numbers, and can anyone count to ten?" Immediately I raised my hand so high up in the air that I almost fell out of my seat.

Teacher asked me my name, and I told her. Then she asked me to count to ten. I stood and began counting. However, I didn't stop at ten. I kept on going until I reached about twenty-five. Then her loud voice commanded me to stop. But I announced to everyone quite proudly that I could count right up to one hundred.

"Is that so?" she responded. When she asked me to come up to the front of the class I honestly thought that she was going to allow me to finish counting up to one hundred. Instead she asked me to be quiet and face the students.

"Look at this show-off!" she said, digging her finger in between my shoulder blades. Teacher told the students hers was not a class for show-offs and continued reprimanding me. "When I ask you to do something, you do it. I said count to ten. I did not give you permission to count any further!"

All the children giggled and a few of them even pointed at me and made faces. After a few moments, she sent me back to my seat and promised to deal with me at another time.

I felt myself blush with shame. I was caught unawares and had no idea that I was doing something wrong. The humiliation brought tears to my eyes, but I swallowed and did not permit myself to cry. In order to cope with my feelings of disgrace, I simply withdrew. I would try never to be so bold again.

All my dreams of impressing the teacher and being rewarded for my hard work were dismissed in an instant.

Teacher took a dislike to me and for the rest of my kindergarten year, I was seldom called upon. When I bravely raised my hand, I was generally ignored. My attendance and behavior were satisfactory to fair. But my grades were always above average. I worked very hard on all my assignments even when I found the lessons boring.

My school was ethnically mixed with the children of immigrants: Italians, Irish, Eastern Europeans, and Greeks. There were also other Latino children, mostly Puerto Rican. A good percentage of the Puerto Rican children did not know English fluently. It was therefore natural for me to speak in Spanish to them. For this I was chastised and punished.

Once when a little girl did not understand the teacher, I forgot my resolution to stay passive and took it upon myself to raise my hand. When Teacher called upon me, I proceeded to translate in Spanish what the teacher meant to my classmate. Before my classmate could respond, Teacher yelled out her disapproval.

"We speak English in the United States of America," she said, and told me that I was not in my old country. Then she addressed the whole class and told us that if everyone acted like me, no one would do any better than their parents. We would all be destined for failure. Where was our gratitude and our loyalty to America, she asked. Of course no one dared respond.

I was put in a corner facing the wall for the rest of the day. A corner which I remember well, with bare pea green walls, for I was sent there numerous times during the year.

I would sit on a chair facing the wall, looking for a discoloration in the paint, a crack in the plaster, or shadows on the surface. In this way I used my eyes and imagination to adjust these imperfections by making them take on other visual forms.

On that wall I remember a variety of scenes, among them trees and a waterfall, part of a schooner sinking at sea, and the profile of a horse. I was able to meditate upon these images and sit under the waterfall or walk in the woods.

Although I was still embarrassed and angry at Teacher, this game helped ease my punishment. At the same time, I enjoyed sharpening my sense of fantasy.

I also began to realize that I must never presume anything in front of Teacher. I must never let Teacher know that I could think for myself. Above all, I must never speak in Spanish, because this would certainly cause Teacher to become furious and punish me.

In class, I learned that it was dangerous to try to speak the language of my parents or my community. Nor was I ever to let Teacher see that I knew more than what she expected of me. As well, I should never introduce another way of doing things, even if, in my own judgment, it was a better way. Any kind of independent behavior meant that I could be publicly humiliated and punished. ...

As a consequence of Teacher's rejection, I became more and more involved in my personal work at home. My mother gave me a small pair of scissors, and I began to do cutouts from cardboard. I used paste and colorful construction paper.

All of my treasures were well kept and organized in my "box of things," a wooden milk crate that contained and protected the contents that I created for the world of my imagination.

I made my own dolls out of cardboard and created pretty paper dresses for them. I made cardboard furniture, buildings, trees, flowers, and animals. In fact, I created a whole world for myself.

A world where I could be outdoors and where my people didn't fight and life did not cause us pain.

In my world only good things were possible.

A Teacher Cares

School was better in The Bronx. There were fewer students in a classroom, and the corridors were not as noisy as my old school. But things remained more or less the same for me until I reached sixth grade. Finally, I encountered one of the few good teachers of my school experience.

Mr. Johnson was a tall person with a head of unruly straw-colored hair. I was becoming more and more bored with school. After the deaths of Papa and Martin, and given the pressures created by changes at home, I became withdrawn and petulant in class and refused to participate in any discussions.

One day, Mr. Johnson had a discussion on special talents and our future. One kid played the clarinet, another played the piano; both were considering musical careers. A black girl said she wanted to become a great singer like Marian Anderson. There was also a boy who liked to draw. I had seen his work and he was not as good as I was, probably because he didn't practice as much as I did. Mr. Johnson said that he knew there were two artists in class and called upon both of us. The boy said he wanted to be a cartoonist. I said I wanted to be an artist who could draw everything in this world and have my work shown in museums.

As soon as I spoke, Mr. Johnson challenged me by asking me to draw something on the black-board. Suddenly I felt stupid, as if everybody was staring at me, and I didn't move. "That's because

IN MY OWN WORDS

Nicholasa Mohr

Growing Up
Inside the Sanctuary
of My Imagination

A Memoir by the Author of
Felita

she can't really draw good," said the boy who wanted to be a cartoonist.

My training, as a member of a large family and the only girl, was to stand up to a provocation, especially when the dare dealt with familiar ground. Now I was determined to show him and the class what I could do. I walked up to the blackboard with total confidence.

I asked Mr. Johnson if he had a special request. Anything I wanted to draw would do, he said. But just then the boy yelled out and dared me to draw a ship with pirates because girls could only draw dolls and baby animals. Everyone laughed, but the teacher said that I was to draw only what *I* wanted. I remained confident, because a ship and pirates doing battle was a favorite scene among the many that I had carefully copied out of adventure books.

I picked up the chalk and carefully drew the bottom of the ship, then the sails and the cannons and, to top it off, a pirate flag with skull and crossbones, followed by the water and clouds. Then I began drawing figures of pirates with swords and guns. I could hear the *oohs* and *aahs* from the class, and this fired me on. I drew another ship in the distance on the attack.

After my demonstration, I enjoyed the attention and admiration I received. Even my antagonist challenger had to admit I could "really draw."

From the very beginning when I put pencil to paper, I recognized my ability to draw as an asset at home, in the street, and in school. This special talent set me apart from most of the other children and gave me an edge, a place from which I was allowed to excel.

Even the most narrow-minded and prejudiced teachers were impressed by my ability. I remember a teacher in third grade who was a frightful bigot. She would not even tolerate a greeting in Spanish between pupils. She'd lecture to us on the virtues of being real Americans and say things like, "Why don't you folks try to speak like Americans?" or "You're all too ungrateful to be allowed in this country." In spite of her low expectations of Latino children, I once overheard this same teacher talking to a colleague about me. "Nicholasa has talent, so she can't be all bad," she remarked.

Mr. Johnson encouraged me to draw posters for the school library for the celebration of Washington's and Lincoln's birthdays. He had me design sets for a class play about Pilgrims landing on Plymouth Rock for Thanksgiving. He told me that I was smart and should definitely go on to college and earn a degree in fine arts. I had only had him for a semester and a quarter when, much to my discouragement, he was transferred to another school. Yet he was one of only two teachers who did their best to help me. The other was an English teacher in high school.

Sadly I can remember no one else caring or helping me during my New York City public school experience.

A Social Worker's Wrath

It was understood that I was going on to college to study art. No matter what we had to do, my mother impressed upon me that I must continue my education. I never doubted for a moment that I would study art. I had my heart set on attending the High School of Music and Art in Manhattan. It was a special school where the students could major in music or in art.

When I inquired at my junior high school, I was informed that I needed a high grade point average to qualify. Some of the kids told me that if a student did exceptionally well at Music and Art, she might receive a scholarship to go on to study art at any number of colleges in the city. As a result, I had been working hard at school to keep up my grades and hard at home doing my artwork. ...

Nicholasa's mother becomes terminally ill with cancer. Sad and distracted, Nicholasa must nonetheless make plans for her education after junior high.

At school, I struggled to keep up my average and was barely making my necessary grades. I was easily distracted. Even when I was outside and saw a mother and daughter walking together, I became depressed. I missed my mother's strength, her energy, and her guidance.

It was already the end of January, and I was going to graduate in June. I was still determined to study art and had made several dates to meet with my guidance counselor at school. However, because there often was no one at home to take care of my mom, I would leave school early or sometimes stay home the entire day. Consequently, these appointments had been canceled.

Finally one afternoon in early February I met with Mrs. Farrell to discuss my application to the High School of Music and Art. She greeted me cordially, told me to sit down, and asked me if I had thought carefully and seriously about which high school I wanted to attend. I was surprised by that question, since I had already made it known to her that I expected to apply to Music and Art. Nonetheless, I made my intentions clear and told Mrs. Farrell that my plans were to graduate from the High School of Music and Art and go on to college to get a degree in fine arts.

Mrs. Farrell reminded me that my grades had been slipping during the past year at school. Except for my close friends and homeroom teacher, I rarely spoke about my mother's illness. But now I told the guidance counselor about my mother's illness and explained that this was the reason for my lower grades. Mrs. Farrell told me she was sorry, but she remained skeptical.

I had always had top grades, I reminded her, except for the past year. Besides, I was only a few points down, and I promised to make them up no matter what. Please, I told her, I really want to go to the high school of my choice.

I clearly remember how she lit up a cigarette and marched back and forth, as if she were deep in thought. She was a tall, handsome woman who was always well dressed. Finally, with a benevolent smile, she informed me that what she was going to tell me was strictly for my own good. She assured me that her decision about my future had come after much thought and concern for my well-being.

In her judgment, the High School of Music and Art was no place for a student like me. I was poor, she reminded me, and if my mother did not survive, the chances of my going on to college were even slimmer than before. No, instead she had chosen a school where I could learn a trade. She decided, she said with a great deal of satisfaction, that I should be a seamstress. This was a skill that would always ensure me some work, she said.

Her own personal seamstress was Puerto Rican, a woman who fixed most of her clothes and even made special dresses for her. She pointed out that the attractive suit she was wearing was made by her valued seamstress. It was a great skill that my people had, she informed me, and I might as well take advantage of this talent.

My heart sank to the pit of my stomach. I hated sewing. I had never sewed. In fact, just the year before my mom had sewn almost an entire apron for me, which was my assignment in home economics class.

I recalled those failed attempts by my mom to teach me embroidery and crocheting when I was little. I was in a state of panic at the thought that I might spend my high school years sewing. It was like facing a nightmare.

Mrs. Farrell continued talking and sounded quite pleased with herself. But I hardly heard her words anymore. I know I interrupted her and pleaded that she not send me to a sewing school. "I can't sew," I implored, "and I hate sewing. Please don't send me there. Please ..."

Suddenly, I forgot all about my determination to get into the high school of my choice and my plans to study art. Now I became so fearful of being punished that my goals were cast aside. I tried to keep my voice steady, but I lost all control and began to cry.

Mrs. Farrell handed me a tissue, saying that there was no need to cry. If I didn't want to go to that school she'd find me another. She suggested a school that would teach me textile design, or perhaps fashion illustration. These skills would allow me to continue with my art career, she reasoned, and when I got out of school I could easily find a job. Meekly, but with some resolve, I brought up Music and Art again. I asked that she please reconsider, because I was determined to go to college and I'd find a way.

But her response was firm. In her analysis, if she allowed me to go there, I would be taking the place of a student who was definite college material. It was not fair of me, she scolded, to deprive another student of that place. No, she asserted, blind ambition was not a wise way for me to proceed.

There have been several times in my life when I felt that the world was crumbling under me and that I was falling into a dark abyss. This was surely one of those times. It never occurred to me to insist upon my rights and demand a school hearing. I was probably the best artist in my school. Everyone was aware of my abilities. My grades had always been in the top ten percent. Yet I had no knowledge that I could take action against this teacher and fight for my rights. As far as I knew, I had no rights.

There was no way I could go home and complain to my brothers.

Everyone was busy tending to my mother. The situation at home was tense at best, and most other times it was chaotic. How could I burden them with this? It would be too selfish. Besides, I was sure it was my fault. I had done something to deserve this decision. I had not worked hard enough—or maybe I just wasn't good enough.

I walked home that gray February day, and I remember the cold drizzle numbing my cheeks as I tried not to cry. I felt ashamed of myself, as if I had let my mother down.

No matter how heartbroken I felt, I decided that I would not tell my mother what had happened. In fact, I was not going to mention it to anyone else, either. ❖

Translating Grandfather's House

E.J. Vega

Julio Marzan

E.J. Vega was born in Cuba and came to the United States with his family in 1968. It was in the New York City schools in third or fourth grade, Vega remembers, that he had the experience on which this poem is based.

Vega currently teaches writing and literature at Palm Beach Community College in Florida. His poetry has appeared in numerous literary journals and several anthologies.

Reprinted from Lori M. Carlson, ed., COOL SALSA: BILINGUAL POEMS ON GROWING UP LATINO IN THE UNITED STATES (New York: Henry Holt & Co.). Collection © 1994 by Lori M. Carlson. Used by permission of Henry Holt & Co., Inc.

According to my sketch,
Rows of lemon & mango
Trees frame the courtyard
Of Grandfather's stone
And clapboard home;
The shadow of a palomino
Gallops on the lip
Of the horizon.

The teacher says
The house is from
Some Zorro
Movie I've seen.

"Ask my mom," I protest.
"She was born there—
Right there on the second floor!"

Crossing her arms she moves on.

Memories once certain as rivets
Become confused as awakenings
In strange places and I question
The house, the horse, the wrens
Perched on the slate roof—
The roof Oscar Jartín
Tumbled from one hot Tuesday,
Installing a new weather vane;
(He broke a shin and two fingers).

Classmates finish drawings of New
  York City
Housing projects on Navy Street.
I draw one too, with wildgrass
Rising from sidewalk cracks like
  widows.
In big round letters I title it:

GRANDFATHER'S HOUSE

Beaming, the teacher scrawls
An A+ in the corner and tapes
It to the green blackboard.

To the green blackboard.
❖

West Indian Girl

Rosa Guy

Rosa Guy was born in Trinidad and came to the United States with her family in 1932. She grew up in New York City's Harlem neighborhood, the setting for much of her fiction. She is a founder of the Harlem Writers Guild and has published novels, short stories and a play for young adults.

Her novel THE FRIENDS was first published in 1973. Set in Harlem, it tells of the complicated friendship between Phyllisia Cathy, whose family immigrated from the Caribbean, and Edith Jackson, an African-American girl.

Excerpted from THE FRIENDS (New York: Bantam Books, 1983). © 1973 by Rosa Guy. Used by permission of Bantam Books, a division of Bantam Doubleday Dell Publishing Group, Inc.

Since my father had sent for us, my sister Ruby who is sixteen and me, two years younger, and set us down in this miserable place called Harlem, New York, this was the first warm day. I, too, had not wanted to come here today. Walking to school, seeing people coming out of their homes with faces softened by smiles, for the first time I had been filled with the desire to run off somewhere, anywhere but to this room. I had not wanted to have to listen to a teacher I did not like, nor to sit among children I liked even less. But where could I go? I knew nothing about this strange city. Going one block out of my way between home and school, and I would be lost. And so I had come, grudgingly, but I had come.

Yet the moment I had entered the classroom, I knew that my instincts had been right. I should not have come today. The same recklessness that had pulled at me in the streets was big in the room, pulling and tugging at the control of the students. Fear cut a zigzag pattern from my stomach to my chest: The students in the class did not like *me*.

They mocked my West Indian accent, called me names—"monkey" was one of the nicer ones. Sometimes they waited after school to tease me, following me at times for several blocks, shouting. But it had been cold and after a time they had been only too glad to hunch their shoulders up to their ears and go home. Winter, as much as I hated it, had protected me. Now it was spring.

* * *

I pulled my attention back into the room just in time to hear Miss Lass throw a question in my direction.

"Can anyone tell me on what continent the country of Egypt is located?" she asked.

I stared fixedly at the blackboard. While it was certain I could not leave school, it was also certain that I did not feel like standing in the full glare of the children's animosity on this warm touchy day to answer any questions.

Teacher waited. The class waited. I waited, praying someone else would know the answer and, barring that, Miss Lass herself would explain. I did not remember her ever discussing Africa before. But I had been the star pupil too long—always jumping up to let others know how smart I was. And so Miss Lass kept looking at me while I kept looking at the blackboard. Finally, after a few minutes, she called: "Phyllisia?"

I did not move. Why did she want to make an example of me to the other children? There were at least thirty others she could call on. "Phyllisia!" I still kept my seat. I kept repeating to myself: I will not stand. I will not answer. I will not.

Then someone snickered, and someone else. My face burned with shame. Sitting there and not answering was like begging. And why should I beg? I had done nothing to anybody. I found myself standing. I heard my voice saying, despite a sixth sense warning me to remain silent, to stay in my seat, "Egypt is in Africa." Once started I kept on talking to dispel any notion that I might be guessing. "It is bordered on the South by the Sudan and on the North by the Mediterranean Sea which opens up into the Nile, which is the longest river in Africa and perhaps the world."

I resumed my seat, a taste of chalk in my mouth, unsatisfied with the display of my brilliance. Nor did I feel any better at the flurry of shuffling feet, the banging of more desks and the sound of contemptuous whispers.

"No it ain't either," a boy shouted from the back of the room. "They got A-rabs in Egypt. Everybody know ain't no A-rabs in Africa."

"That's where you are wrong," Miss Lass shrilled. "Egypt *is* a country in Africa. If some of you would follow Phyllisia's example and study your books, then perhaps the intelligence rate in this room might zoom up to zero."

Silently I groaned. Miss Lass had to know better. She had to know that she was setting me up as a target. Any fool would feel the agitation in the room. But that was exactly what she wanted!

I knew it suddenly. Standing in front of the room, her blond hair pulled back to emphasize the determination of her face, her body girdled to emphasize the determination of her spine, her eyes holding determinedly to anger, *Miss Lass was*

afraid!! She was afraid and she was using *me* to keep the hatred of the children away from *her*. I was the natural choice because I was a stranger and because I was proud.

The thought seemed to be so loud that it drew her attention, and for one moment we stared startled into each other's eyes. Her face turned a beet red and she shifted her gaze.

I felt a dozen needles sticking in my stomach. I leaned back in my seat. The fingernails of the girl behind me dug into my back. "Teacher's pet," she hissed. I pulled away, but as I did my head magnetically turned and I found myself staring into the eyes of the thick-muscled girl with the breasts. She had turned completely around in her seat so that her back faced the teacher while she stared at me. As our stares locked, she balled up her fist, put it first over one eye and then the other. The needles in my stomach multiplied by thousands.

* * *

A crowd was waiting for me when I walked down the outside steps of the school. They had gathered as though the entire school had been given notice that a rumble was on. Leaving no doubt that I was the intended victim, a bloody roar rose when I appeared on the steps.

Glancing through the crowd with pretended casualness, I picked out some of my classmates. Most were standing in front, with big-breasted Beulah first, her evil intentions plastered over her face. The thin girl who had dug her fingernails in my back stood behind her, whispering excitedly in her ear.

On stoops around the school and across the street, grownups stood looking at the yelling mob. At windows of buildings more adults adjusted themselves to get a better view. Was there one who might come down to help a young girl, desperate with fear, ready to be set upon by a mob? I knew the answer. No.

My pride was crumbling. To preserve some of it, I had to move quickly. So, holding my book bag tightly to my chest, I stuck my head up, walked down the steps and pushed boldly past Beulah, with her big breasts pushed aggressively out.

LIFE IS TOUGH.
LIFE IS REAL.
FRIENDSHIP
IS BEAUTIFUL.

THE AWARD-WINNING NOVEL THE
NEW YORK TIMES CALLS "A HEART-SLAMMER"

THE
FRIENDS

BY ROSA GUY
AUTHOR OF *RUBY* AND *EDITH JACKSON*

But my back quivered as I passed as though it had eyes and actually did see the powerful hands reach out and push me. Push me toward a little boy who stepped cunningly out of my way. And there I was face to face with the girl who sat behind me in class.

This girl was tall and as thin as I. I knew I could match her strength. But what if I started to fight her and Beulah jumped in too? While trying to make up my mind, the thin girl quickly shoved me back into the waiting leathery arms of the girl I feared the most.

"You dirty West Indian," she hissed in my ear. "You ain't rapping so big out here, is you? No, you ain't rapping so big out here. We should get Miss Lassy-assy out so she can see how you ain't doing no big-time talking and acting better than anybody."

"West Indian?" A boy called out. "My Ma call them monkey chasers."

"Monkey chaser, monkey chaser, bring monkey soup for your monkey father."

Someone else shouted in a mock West Indian accent: "Run her into the sea, mahn. What she want here nohow? We ain't got no trees to swing from."

My dry tongue licked drier lips, my knees buckled as I tried once again to push through the dense crowd. Blocking my way was a boy who stuck his hand under my chin. "Best man hit this." It was their idea of fair play: If I was a "good sport," I would hit the boy's hand, the boy would then hit Beulah, who would complete the cycle by hitting me to start the fight.

I pretended I did not see the hand.

"West Indian ain't gonna hit shit," Beulah sneered. "I'll hit it." She hit the hand. The hand in turn hit me. I was now supposed to hit Beulah to complete the cycle. My body quaked. I clutched my book bag to my chest and again tried to shoulder my way through.

"Pardon me," I said, forcing politeness. "I ..."

"Dig that rap," the thin girl jeered. "Pardon me. Who the hell she think she is?"

"Always trying to act better than the folks," Beulah sneered. Then with her thick, strong hands she spun me around punching her fist against my nose. "Don't push me," she yelled at the same time. "You see she pushed me?" Not expecting any answer she kept on punching and punching.

Blood ran from my nose and I tasted more in my mouth. I encircled my head with my arms. A blow caught me in my ribs. I doubled over, put my book bag to protect my stomach, and the fists pounded my face again.

"Old Big-Tits sure can fight."

"Yeah. She gonna smash that monkey into a African monkey stew."

I crouched trying to arouse pity. If not in the children, certainly in some of the grownups looking on. That was a mistake. At my look of utter helplessness the children jeered. "Let's finish her off," someone yelled. They moved in around me.

In terror I leveled my head, rammed it in the direction of the jabbing fists. It contacted with the fleshy chest. The girl staggered. I backed up, rammed forward again. This time the thick, tough girl sprawled backwards to the sidewalk and lay there squirming in pain. I ran over her, kicked her face out of the way of my flying feet, hit the person in front of me with my shoulder—the crowd opened up and I ran for my life.

*   *   *

Rushing into the apartment, planning to hide in my room, I ran right into my mother's arms. *"Bon Dieu,"* she cried after one look at my face. "What is this? What have they done to you?"

The look of my mother—tall, and an olive complexion with black, black eyes—has always awed me. As I saw her now, heard her voice, rich, deep, softened by the French Creole of The Island— it tickled the pores of my skin, thickened my throat with unshed tears and jumbled my words as they fell thick and heavy from my swollen lips.

"Al—all the chi—child—ren bunch up and wa—ant to fi—fight me."

"Want to? From the look of your face I would say they did fight you." She called to my sister. "Ruby, Ruby, bring me a basin of water and a rag." Then pulling me into the living room, she sat on the couch holding me to her knees. "Tell me, Phyllisia, why? Don't the children like you?"

The pity in her voice pushed me to the brink of hysterics. "No. They hate me! Everybody hates me!"

"But how so?"

"I an—swer the que—questions the teach—er asks and—and the gi—girl be—hind says that I— I'm teacher's pet. And wh—hen I co—me down— stairs th—they all stand a-round wait—ing ..."

"How long has this been going on?"

"Si—ince the be—begin—ning. They say all ki—kinds of nas—ty things to—to me."

"Nasty things like what?"

"They—they call me mon—monkey chaser."

Ruby had come into the room with the basin of water. Mother turned to her: "Do you have trouble like this, Ruby?"

"No, Mother."

"Why is that? Is it because the children are older in your school?"

"It is because I don't stick my hand in the air all the time and try to prove how smart I am." Ruby spoke in her usual, vain, airy manner. "After all, Mother, you know how Phyllisia is. If she did not try to act so smart and know-it-all, she would not be opening up her mouth and continually be reminding the children where she comes from."

All of my self-pity turned into a need for revenge. But I held myself at Mother's knees not to rush up and scratch at her pretty face.

Mother's eyes had widened. A pulse beat rapidly at her delicate throat. "Ruby, are you standing there telling me that you do not answer questions in class because you are ashamed of where you come from?"

Ruby did not notice the reproach in Mother's voice and went on in the same manner, "Well, the children don't like it and the teachers don't demand it, so why call attention to oneself? Sometimes when the children don't know the answer, I even slip it to them."

Aghast, Mother cried: "Is so? For shame, for shame, Ruby. I did not know that you were ashamed of yourself."

"I am not ashamed of myself, Mother." Ruby hated to be scolded. Tears rose quickly to her eyes. "But I want people to like me."

"Ruby, you are a nice-looking girl. You are well-mannered. If you can also add intelligence to that list, then you must look elsewhere for the reasons people don't like you."

Mother's displeasure gave me new confidence. "Mother," I pleaded, "I don't want to go back to that school tomorrow. Please, don't make me go back to that school."

"You have to," she said quietly. "You are a West Indian girl going to school in New York and you are proud. What happens in this school will happen in any other. So if you must fight, you must." ❖

A Question of Identity

Julio Morales

Julio Morales was born in Puerto Rico and moved to New York with his family when he was ten. A social worker and writer, he has written and lectured widely on the Puerto Rican migrant experience. He teaches at the University of Connecticut School of Social Work in Hartford.

Thirty-five years ago, as a college student, Morales wrote "A Question of Identity." He presented the speech to the fifth annual youth conference of the Puerto Rican Association for Community Affairs (PRACA) on February 12, 1963. PRACA, based in New York, was one of the first Puerto Rican civic associations in the country. It still exists and today concentrates on human and family services.

"A Question of Identity" is used by permission of the author. Essay © 1963, afterword © 1998, by Julio Morales.

As I stand here behind this lectern, speaking into these microphones, I recall that three years ago I was sitting where you are, listening to a group of Puerto Rican speakers. I felt extremely happy that day because I had come to a Puerto Rican youth conference and had found over two hundred Puerto Ricans who were my age and who had the same aspirations and the same problems I had.

The speakers were very intelligent Puerto Rican leaders, and as they spoke about my culture and about my people, I discovered that there was much I didn't know or had forgotten about myself. I felt pride and happiness at PRACA's Second Youth Conference, but I also felt shame. Before that day I had been out to prove to the world and to myself that I, Julio Morales, could be as good or better than the continental American. Until then I had imagined myself as one of the very few Puerto Ricans who would amount to anything. Until that time I had been Puerto Rican and had never denied it, but I had accepted the stereotyped ideas that non–Puerto Rican New Yorkers held of us, and I had seen myself as they saw me—as an exception.

I think that if I tell you a little about myself, you might understand why I felt as I did and perhaps you will discover that you and I have certain things in common. I was born on a little island called Vieques, which although 18 miles from the main island, is one of Puerto Rico's 76 municipalities. Thinking back, I remember two things more than anything else. The first is an old fort built by the Spaniards. In it were prisons, torture chambers, cannons, and all the other things one expects to find in a military fort. This very old Spanish fort, to the people of Vieques, serves as a reminder of their Spanish inheritance.

The second thing that stands out in my mind is *el Cerro del Tamarindo*, a small hill which was very near our home. At the very top of this hill, a tamarind tree stands all by itself. From the summit of el Cerro I used to see the boats floating in the Caribbean and I remember running up the hill every day at about six so that I could see the ferry boat coming into the port to bring mail and passengers from Fajardo, the town in Puerto Rico nearest to Vieques. If I close my eyes I can visualize a little boy all by

CARIBBEAN CONNECTIONS: MOVING NORTH   123

Julio Morales

We left Vieques, the six of us—my parents, my brother, my two sisters and I. We moved into the welcoming grounds of Spanish Harlem, also known as El Barrio.

I remember climbing six flights of stairs to get to our three-room apartment. Since then we have moved several times, but the image of our first home in New York City will always be clear in my mind. It wasn't much, for it was small and uncomfortable. My brother, my sisters, and I had no *batey* in which we could play, but across the street there was a school yard we could use. We had no Cerro de Tamarindo, but in the summer we climbed one more flight of stairs and we were on the roof. We did not see the blueness of the sea and the sky, or the beauty of Vieques, but we had fun laughing at the hundreds of people sitting on the stoops of the buildings trying to get some fresh air. There were many hardships at first, many more than in Vieques, because there were six of us and living was expensive, but my father worked hard for his family and we always had a sense of love and security.

I had been born in Puerto Rico, so I identified with Puerto Ricans and felt at home in Spanish Harlem, where people around me spoke in Spanish and ate rice and beans as they had done in Vieques. However, when I started going to school and learning the English language, some of the American element started to rub off on me and I started to change.

I was placed in an "Opportunity Class" at the beginning of my schooling in New York. This was a class for slow learners and was composed mainly of Puerto Rican youngsters. After seven months I was able to speak, read, and write well enough to be placed in a regular class. I think it was the day I changed classes that I, Julio Morales, really started to become someone else. I can recall that spring morning quite clearly. My teacher, whom I liked very much, said that I was to be placed in a different class—a "better class," she told me. I walked into the new classroom and noticed that there were very few Puerto Rican children in it. The person in charge asked my teacher if she thought I should be placed with the

himself, next to a tamarind tree, looking at all of Vieques' beauty. The blue of the Caribbean and the blue of the sky blended into one as they appeared to unite in the distance. Most of my memories from Vieques, like this one, are pleasant ones, and when I think back to them they bring a smile to my lips.

On my tenth birthday my family packed up and left Vieques. It did not come as a total surprise to me because my parents had been discussing the journey for a long time. My grandparents, uncles, aunts, and cousins had all left Vieques and were living in New York. We migrated as they did to the land of opportunity, hoping for a better future than the one Vieques offered us. It was the first time I had ever gone outside my little island, and although I feared the thought of leaving the place of my birth, I was thrilled and excited. The thought of a plane ride delighted me, although it seemed to frighten my parents.

slow readers. My teacher looked at me and smiled, then said, "No, Julio is different from other Puerto Rican children; he is very intelligent and can read very well."

I was different—I could read well: those were her exact words.

That day I got out of school several minutes earlier and as usual I waited for my sister, so we could go home together. I was dying to tell her about my change in class. A couple of minutes later, a group of about six non-Puerto Rican children came up to me and asked if I were Puerto Rican. I said "yes." The next instant I was being beaten by these six older boys. "Hit the dirty spic," they cried out as they beat me. *Mira, mira,* they yelled and laughed as they kicked me.

Some minutes later, Teresa, my sister, came out of school and saw that I was being beaten. In confusion she started screaming and crying and then rushed back into the school shouting for help. Several teachers ran out and the boys quickly disappeared, but I was hurt so badly that I had to be carried home.

Two things happened that unforgettable day which were to deeply affect me. I had been called an exception, and I had been beaten up for being a Puerto Rican. That evening I spent a couple of hours on the roof without speaking to anyone. I just observed my environment and I thought. I saw the people on the stoops and heard the screaming and the yelling of the teenagers as they ran around in the vacant lots, I saw the dirty youngsters playing in the street, and at a distance I remember seeing a fist fight. These were my people, but— "Am I like them?" I asked myself. No! I was different; I was an exception; my teacher had said so that morning. The boys beat me because they hadn't realized that I wasn't like other Puerto Ricans. I was clean, I didn't fight, I loved school, I wanted to learn, and I wanted to become someone important when I grew up. I realized that being Puerto Rican in New York meant being different and it meant not being as good as the other Americans, for if not, why had I been beaten? I wanted to be an American and to belong to the group which was best, because I refused to believe that I was inferior to anyone.

I was then eleven years old and for nearly seven years I reasoned the same way. When I saw the rats and roaches in Puerto Rican homes, when I saw Puerto Ricans yelling in the subways or drunk in the streets, or when I read in the newspapers that Rivera or Martines or Velásquez or Quiñones had stolen or killed, I felt ashamed and humiliated. I thought, like the average non-Puerto Rican, that my people were noisy, dirty, and potential criminals. I looked at my family and some of my friends and realized that they were good, but I was blinded by prejudice towards Puerto Ricans and reasoned that my family and friends, like myself, were exceptions.

No one would believe that there were some good Puerto Ricans, so I was out to show the world that, yes, I was Puerto Rican, I had been born in Vieques in a house near a hill with a lonely tamarindo tree, but I was good. I wanted everyone to know that there was at least one decent Puerto Rican. I studied harder, kept myself and my clothing cleaner, and bent over backwards to please people, and when I heard them say, "Such a nice Puerto Rican boy," I would smile and feel that I was doing well.

I remember how happy I was when I graduated with many honors from James Fenimore Cooper Junior High School, and when I entered the High School of Commerce I went in thinking that good grades were not enough; I had to be well known and well liked. I joined all the clubs and activities I could, and in my senior year I became Commerce's first elected Puerto Rican student body president.

I was in the Honor School, and there my stereotyped ideas were further enhanced. Very few Puerto Ricans were in the honor classes, and many of those who were, dropped out after the first few terms. Very few, if any, tried out for clubs and teams, and too many of them ended up in the Dean's office for causing trouble.

One day a notice came to the student organization office advertising a Puerto Rican youth conference. I was asked to select two students to represent our school. I thought it would be a waste of time, but I was curious as to what the conference would be like and so I asked if I could be one of the two representatives. I attended PRACA's second youth conference, and as I told you before, I felt pride and shame. Perhaps now, you can see why. My stereotyped ideas about the Puerto Rican New Yorkers were destroyed, shattered. I now felt guilty and thought that I had found something I needed, because for seven years I had not been Julio Morales, and although I had been accepted by the continental New Yorker, I had rejected myself.

I went home that day filled with emotion and deeply disturbed. I heard yelling in the subways and realized that Puerto Ricans were not the only ones who were noisy, for the noise was coming from a group of non-Puerto Ricans. Puerto Ricans were not the only drunks that one saw in the streets, and I had been told that the Puerto Rican crime rate was lower than the crime rates of other groups in New York. The rats and the roaches had been in New York City long before the Puerto Ricans; when we migrated from Puerto Rico we did not pack them in our suitcases to import them. These were American roaches, these were American rats. No, I felt sure that the slums were slums before we moved in, and that we moved into them because nothing better was offered us.

That night before going to bed, I kissed my mother and said, *"Bendición, mami, bendición, papi,"* walked into my room and prayed to God in Spanish. *Bendición*—bless me—I had said to my parents, and to me God still understood my first language. Here was something I had not rejected. Here was something in my culture which was beautiful. The speakers that morning had pointed things to me that in my escape I had chosen to forget, and as I thought back to my days in Puerto Rico, I began to realize that we did have a beautiful culture. I remembered many of the lovely traditions which were typically Puerto Rican, and realized that I had denied a culture which was in existence before the Mayflower reached Plymouth Rock.

I had been confused and misinformed, but I was eager to change. I wanted to meet Puerto Ricans who could advise me, Puerto Ricans I could admire and who could tell me what I needed to be told. Through PRACA, I was exposed to a different type of environment. I saw education and organization among Puerto Ricans. I met social workers, doctors, lawyers and teachers in the Puerto Rican community. Needless to say, I once again became the Julio Morales that had left Vieques eight years before.

Upon entering Hunter College, where I am now a junior, I met Puerto Rican students like myself. I still wanted good grades and wanted to be active in school organizations, but now I had different reasons. Now I was really part of a community; I belonged without feeling hostility or shame. I did not feel that I had to prove myself to anyone or that I was an exception—now, I was one of many.

I am different; but only because I am an individual and everyone is different from everyone else. But I am not better than other Puerto Ricans. I have learned to accept myself. Have you? Have you asked yourself, "Who am I? What am I? What are my goals? Where am I going? Would I like to be someone else?"

There was a program on television several weeks ago about a Puerto Rican student nurse who was ashamed of her nationality. Her name was Teresa Colon, and she fooled the world by changing it to Terry Collins. I, in many respects, was like her for seven years. Unfortunately I know too many Terry Collinses and would not be surprised to find some sitting out there in the audience. Terry Collins and I found out that if we try to be what we are not, we fail ourselves and those we love. If we become someone else we become ghosts. In our efforts to deny our heritage without being able to identify with something else, we become nothing.

You might say, "But we are New Yorkers. Should we walk around with a sign on our backs which reads 'I am a Puerto Rican'?" No! This is wrong. What I do say is that you must know who you are. Don't think that by doing what I did you will become more successful. We are all part of a group, and the strength of a group is found in that group's cultural heritage. It is true that we are also individuals, but individuals will get as far as the group from which they come, and an individual is respected as much as his group is respected. I say, be New Yorkers, but don't forget that you are Puerto Ricans also. Let us aspire, let us attain, let us give of ourselves, let us take and enrich ourselves. But in this process of giving and taking, let us not lose what we started out with. Let us keep our language and our traditions, let us keep our heritage alive. Let us not lose our identity.

Let us be a bridge between the Puerto Rican community and other New Yorkers. Let us educate ourselves and encourage our friends to do the same, for only through education can we as Puerto Ricans assume our responsibility as leaders and constructively contribute to the future of this city. Let us be New Yorkers; but first let us accept ourselves as Puerto Ricans. With the strength and inspiration of our cultural heritage, we are better prepared to face the future. ❖

> **continental American:** someone from the "lower 48," the contiguous or mainland United States
> **el Cerro del Tamarindo:** Tamarind Hill. Tamarind trees bear long pods with flat seeds and a sour pulp.
> **El Barrio:** East Harlem section of New York City
> **batey:** back yard

Afterword by Dr. Morales

I wrote this speech 35 years ago, but it still rings true today. Most of us—young Puerto Ricans born or raised in the United States—were struggling with putting two cultures together. We had to live simultaneously in two cultures that at times were in conflict with each other. That's still how it is for many young Puerto Ricans.

At the School of Social Work, I supervise graduate students who work with young people in schools and family agencies in Connecticut. We see Puerto Rican youngsters, the first generation born or raised in the States, who are under great stress. They feel pressure from the schools and their friends to act "American," and they feel pressure from their parents to conform to Puerto Rican expectations. It causes conflict in families very often.

This has been an issue for other ethnic groups in this country's history as well. What I said in my speech could have been said by an Italian child a hundred years ago, or by a Haitian child today. We have never understood, as a society, how to benefit from the richness of the cultures that immigrants bring. We need to help people learn English but also encourage them to remain bilingual and bicultural. If they love themselves and their culture, they will be better prepared to contribute to American society. ❖

Daughter of Invention

Julia Alvarez

Julia Alvarez was born in New York City to Dominican parents and spent her early childhood in the Dominican Republic. In 1960, when she was ten, her family had to flee their homeland. Her father, a prominent physician, was involved in a plot to overthrow Trujillo that was uncovered by the dictator's secret police.

The family settled in New York. After obtaining degrees from Middlebury College and Syracuse University, Alvarez taught creative writing in schools, prisons and old-age homes. The author of three novels and two books of poems, she teaches literature and creative writing at Middlebury College in Vermont.

HOW THE GARCÍA GIRLS LOST THEIR ACCENTS is Alvarez's first novel. The fictional Garcías—four sisters, their mother, and their physician father—flee the Dominican Republic under circumstances much like those in the author's real past. Arriving in New York, they

(continued on next page)

For a period after they arrived in this country, Laura García tried to invent something. Her ideas always came after the sightseeing visits she took with her daughters to department stores to see the wonders of this new country. On his free Sundays, Carlos carted the girls off to the Statue of Liberty or the Brooklyn Bridge or Rockefeller Center, but as far as Laura was concerned, these were men's wonders. Down in housewares were the true treasures women were after.

Laura and her daughters would take the escalator, marveling at the moving staircase, she teasing them that this might be the ladder Jacob saw with angels moving up and down to heaven. The moment they lingered by a display, a perky saleslady approached, no doubt thinking a young mother with four girls in tow fit the perfect profile for the new refrigerator with automatic defrost or the heavy duty washing machine with the prewash soak cycle. Laura paid close attention during the demonstrations, asking intelligent questions, but at the last minute saying she would talk it over with her husband. On the drive home, try as they might, her daughters could not engage their mother in conversation, for inspired by what she had just seen, Laura had begun inventing.

She never put anything actual on paper until she had settled her house down at night. On his side of the bed her husband would be conked out for an hour already, his Spanish newspapers draped over his chest, his glasses propped up on his bedside table, looking out eerily at the darkened room like a disembodied bodyguard. In her lighted corner, pillows propped behind her, Laura sat up inventing. On her lap lay one of those innumerable pads of paper her husband brought home from his office, compliments of some pharmaceutical company, advertising tranquilizers or antibiotics or skin cream. She would be working on a sketch of something familiar but drawn at such close range so she could attach a special nozzle or handier handle, the thing looked peculiar. Her daughters would giggle over the odd doodles they found in kitchen drawers or on the back shelf of the downstairs toilet. Once Yoyo was sure her mother had drawn a picture of a man's you-know-what; she showed her sisters her find, and with coy, posed faces they inquired of their mother what she was up to. *Ay*, that was one of her failures, she explained to them, a child's double-compartment drinking glass with an outsized, built-in straw.

Her daughters would seek her out at night when she seemed to have a moment to talk to them: they were having trouble at school or they wanted her to persuade their father to give them permission to go into the city or to a shopping mall or a movie—in broad daylight, Mami! Laura would wave them out of her room. "The problem with you girls ..." The problem boiled down to the fact that they wanted to become Americans and their father—and their mother, too, at first—would have none of it.

"You girls are going to drive me crazy!" she threatened, if they kept nagging. "When I end up in Bellevue, you'll be safely sorry!"

She spoke in English when she argued with them. And her English was a mishmash of mixed-up idioms and sayings that showed she was "green behind the ears," as she called it.

If her husband insisted she speak in Spanish to the girls so they wouldn't forget their native tongue, she'd snap, "When in Rome, do unto the Romans."

Yoyo, the Big Mouth, had become the spokesman for her sisters, and she stood her ground in that bedroom. "We're not going to that school anymore, Mami!"

"You have to." Her eyes would widen with worry. "In this country, it is against the law not to go to school. You want us to get thrown out?"

"You want us to get killed? Those kids were throwing stones today!"

"Sticks and stones don't break bones," she chanted. Yoyo could tell, though, by the look on her face, it was as if one of those stones the kids had aimed at her daughters had hit her. But she always pretended they were at fault. "What did you do to provoke them? It takes two to tangle, you know."

"Thanks, thanks a lot, Mom!" Yoyo stormed out of that room and into her own. Her daughters never called her *Mom* except when they wanted her to feel how much she had failed them in this country. She was a good enough Mami, fussing and scolding and giving advice, but a terrible girlfriend parent, a real failure of a Mom.

Back she went to her pencil and pad, scribbling and tsking and tearing off sheets, finally giving up, and taking up her *New York Times*. Some nights, though, if she got a good idea, she rushed into Yoyo's room, a flushed look on her face, her tablet of paper in her hand, a cursory knock on the door she'd just thrown open. "Do I have something to show you, Cuquita!"

This was Yoyo's time to herself, after she finished her homework, while her sisters were still downstairs watching TV in the basement. Hunched over her small desk, the overhead light turned off, her desk lamp poignantly lighting only her paper, the rest of the room in warm, soft, uncreated darkness, she wrote her secret poems in her new language.

"You're going to ruin your eyes!" Laura began, snapping on the overly bright overhead light, scaring off whatever shy passion Yoyo, with the blue thread of her writing, had just begun coaxing out of a labyrinth of feelings.

struggle to adapt to life in the United States. "Daughter of Invention" is told from the perspective of Yoyo, the third sister.

Excerpted from HOW THE GARCÍA GIRLS LOST THEIR ACCENTS, published by Plume, a division of Penguin USA Inc.; originally published in hardcover by Algonquin Books of Chapel Hill. © 1991 by Julia Alvarez. Used by permission of Susan Bergholz Literary Services, New York. All rights reserved.

"A major achievement...a family presented with such eloquence and such profound honesty you'll want to claim them as yours."
—Gloria Naylor

"Oh, Mami!" Yoyo cried out, her eyes blinking up at her mother. "I'm writing."

"*Ay, Cuquita.*" That was her communal pet name for whoever was in her favor. "Cuquita, when I make a million, I'll buy you your very own typewriter." (Yoyo had been nagging her mother for one just like the one her father had bought to do his order forms at home.) "Gravy on the turkey" was what she called it when someone was buttering her up. She buttered and poured. "I'll hire you your very own typist."

Down she plopped on the bed and held out her pad. "Take a guess, Cuquita?" Yoyo studied the rough sketch a moment. Soap sprayed from the nozzle head of a shower when you turned the knob a certain way? Instant coffee with creamer already mixed in? Time-released water capsules for your potted plants when you were away? A keychain with a timer that would go off when your parking meter was about to expire? (The ticking would help you find your keys easily if you mislaid them.) The famous one,

famous only in hindsight, was the stick person dragging a square by a rope—a suitcase with wheels? "Oh, of course," Yoyo said, humoring her. "What every household needs: a shower like a car wash, keys ticking like a bomb, luggage on a leash!" By now, it had become something of a family joke, their Thomas Edison Mami, their Benjamin Franklin Mom.

Her face fell. "Come on now! Use your head." One more wrong guess, and she'd show Yoyo, pointing with her pencil to the different highlights of this incredible new wonder. "Remember that time we took the car to Bear Mountain, and we re-ah-lized that we had forgotten to pack an opener with our pick-a-nick?" (Her daughters kept correcting her, but she insisted this was how it should be said.) "When we were ready to eat we didn't have any way to open the refreshments cans?" (This before fliptop lids, which she claimed had crossed her mind.) "You know what this is now?" Yoyo shook her head. "Is a car bumper, but see this part is a removable can opener. So simple and yet so necessary, eh?"

"Yeah, Mami. You should patent it." Yoyo shrugged as her mother tore off the scratch paper and folded it, carefully, corner to corner, as if she were going to save it. But then, she tossed it in the wastebasket on her way out of the room and gave a little laugh like a disclaimer. "It's half of one or two dozen of another."

None of her daughters was very encouraging. They resented her spending time on those dumb inventions. Here they were trying to fit in America among Americans; they needed help figuring out who they were, why the Irish kids whose grandparents had been micks were calling them spics. Why had they come to this country in the first place? Important, crucial, final things, and here was their own mother, who didn't have a second to help them puzzle any of this out, inventing gadgets to make life easier for the American Moms.

Sometimes Yoyo challenged her. "Why, Mami? Why do it? You're never going to make money. The Americans have already thought of everything, you know that."

"Maybe not. Maybe, just maybe, there's something they've missed that's important. With patience and calm, even a burro can climb a palm."

This last was one of her many Dominican sayings she had imported into her scrambled English.

"But what's the point?" Yoyo persisted.

"Point, point, does everything need a point? Why do you write poems?"

Yoyo had to admit it was her mother who had the point there. Still, in the hierarchy of things, a poem seemed much more important than a potty that played music when a toilet-training toddler went in its bowl.

They talked about it among themselves, the four girls, as they often did now about the many puzzling things in this new country.

"Better she reinvents the wheel than be on our cases all the time," the oldest, Carla, observed. In the close quarters of an American nuclear family, their mother's prodigious energy was becoming a real drain on their self-determination. Let her have a project. What harm could she do, and besides, she needed that acknowledgement. It had come to her automatically in the old country from being a de la Torre. "García de la Torre," Laura would enunciate carefully, giving her maiden as well as married name when they first arrived. But the blank smiles had never heard of her name. She would show them. She would prove to these Americans what a smart woman could do with a pencil and pad.

She had a near miss once. Every night, she liked to read *The New York Times* in bed before turning off her light, to see what the Americans were up to. One night, she let out a yelp to wake up her husband beside her. He sat bolt upright, reaching for his glasses which in his haste, he knocked across the room. "*¿Que pasa? ¿Que pasa?*" What is wrong? There was terror in his voice, the same fear she'd heard in the Dominican Republic before they left. They had been watched there; he was followed. They could not talk, of course, though they had whispered to each other in fear at night in the dark bed. Now in America, he was safe, a success even; his Centro de Medicina in the Bronx was thronged with the sick and the homesick yearning to go home again. But in dreams, he went back to those awful days and long nights, and his wife's screams confirmed his secret fear: they had not gotten away after all; the SIM had come for them at last.

"*Ay*, Cuco! Remember how I showed you that suitcase with little wheels so we should not have to carry those heavy bags when we traveled? Someone stole my idea and made a million!" She shook the paper in his face. "See, see! This man was no *bobo*! He didn't put all his pokers on a back burner. I kept telling you, one of these days my ship would pass me by in the night!" She wagged her finger at her husband and daughters, laughing all the while, one of those eerie laughs crazy people in movies laugh. The four girls had congregated in her room. They eyed their mother and each other. Perhaps they were all thinking the same thing, wouldn't it be weird and sad if Mami did end up in Bellevue?

"*¡Ya, ya!*" She waved them out of her room at last. "There is no use trying to drink spilt milk, that's for sure."

It was the suitcase rollers that stopped Laura's hand; she had weathervaned a minor brainstorm. And yet, this plagiarist had gotten all the credit, and the money. What use was it trying to compete with the Americans: they would always have the head start. It was their country, after all. Best stick close to home. She cast her sights about—her daughters ducked—and found her husband's office in need. Several days a week, dressed professionally in a white smock with a little name tag pinned on the lapel, a shopping bag full of cleaning materials and rags, she rode with her husband in his car to the Bronx. On the way, she organized the glove compartment or took off the address stickers from the magazines for the waiting room because she had read somewhere how by means of these stickers drug addict patients found out where doctors lived and burglarized their homes looking for syringes. At night, she did the books, filling in columns with how much money they had made that day. Who had time to be inventing silly things!

* * *

She did take up her pencil and pad one last time. But it was to help one of her daughters out. In ninth grade, Yoyo was chosen by her English teacher, Sister Mary Joseph, to deliver the Teacher's Day address at the school assembly. Back in the Dominican Republic growing up, Yoyo had been a terrible student. No one could ever get her to sit down to a book. But in New York, she needed to settle somewhere, and since the natives were unfriendly, and the country inhospitable, she took root in the language. By high school, the nuns were reading her stories and compositions out loud in English class.

But the spectre of delivering a speech brown-nosing the teachers jammed her imagination. At first she didn't want to and then she couldn't seem to write that speech. She should have thought of it as "a great honor," as her father called it. But she was mortified. She still had a slight accent, and she did not like to speak in public, subjecting herself to her classmates' ridicule. It also took no great figuring to see that to deliver a eulogy for a convent full of crazy, old, overweight nuns was no way to endear herself to her peers.

But she didn't know how to get out of it. Night after night, she sat at her desk, hoping to polish off some quick, noncommittal little speech. But she couldn't get anything down.

The weekend before the assembly Monday morning Yoyo went into a panic. Her mother would just have to call in tomorrow and say Yoyo was in the hospital, in a coma.

Laura tried to calm her down. "Just remember how Mister Lincoln couldn't think of anything to say at the Gettysburg, but then, bang! *Four score and once upon a time ago,*" she began reciting. "Something is going to come if you just relax. You'll see, like the Americans say, *Necessity is the daughter of invention.* I'll help you."

That weekend, her mother turned all her energy towards helping Yoyo write her speech. "Please, Mami, just leave me alone, please," Yoyo pleaded with her. But Yoyo would get rid of the goose only to have to contend with the gander. Her father kept poking his head in the door just to see if Yoyo had "fulfilled your obligations," a phrase he had used when the girls were younger and he'd check to see whether they had gone to the bathroom before a car trip. Several times that weekend around the supper table, he recited his own high school valedictorian speech. He gave Yoyo pointers on delivery, notes on the great orators and their tricks. (Humbleness and praise and falling silent with great emotion were his favorites.)

Laura sat across the table, the only one who seemed to be listening to him. Yoyo and her sisters were forgetting a lot of their Spanish, and their father's formal, florid diction was hard to understand. But Laura smiled softly to herself, and turned the lazy Susan at the center of the table around and around as if it were the prime mover, the first gear of her attention.

That Sunday evening, Yoyo was reading some poetry to get herself inspired: Whitman's poems in an old book with an engraved cover her father had picked up in a thrift shop next to his office. *I celebrate myself and sing myself.... He most honors my style who learns under it to destroy the teacher.* The poet's words shocked and thrilled her. She had gotten used to the nuns, a literature of appropriate sentiments, poems with a message, expurgated texts. But here was a flesh and blood man, belching and laughing and sweating in poems. *Who touches this book touches a man.*

That night, at last, she started to write, recklessly, three, five pages, looking up once only to see her father passing by the hall on tiptoe. When Yoyo was done, she read over her words, and her eyes filled. She finally sounded like herself in English!

As soon as she had finished that first draft, she called her mother to her room. Laura listened attentively while Yoyo read the speech out loud, and in the end, her eyes were glistening too. Her face was soft and warm and proud. "Ay, Yoyo, you are going to be the one to bring our name to the headlights in this country! That is a beautiful, beautiful speech I want for your father to hear it before he goes to sleep. Then I will type it for you, all right?"

Down the hall they went, mother and daughter, faces flushed with accomplishment. Into the master bedroom where Carlos was propped up on his pillows, still awake, reading the Dominican papers, already days old. Now that the dictatorship had been toppled, he had become interested in his country's fate again. The interim government was going to hold the first free elections in thirty years. History was in the making, freedom and hope were in the air again! There was still some question in his mind whether or not he might move his family back. But Laura had gotten used to the life here.

She did not want to go back to the old country where, de la Torre or not, she was only a wife and a mother (and a failed one at that, since she had never provided the required son). Better an independent nobody than a high-class houseslave. She did not come straight out and disagree with her husband's plans. Instead, she fussed with him about reading the papers in bed, soiling their sheets with those poorly printed, foreign tabloids. "*The Times* is not that bad!" she'd claim if her husband tried to humor her by saying they shared the same dirty habit.

The minute Carlos saw his wife and daughter filing in, he put his paper down, and his face brightened as if at long last his wife had delivered the son, and that was the news she was bringing him. His teeth were already grinning from the glass of water next to his bedside lamp, so he lisped when he said, "Eh-speech, eh-speech!"

"It is so beautiful, Cuco," Laura coached him, turning the sound on his TV off. She sat down at the foot of the bed. Yoyo stood before both of them, blocking their view of the soldiers in helicopters landing amid silenced gun reports and explosions. A few weeks ago it had been the shores of the Dominican Republic. Now it was the jungles of Southeast Asia they were saving. Her mother gave her the nod to begin reading.

Yoyo didn't need much encouragement. She put her nose to the fire, as her mother would have said, and read from start to finish without looking up. When she concluded, she was a little embarrassed at the pride she took in her own words. She pretended to quibble with a phrase or two, then looked questioningly to her mother. Laura's face was radiant. Yoyo turned to share her pride with her father.

The expression on his face shocked both mother and daughter. Carlos's toothless mouth had collapsed into a dark zero. His eyes bored into Yoyo, then shifted to Laura. In barely audible Spanish, as if secret microphones or informers were all about, he whispered to his wife, "You will permit her to read *that*?"

Laura's eyebrows shot up, her mouth fell open. In the old country, any whisper of a challenge to authority could bring the secret police in their

black V.W.'s. But this was America. People could say what they thought. "What is wrong with her speech?" Laura questioned him.

"What ees wrrrong with her eh-speech?" Carlos wagged his head at her. His anger was always more frightening in his broken English. As if he had mutilated the language in his fury—and now there was nothing to stand between them and his raw, dumb anger. "What is wrong? I will tell you what is wrong. It show no gratitude. It is boastful. *I celebrate myself? The best student learns to destroy the teacher?*" He mocked Yoyo's plagiarized words. "That is insubordinate. It is improper. It is disrespecting of her teachers—" In his anger he had forgotten his fear of lurking spies: each wrong he voiced was a decibel higher than the last outrage. Finally, he shouted at Yoyo, "As your father, I forbid you to make that eh-speech!"

Laura leapt to her feet, a sign that *she* was about to deliver her own speech. She was a small woman, and she spoke all her pronouncements standing up, either for more projection or as a carry-over from her girlhood in convent schools where one asked for, and literally, took the floor in order to speak. She stood by Yoyo's side, shoulder to shoulder. They looked down at Carlos. "That is no tone of voice—" she began.

But now, Carlos was truly furious. It was bad enough that his daughter was rebelling, but here was his own wife joining forces with her. Soon he would be surrounded by a houseful of independent American women. He too leapt from the bed, throwing off his covers. The Spanish newspapers flew across the room. He snatched the speech out of Yoyo's hands, held it before the girl's wide eyes, a vengeful, mad look in his own, and then once, twice, three, four, countless times, he tore the speech into shreds.

"Are you crazy?" Laura lunged at him. "Have you gone mad? That is her speech for tomorrow you have torn up!"

"Have *you* gone mad?" He shook her away. "You were going to let her read that ... that insult to her teachers?"

"Insult to her teachers!" Laura's face had crumpled up like a piece of paper. On it was written a love note to her husband, an unhappy, haunted man. "This is America, Papi, America! You are not in a savage country anymore!"

Meanwhile, Yoyo was on her knees, weeping wildly, collecting all the little pieces of her speech, hoping that she could put it back together before the assembly tomorrow morning. But not even a sibyl could have made sense of those tiny scraps of paper. All hope was lost. "He broke it, he broke it," Yoyo moaned as she picked up a handful of pieces.

Probably, if she had thought a moment about it, she would not have done what she did next. She would have realized her father had lost brothers and friends to the dictator Trujillo. For the rest of his life, he would be haunted by blood in the streets and late night disappearances. Even after all these years, he cringed if a black Volkswagen passed him on the street. He feared anyone in uniform: the meter maid giving out parking tickets, a museum guard approaching to tell him not to get too close to his favorite Goya.

On her knees, Yoyo thought of the worst thing she could say to her father. She gathered a handful of scraps, stood up, and hurled them in his face. In a low, ugly whisper, she pronounced Trujillo's hated nickname: "Chapita! You're just another Chapita!"

It took Yoyo's father only a moment to register the loathsome nickname before he came after her. Down the halls they raced, but Yoyo was quicker than he and made it into her room just in time to lock the door as her father threw his weight against it. He called down curses on her head, ordered her on his authority as her father to open that door! He throttled that doorknob, but all to no avail. Her mother's love of gadgets saved Yoyo's hide that night. Laura had hired a locksmith to install good locks on all the bedroom doors after the house had been broken into once while they were away. Now if burglars broke in again, and the family were at home, there would be a second round of locks for the thieves to contend with.

"Lolo," she said, trying to calm him down. "Don't you ruin my new locks."

Finally he did calm down, his anger spent. Yoyo heard their footsteps retreating down the hall. Their door clicked shut. Then, muffled voices, her mother's rising in anger, in persuasion, her father's deeper murmurs of explanation and self-defense. The house fell silent a moment, before Yoyo heard, far off, the gun blasts and explosions, the serious, self-important voices of newscasters reporting their TV war.

A little while later, there was a quiet knock at Yoyo's door, followed by a tentative attempt at the door knob. "Cuquita?" her mother whispered. "Open up, Cuquita."

"Go away," Yoyo wailed, but they both knew she was glad her mother was there, and needed only a moment's protest to save face.

Together they concocted a speech: two brief pages of stale compliments and the polite commonplaces on teachers, a speech wrought by necessity and without much invention by mother and daughter late into the night on one of the pads of paper Laura had once used for her own inventions. After it was drafted, Laura typed it up while Yoyo stood by, correcting her mother's misnomers and mis-sayings.

Yoyo came home the next day with the success story of the assembly. The nuns had been flattered, the audience had stood up and given "our devoted teachers a standing ovation," what Laura had suggested they do at the end of the speech.

She clapped her hands together as Yoyo recreated the moment. "I stole that from your father's speech, remember? Remember how he put that in at the end!" She quoted him in Spanish, then translated for Yoyo into English.

That night, Yoyo watched him from the upstairs hall window, where she'd retreated the minute she heard his car pull up in front of the house. Slowly, her father came up the driveway, a grim expression on his face as he grappled with a large, heavy cardboard box. At the front door, he set the package down carefully and patted all his pockets for his house keys. (If only he'd had Laura's ticking key chain!) Yoyo heard the snapping open of locks downstairs. She listened as he struggled to maneuver the box through the narrow doorway. He called her name several times, but she did not answer him.

"My daughter, your father, he love you very much," he explained from the bottom of the stairs. "He just want to protect you." Finally, her mother came up and pleaded with Yoyo to go down and reconcile with him. "Your father did not mean to harm. You must pardon him. Always it is better to let bygones be forgotten, no?"

Downstairs, Yoyo found her father setting up a brand new electric typewriter on the kitchen table. It was even better than her mother's. He had outdone himself with all the extra features: a plastic carrying case with Yoyo's initials decaled below the handle, a brace to lift the paper upright while she typed, an erase cartridge, an automatic margin tab, a plastic hood like a toaster cover to keep the dust away. Not even her mother could have invented such a machine!

But Laura's inventing days were over just as Yoyo's were starting up with her school-wide success. Rather than the rolling suitcase everyone else in the family remembers, Yoyo thinks of the speech her mother wrote as her last invention. It was as if, after that, her mother had passed on to Yoyo her pencil and pad and said, "Okay, Cuquita, here's the buck. You give it a shot." ❖

SIM: Trujillo's secret police

The One-and-a-Half Generation

Gustavo Pérez Firmat

Gustavo Pérez Firmat was born in Cuba. He moved to the United States with his family in 1960, at age 11, and spent the next 13 years in the Little Havana section of Miami. He is professor of Spanish-American literature at Duke University in North Carolina.

Through his poetry, essays and literary criticism, Pérez Firmat explores Cuban-American culture and identity. He is particularly interested in the experience of being bilingual and bicultural. This experience often finds its strongest expression in people who left their country of birth as older children or teenagers and grew to adulthood in their adopted country—what he calls "the one-and-a-half generation."

Excerpted from NEXT YEAR IN CUBA: A CUBANO'S COMING-OF-AGE IN AMERICA (New York: Doubleday). © 1995 by Gustavo Pérez Firmat. Used by permission of Doubleday, a division of Bantam Doubleday Dell Publishing Group, Inc.

'm Cuban-American, a member of what has been called the "one-and-a-half" generation, that is, Cubans who were born on the island and came to the United States as children or adolescents. I arrived in this country 34 years ago, when I was 11 years old, after the triumph of the Castro Revolution. As a one-and-a-halfer, I'm too old to be entirely American, but too young to be anything else—a condition that I share with many other Hispanic Americans as well as with immigrants from other cultures and lands. Born in Cuba but made in the U.S.A., I can no longer imagine living outside American culture and the English language. And yet Cuba remains my true home, the place that decisively shaped my character and my values. My life is a delicate balancing act between two countries, two cultures, two languages. Ask me where I really belong, in Cuba or in America, and I wouldn't be able to tell you, because I belong in both. ...

As an exile, my experience is different from that of immigrants in that I came to this country fully intending to return to my homeland as soon as possible. As a *Cuban* exile, I grew up in a foreign land, but was surrounded by the language and culture of my birth. Cuban culture runs deep in me. Although I have lived three-fourths of my life in this country, I have lived less than half of it outside what I would term "Greater Havana," an extended urban area that encompasses both Havana and Miami. Indeed, with a Cuban population of over half a million, Miami is second only to Havana as the largest Cuban city. For over three decades *regreso* has been this community's magical, monotonous mantra. The Cuban version of the Jewish promise "Next year in Jerusalem" is *El año que viene en Cuba,* "Next year in Cuba," a toast that I have heard and uttered every Christmas Eve since 1960. But even if my Cuban self, my *yo cubano,* resists the refusal of *regreso,* my American me suspects that return may not be feasible. The truth may well be that once an exile, always an exile.

Members of the one-and-a-half generation occupy a unique intermediate position. For my parents and my children, the options are more limited than they are for me. My father, who is now in his seventies, has no choice but to be Cuban. The thirty years of living and working in the

United States seem to have had little impact on his Cuban ways. His English is a little better than when he first got here, but he still views *los americanos* with the same mixture of awe, disdain, and incomprehension that he did upon his arrival. The fact that my mother and all of his children and grandchildren are now American citizens seems not to have reduced his distance from U.S. culture. He will never be an *americano,* either legally or in spirit. No matter how many years he has resided away from the island—and if he survives a few more years there will come a time when he too will have lived longer in Miami than he did in Havana—he remains as unassimilated today as he was on the day in October 1960 when he got off the ferry at Key West.

My children, who were born in this country of Cuban parents and in whom I have tried to inculcate some sort of *cubanía,* are American through and through. They can be "saved" from their Americanness no more than my father can be "saved" from his Cubanness. Although they belong to the so-called ABC generation (American-born Cubans), they are Cubans in name only, in last name. A better abbreviation for them would be the reverse, the CBA generation (Cuban-bred Americans). Like other second-generation Americans, my children maintain a connection to their parents' homeland, but it's a bond forged by my experiences rather than their own. For David and Miriam, who are twelve and nine years old, Cuba is an endearing, hopefully an enduring fiction—as ethereal as the smoke and as persistent as the smell of their grandfather's cigars (which these days are not even Cuban but Miamian).

Like my father, I too smoke cigars, except that I buy them a couple at a time from a yuppie tobacconist in Chapel Hill, whereas my father buys his by the box from the factory in Little Havana. If smoking cigars is a token of Cuban maleness, then I'm an occasional Cuban, a Friday-night *cubanazo,* for I light up a couple of evenings a week after dinner. While my children watch TV sitcoms, I observe my roots go up in smoke. If for my father Cuba is a burdensome fact, and if for my children it's an endearing fiction, for one-and-a-halfers like me, the country of my birth is a blend of both fact and fiction. Since my recollections of the island are an indeterminate mix of eyewitness and hearsay, what I know is mixed in with what I have been told. My memories merge with others' dreams.

Spiritually tied to Cuba, yet firmly rooted in the United States, I belong to a rare group of exiles that could, should Castro be overthrown in the near future, genuinely choose whether to return or stay. My father does not have this choice; in a sense, he never left. My children also do not have the choice; they cannot even speak the Spanish language. My son occasionally brags to his friends that he is Cuban—but he can only assert his Cubanness in English. Wedged between the first and second generations, the one-and-a-halfer shares the nostalgia of his parents and the forgetfulness of his children. For me, homecoming would feel like departure. ❖

regreso: return
los americanos: the Americans
cubanía: Cubanness

The Myth of the Latin Woman: I Just Met a Girl Named María

Judith Ortiz Cofer

Rick O'Quinn

Judith Ortiz Cofer was born in Puerto Rico. Her father, one of many Puerto Ricans to serve in the U.S. armed forces, was a Navy man assigned to a ship based at Brooklyn Navy Yard in New York City. In 1955, when Ortiz Cofer was three, the family moved from Puerto Rico to Paterson, New Jersey, across the Hudson River from New York. They continued to shuttle between New Jersey and the Island according to the father's tours of duty.

In Paterson, the family lived in a tenement dubbed "El Building" by its mostly Puerto Rican residents. Ortiz Cofer remembers, "I lived in a bubble created by my

(continued on next page)

On a bus trip to London from Oxford University, where I was earning some graduate credits one summer, a young man, obviously fresh from a pub, spotted me and as if struck by inspiration went down on his knees in the aisle. With both hands over his heart he broke into an Irish tenor's rendition of "María" from *West Side Story*. My politely amused fellow passengers gave his lovely voice the round of gentle applause it deserved. Though I was not quite as amused, I managed my version of an English smile: no show of teeth, no extreme contortions of the facial muscles—I was at this time of my life practicing reserve and cool. Oh, that British control, how I coveted it. But María had followed me to London, reminding me of a prime fact of my life: you can leave the Island, master the English language, and travel as far as you can, but if you are a Latina, especially one like me who so obviously belongs to Rita Moreno's gene pool, the Island travels with you.

This is sometimes a very good thing—it may win you that extra minute of someone's attention. But with some people, the same things can make *you* an island—not so much a tropical paradise as an Alcatraz, a place nobody wants to visit. As a Puerto Rican girl growing up in the United States and wanting like most children to "belong," I resented the stereotype that my Hispanic appearance called forth from many people I met.

Our family lived in a large urban center in New Jersey during the sixties, where life was designed as a microcosm of my parents' casas on the island. We spoke in Spanish, we ate Puerto Rican food bought at the bodega, and we practiced strict Catholicism complete with Saturday confession and Sunday mass at a church where our parents were accommodated into a one-hour Spanish mass slot, performed by a Chinese priest trained as a missionary for Latin America.

As a girl, I was kept under strict surveillance, since virtue and modesty were, by cultural equation, the same as family honor. As a teenager I was instructed on how to behave as a proper señorita. But it was a conflicting message girls got, since the Puerto Rican mothers also encouraged their daughters to look and act like women and to dress in clothes our Anglo friends and their mothers found too "mature" for our age. It was, and is, cultural, yet I often felt humiliated when I appeared at an American friend's party wearing a dress more suitable to a semiformal than to a playroom birthday celebration. At Puerto Rican festivities, neither the music nor the colors we wore could be too loud. I still experience a vague sense of letdown when I'm invited to a "party" and it turns out to be a marathon conversation in hushed tones rather than a fiesta with salsa, laughter, and dancing—the kind of celebration I remember from my childhood.

I remember Career Day in our high school, when teachers told us to come dressed as if for a job interview. It quickly became obvious that to the barrio girls, "dressing up" sometimes meant wearing ornate jewelry and clothing that would be more appropriate (by mainstream standards) for the company Christmas party than as daily office attire. That morning, I had agonized in front of my closet, trying to figure out what a "career girl" would wear because, essentially, except for Marlo Thomas on TV, I had no models on which to base my decision. I knew how to dress for school: at the Catholic school I attended we all wore uniforms; I knew how to dress for Sunday mass, and I knew what dresses to wear for parties at my relatives' homes. Though I do not recall the precise details of my Career Day outfit, it must have been a composite of the above choices. But I remember a comment my friend (an Italian-American) made in later years that coalesced my impressions of that day. She said that at the business school she was attending, the Puerto Rican girls always stood out for wearing "everything at once." She meant, of course, too much jewelry, too many accessories. On that day at school, we were simply made the negative models by the nuns who were themselves not credible fashion experts to any of us. But it was painfully obvious to me that to the others, in their tailored skirts and silk blouses, we must have seemed "hopeless" and "vulgar." Though I now know that most adolescents feel out of step much of the time, I also know that for the Puerto Rican girls of my generation that sense was intensified. The way our teachers and class-mates looked at us that day in school was just a taste of the culture clash that awaited us in the real world, where prospective employers and men on the street would often misinterpret our tight skirts and jingling bracelets as a come-on.

Mixed cultural signals have perpetuated certain stereotypes—for example, that of the Hispanic woman as the "Hot Tamale" or sexual firebrand. It is a one-dimensional view that the media have found easy to promote. In their special vocabulary, advertisers have designated "sizzling" and "smoldering" as the adjectives of choice for describing not only the foods but also the women of Latin America. From conversations in my house, I recall hearing about the harassment that Puerto Rican women endured in factories where the "boss men" talked to them as if sexual innuendo was all they understood, and worse, often gave them the choice of submitting to advances or being fired.

It is custom, however, not chromosomes, that leads us to choose scarlet over pale pink. As young girls, we were influenced in our decisions about clothes and colors by the women—older sisters and mothers who had

Puerto Rican parents in a home where two cultures and languages became one."

Ortiz Cofer is the author of a novel, a memoir, two books of poetry, and a poetry-prose collection. She teaches English and creative writing at the University of Georgia.

Reprinted from THE LATIN DELI: PROSE & POETRY (Athens, Ga.: University of Georgia Press). © 1993 by Judith Ortiz Cofer. Used by permission of the University of Georgia Press.

grown up on a tropical island where the natural environment was a riot of primary colors, where showing your skin was one way to keep cool as well as to look sexy. Most important of all, on the island, women perhaps felt freer to dress and move more provocatively, since, in most cases, they were protected by the traditions, mores, and laws of a Spanish/Catholic system of morality and machismo whose main rule was: *You may look at my sister, but if you touch her I will kill you.* The extended family and church structure could provide a young woman with a circle of safety in her small pueblo on the island; if a man "wronged" a girl, everyone would close in to save her family honor.

This is what I have gleaned from my discussions as an adult with older Puerto Rican women. They have told me about dressing in their best party clothes on Saturday nights and going to the town's plaza to promenade with their girlfriends in front of the boys they liked. The males were thus given an opportunity to admire the women and to express their admiration in the form of *piropos:* erotically charged street poems they composed on the spot. I have been subjected to a few piropos while visiting the Island, and they can be outrageous, although custom dictates that they must never cross into obscenity. This ritual, as I understand it, also entails a show of studied indifference on the woman's part; if she is "decent," she must not acknowledge the man's impassioned words. So I do understand how things can be lost in translation. When a Puerto Rican girl dressed in her idea of what is attractive meets a man from the mainstream culture who has been trained to react to certain types of clothing as a sexual signal, a clash is likely to take place. The line I first heard based on this aspect of the myth happened when the boy who took me to my first formal dance leaned over to plant a sloppy overeager kiss painfully on my mouth, and when I didn't respond with sufficient passion, said in a resentful tone: "I thought you Latin girls were supposed to mature early"—my first instance of being thought of as a fruit or vegetable—I was supposed to *ripen*, not just grow into womanhood like other girls.

It is surprising to some of my professional friends that some people, including those who should know better, still put others "in their place." Though rarer, these incidents are still commonplace in my life. It happened to me most recently during a stay at a very classy metropolitan hotel favored by young professional couples for their weddings. Late one evening after the theater, as I walked toward my room with my new colleague (a woman with whom I was coordinating an arts program), a middle-aged man in a tuxedo, a young girl in satin and lace on his arm, stepped directly into our path. With his champagne glass extended toward me, he exclaimed, "Evita!"

Our way blocked, my companion and I listened as the man half-recited, half-bellowed, "Don't Cry for Me, Argentina." When he finished, the young girl said, "How about a round of applause for my daddy?" We complied, hoping this would bring the silly spectacle to a close. I was becoming aware that our little group was attracting the attention of the other guests. "Daddy" must have perceived this too, and he once more barred the way as we tried to walk past him. He began to shout-sing a ditty to the tune of "La Bamba"—except the lyrics were about a girl named María whose exploits all rhymed with her name and gonorrhea. The girl kept saying "Oh, Daddy" and looking at me with pleading eyes. She wanted me to laugh along with the others. My companion and I stood silently waiting for the man to end his offensive song. When he finished, I looked not at him but at his daughter. I advised her calmly never to ask her father what he had done in the army. Then I walked between them and to my room. My friend complimented me on my cool handling of the situation. I confessed to her that I really had wanted to push the jerk into the swimming pool. I knew that this same man— probably a corporate executive, well-educated, even worldly by most standards—would not have been likely to regale a white woman with a dirty song in public. He would perhaps have checked his impulse by assuming that she could be somebody's wife or mother, or at least *somebody* who might take offense. But to him, I was just an Evita or a María: merely a character in his cartoon-populated universe.

Because of my education and my proficiency with the English language, I have acquired many mechanisms for dealing with the anger I experience. This was not true for my parents, nor is it true for the many Latin women working at menial jobs who must put up with stereotypes about our ethnic group such as: "They make good domestics." This is another facet of the myth of the Latin woman in the United States. Its origin is simple to deduce. Work as domestics, waitressing, and factory jobs are all that's available to women with little English and few skills. The myth of the Hispanic menial has been sustained by the same media phenomenon that made "Mammy" from *Gone with the Wind* America's idea of the black woman for generations; María, the housemaid or counter girl, is now indelibly etched into the national psyche. The big and the little screens have presented us with the picture of the funny Hispanic maid, mispronouncing words and cooking up a spicy storm in a shiny California kitchen.

This media-engendered image of the Latina in the United States has been documented by feminist Hispanic scholars, who claim that such portrayals are partially responsible for the denial of opportunities for upward mobility among Latinas in the professions. I have a Chicana friend working on a Ph.D. in philosophy at a major university. She says her doctor still shakes his head in puzzled amazement at all the "big words" she uses. Since I do not wear my diplomas around my neck for all to see, I too have on occasion been sent to that "kitchen," where some think I obviously belong.

One such incident that has stayed with me, though I recognize it as a minor offense, happened on the day of my first public poetry reading. It took place in Miami in a boat-restaurant where we were having lunch before the event. I was nervous and excited as I walked in with my notebook in my hand. An older woman motioned me to her table. Thinking (foolish me) that she wanted me to autograph a copy of my brand new slender volume of verse, I went over. She ordered a cup of coffee from me, assuming that I was the waitress. Easy enough to mistake my poems for menus, I suppose. I know that it wasn't an intentional act of cruelty, yet of all the good things that happened that day, I remember that scene most clearly, because it reminded me of what I had to overcome before anyone would take me seriously. In retrospect I understand that my anger gave my reading fire, that I have almost always taken doubts in my abilities as a challenge—and that the result is, most times, a feeling of satisfaction at having won a convert when I see the cold, appraising eyes warm to my words, the body language change, the smile that indicates that I have opened some avenue for communication. That day, I read to that woman and her lowered eyes told me that she was embarrassed at her little faux pas, and when I willed her to look up at me, it was my victory, and she graciously allowed me to punish her with my full attention. We shook hands at the end of the reading, and I never saw her again. She has probably forgotten the whole thing, but maybe not.

Yet I am one of the lucky ones. My parents made it possible for me to acquire a stronger footing in the mainstream culture by giving me the chance at an education. And books and art have saved me from the harsher forms of ethnic and racial prejudice that many of my Hispanic *compañeras* have had to endure. I travel a lot around the United States, reading from my books of poetry and my novel, and the reception I most often receive is one of positive interest by people who want to know more about my culture. There are, however, thousands of Latinas without the privilege of an education or the entrée into society that I have. For them life is a struggle against the misconceptions perpetuated by the myth of the Latina as whore, domestic or criminal. We cannot change this by legislating the way people look at us. The transformation, as I see it, has to occur at a much more individual level. My personal goal in my public life is to try to replace the old pervasive stereotypes and myths about Latinas with a much more interesting set of realities. Every time I give a reading, I hope the stories I tell, the dreams and fears I examine in my work, can achieve some universal truth which will get my audience past the particulars of my skin color, my accent, or my clothes.

I once wrote a poem in which I called us Latinas "God's brown daughters." This poem is really a prayer of sorts, offered upward, but also, through the human-to-human channel of art, outward. It is a prayer for communication, and for respect. In it, Latin women pray "in Spanish to an Anglo God/with a Jewish heritage," and they are "fervently hoping/that if not omnipotent,/at least He be bilingual." ❖

Black Hispanics: The Ties that Bind

Vivian Brady

Vivian Brady was born in the Bronx, New York. She was a student at Hunter College, City University of New York, when she wrote this essay. She graduated from New York University Law School and is now a lawyer in private practice.

Reprinted from CENTRO, the bulletin of the Centro de Estudios Puertorriqueños, Hunter College, Vol. II, No. 3, Spring 1988. © 1988 by Vivian Brady. Used by permission of the Centro de Estudios Puertorriqueños and Vivian Brady.

At the bottom of my course selection sheet is an optional question: Students are requested to supply the college with their ethnicity for federal reporting requirements. Six categories are provided: White non-Hispanic, Black non-Hispanic, Puerto Rican, Hispanic other, Asian/Pacific Islander and Native American/Alaskan. Students must choose only one category, the one that best describes them.

As someone who describes herself as a Black–Puerto Rican, I have always found the restriction to only one choice incredibly frustrating. There never seems to be any category that acknowledges the strong African heritage of Hispanic people in the Caribbean and Latin America. We, as Hispanics, are isolated as if we were a separate race unto ourselves. Unlike English and French-speaking people of the Caribbean, the kinship ties of Puerto Ricans to the Black American community are often ignored or denied. Our common bond of African heritage, as people of color in this hemisphere, and our implicit sisterhood and brotherhood are often left unrecognized, even on my course selection sheet.

My recognition of myself as a Black–Puerto Rican may be facilitated by the fact that my parents come from two different islands. My mother is from Puerto Rico and my father from St. Thomas, in the U.S. Virgin Islands. But I have met many Hispanics who do not have mixed parentage who see themselves as I do.

My mother emigrated to this country from Puerto Rico when she was three years old. Her family came to find a better life, settling in El Barrio, East Harlem.

She has always viewed herself as a Black woman, a brave and independent stance to take in the 1940s and 1950s. To my mother, separating the communities was a dangerous thing. She believes that it strengthens us to find our commonalities and stand united, because the price of separation can be great in the face of racist oppression.

The "West Side Story" of my mother's time was more the relationship between the newly-arrived Puerto Ricans and the American Blacks than the romanticized tensions between the Italians and Puerto Ricans of that musical's fame. An imaginary line was drawn on Lenox Avenue creating two insular communities, one Black and one Puerto Rican. Even though their lives and experiences were startlingly similar, there was ambivalence. This ambivalence still divides us today.

Both groups fell into the trap of believing the racist dogma of the day. Many Puerto Ricans accepted at face value that Black was synonymous with inferiority. They believed the stereotypes about Blacks being "bad" and shied away from building a relationship with them, not wanting to be tainted by their status. Black Americans also fell into the mire of white racism: Puerto Ricans were loud, heavy drinkers and the men were womanizing Latinos. It seems funny to list these ridiculous images, yet they live on. I know because I have lived on both sides of the issue, red-faced and embarrassed at how glibly we apply these stereotypes to each other.

We live together in some of the poorest communities, racked by a drug epidemic, inadequate housing, and an educational system that leaves us intellectually stifled. We ride the subways together every day, feeling much the same anger and despair, yet there is uncertainty between us. We see our cultural differences as insurmountable even though we have a shared heritage.

My grandmother lives in Ceiba, a sleepy town near the U.S. Navy base in Puerto Rico where all the houses are painted in tropical pastels and one can hear the war games being executed along the coast. I see in her brown face my African heritage. Slaves were imported into Puerto Rico, as to other neighboring islands, for their cheap labor. They were exploited in the sugar cane fields under the hot sun. They brought with them their music, spirit and culture, enriching Puerto Rico.

Black people in the Spanish-speaking Caribbean and Latin America have left us with great legacies. They include the *quilombo* leader Ganga Zambi in Brazil, the African rhythms of the merengue, and the spiritual influences in our religions.

My grandmother would never call herself black, though; she is firstly and lastly Puerto Rican. Most Puerto Ricans describe their country like a rainbow, a mixture and blend of African, European and Indian. I have often heard Black Americans alienated by this concept; they see a woman as dark as my grandmother not identifying herself as Black and conclude that "Puerto Ricans don't know what they are," or that they seek to deny their blackness. Sadly enough this is true for some. I certainly don't wish to obscure the issues of race, color and class among Puerto Ricans. But it is Puerto Rican to recognize our mixed heritage. It is a mulatto country, not the stark black and white of the United States.

When I learn about African-American history I treat it as my own, as part of my identity as a Black woman. I see the accomplishments and survival of Black Americans as a testimony to all people of color. I hope that Black Americans can find pride and strength in Puerto Rican and other Afro-Latin histories, but I know that it will take time.

Things are not simple, and viewing the situation perched on the edge of both communities, I see that though we may socialize, form committees and lobby together, we must learn more about each other to see the merits of standing non-judgementally side by side.

I recently asked some of my Black American friends, "What if Michael Griffith were Puerto Rican? Would you fight racist aggression in Howard Beach if the lynch mob were out to kill 'dirty spics' with bats and pipes?" Most said their response would have been tempered by the fact that the victim was Hispanic and that they would not be as passionate. By the same token I would have liked to see a stronger voice by the Hispanic community during the Howard Beach case. We do not yet see that the enemy and the issue are the same; we must both be energized to see the struggle.

I have been told that it is impossible for me to continue being both Puerto Rican and Black and that I will inevitably need to choose sides. But I, like many other Hispanics, know that the blood I share with African-Americans links me to the survival and work necessary in both communities equally. There is a wealth of strength that can help us discard the pervasive racism our country is shackled to, but it must be a combined effort. ❖

quilombo: rebel community formed by Africans who escaped from slavery in 19th-century Brazil
Howard Beach: In Howard Beach, N.Y., in 1986, a gang of white youths chased a black man, Michael Griffith, onto a highway, where he was struck by a car and killed.

Fighting for Justice: Brooklyn to Washington

Shirley Chisholm

Shirley Chisholm is the first black woman ever elected to the U.S. Congress. She served in the House of Representatives from 1968 to 1982, representing New York's 12th Congressional District.

Chisholm was born in Brooklyn. Her mother was from Barbados; her father, born in Guyana, grew up in Cuba and Barbados. They had emigrated as part of the first wave of West Indians to settle in New York in the 1920s. When Chisholm was four, she was sent to live on her grandmother's farm in Barbados. She returned at age ten to rejoin her parents in Brooklyn.

The following excerpts are from Chisholm's memoir, UNBOUGHT AND UNBOSSED (Boston: Houghton Mifflin). © 1970 by Shirley Chisholm. Used by permission of the author. Italicized transitions have been added.

My father was working then as a helper in a big cake bakery. I idolized him, his good looks, his extensive vocabulary, and his intelligence. A tall, thin, handsome man with white hair (it turned in his early twenties), brown skin, and a straight, Grecian nose, he would have been a brilliant scholar if he had been able to go to college. He was an omnivorous reader. Even during the Depression, he always bought two or three newspapers a day. Mother never understood his spending the money; she thought he could get all the news from one. Papa read everything within reach. If he saw a man passing out handbills, he would cross the street to get one and read it. The result was that, although he only finished the equivalent of fifth grade, he seemed to know a little about almost everything.

A tireless talker, he had dozens of friends whom he brought home in the evenings for the sake of their conversation. ... Lying in bed, we could hear them talk about the islands and their politics. Papa and his friends traded story after story showing how Britain was oppressing the colonial peoples of the world. He would speak scornfully of "the divine right of kings."

Papa was a Garveyite, too, a follower of Marcus Garvey, the Jamaican who originated many of the ideas that characterize today's militant black separatists. ... Garvey declared in the 1920s that "black is beautiful" and called on blacks to preserve their racial purity by becoming separate. His goal was to unite American blacks and return them to Africa, where they would become the equals of any man, in independent isolation. I think this appealed to my father because he, too, was very proud black man. He instilled pride in his children, a pride in ourselves and our race that was not as fashionable at that time as it is today.

Much of the kitchen-table talk had to do with unions. Papa belonged to the Confectionery and Bakers International Union, and there was nothing he was more proud of than being a union man. He brought labor newspapers home and read from them to his friends. When he was elected a shop steward at the bakery, you would have thought he had been made a king. ...

Dinner together every night was an inflexible rule in our family. The table had to be set when Papa got there. We waited for him to say a blessing before anything was passed. Then he would lead the conversation, telling Mother about the events of his day and asking the children the inevitable question, "What did you learn in school?" It was no idle query; he wanted an answer. Papa harped on the theme, "You must make something of yourselves. You've got to go to school, and I'm not sending you to play either. Study and make something of yourselves. Remember, only the strong people survive in this world. God gave you a brain; use it."

After graduating from Brooklyn College in 1946, Chisholm worked as a teacher and an educational administrator, and earned a master's degree from Columbia University.

She also became involved in local politics. Although her Brooklyn neighborhood, Bedford-Stuyvesant, was at least two-thirds black and Latino, white politicians had long controlled political power in the area. Chisholm helped build a grassroots movement to elect black candidates to represent Brooklyn in Congress and the New York state assembly. After years of hard work—registering new voters, canvassing house to house, using volunteer poll watchers—the Unity Democratic Club broke the hold of the white political machine.

Endorsed by the club, Chisholm stood for election to the state assembly and won. Among the bills she introduced which became state law were one to help disadvantaged students go to college, and another to set up the state's first unemployment insurance fund for domestic employees.

Three years later, Chisholm ran for Congress on the Democratic ticket. Her campaign slogan was "Fighting Shirley Chisholm: Unbought and Unbossed." She writes of the crucial role that women played in her congressional campaign:

Men always underestimate women. They underestimated me, and they underestimated the women like me. If they had thought about it, they would have realized that many of the homes in black neighborhoods are headed by women. They stay put, raise their families—and register to vote in greater numbers. The women are always organizing for something, even if it is only a bridge

club. They run the PTA, they are the backbone of the social groups and civic clubs, more than the men. So the organization was already there. All I had to do was get its help. I went to the presidents and leaders and asked, "Can you help me?" If I succeeded in convincing them, they were ready to help—and able.

It was not my original strategy to organize womanpower to elect me; it was forced on me by the time, place, and circumstances. I never meant and never mean to start a war between women and men. It is true that women are second-class citizens, just as black people are. ...

Discrimination against women in politics is particularly unjust, because no political organization I have seen could function without women. They do the work that the men won't do. I know, because I have done it all. For years I stayed in the wings and worked to put men in office, even writing their speeches and cuing them on how to answer questions. They would still be exploiting my abilities if I had not rebelled. Increasingly, other women are reaching the same conclusion.

Running for Congress, Chisholm was an outsider in more than one way: black, female, and also West Indian.

An inescapable fact, but one I have never liked to discuss because of the senseless bad feeling it can cause, is that a surprising number of the successful black politicians of our time are of West Indian descent. ... Other black people will say, "Why don't those monkeys get back on a banana boat?" There is a strong undercurrent of resentment, at least in New York, where most of the islanders migrated. It has never come out in the open against me, but sometimes I can sense it.

It is wrong, because the accident that my ancestors were brought as slaves to the islands while black mainland natives' ancestors were brought as slaves to the States is really not important, compared to the common heritage of black brotherhood and unity in the face of oppression that we have.

After a successful campaign, Chisholm arrived in Washington in January 1968. She was dismayed by the power games, influence-peddling and snobbery she found in Congress, whose members seemed to act mainly in their own self-interest.

The United States was becoming entangled in Vietnam, pouring billions of tax dollars into an unjust and unwinnable war. Yet the nation's lawmakers were reluctant to spend resources improving the lives of poor Americans in the inner cities. Chisholm had to speak up.

Now, I am not a pacifist. Ending the war had not been a major theme of my campaign; it was ninth on a list of nine goals that I had pledged to fight for if I were elected, behind jobs, job training, equality education, adequate housing, enforcement of anti-discrimination laws, support for day care centers, and several other items. But when President Nixon announced, on the same day, that he had decided that the United States would not be safe until we started to build an ABM [anti-ballistic missile] system, and that the Head Start program in the District of Columbia was to be cut back for lack of money, that was enough for me. ... I had to tell the world that it was wrong to plan to spend billions on an elaborate and unnecessary weapons system when disadvantaged children were getting nothing.

The juxtaposition of the two presidential announcements was the theme of my speech, but there were dozens of other indications of the administration's intentions that I could have seized on. Nor was the bias in favor of weapons of death and against programs for peace all at the White House end of Pennsylvania Avenue. There was the case of Pride, Incorporated. This is a vigorous and successful black organization that grew up spontaneously among young men in the inner city of the District of Columbia. Originally its program was to kill rats and clean up litter; it was so successful that it earned a million-dollar federal grant to continue its program and expand into new fields, particularly the creation of jobs for young, unemployed black men. Its enemies on the Hill turned a team of at least six auditors from the General Accounting Office loose on Pride. They worked seven months and spent more than $100,000. At last they reported they had uncovered a fraud—it involved a little less than $2,100. In the same seven months billions of dollars were spent by the Department of Defense. How many auditors

Shirley Chisholm

were checking up on the cozy, classified, negotiated contracts on which the billions were spent? Just five.

But more important was the contrast that was so plain to me that I could not understand why it was not plain to everyone, including the other members of Congress. While we gave the military a blank check to dream up new weapons, following up revelations of their worthlessness and wasteful-ness with decisions to spend more on them, we were merciless with the failures of social programs. Take the Job Corps. Its shortcomings and mistakes were criticized at length, although the amounts involved were trivial compared to military spending waste. Its accomplishments were greater than its failures, and its promise greater still. If it had been a research and development program creating better ways to kill, it would have been pronounced invaluable, and billions would have been poured into it.

It seemed to me that there was only one possible course for me to take. I could not vote for money for war while funds were being denied to feed, house, and school Americans. ...

"We Americans," I said in my maiden speech late in March, "have come to feel that it is our mission to make the world free. We believe that we are the good guys, everywhere, in Vietnam, in Latin America, wherever we go. We believe we are good guys at home, too. When the Kerner Commission told white America what black America has always known, that prejudice and hatred built the nation's slums, maintains them and profits by them, white America could not believe it. But it is true. Unless we start to fight and defeat the enemies in our own country, poverty and racism, and make our talk of equality and opportunity ring true, we are exposed in the eyes of the world as hypocrites when we talk about making people free.

"I am deeply disappointed at the clear evidence that the number one priority of the new administration is to buy more and more and more weapons of war, to return to the era of the Cold War and to ignore the war we must fight here, the war that is not optional. There is only one way, I believe, to turn these policies around. The Congress must respond to the mandate that the American people have clearly expressed. They have said, 'End this war. Stop the waste. Stop the killing. Do something for our own people first.'..."

I concluded, "We must force the administration to rethink its distorted, unreal scale of priorities. Our children, our jobless men, our deprived, rejected, and starving fellow citizens must come first. For this reason, I intend to vote 'no' on every money bill that comes to the floor of this House that provides any funds for the Department of Defense. Any bill whatsoever, until the time comes when our values and priorities have been turned right-side up again, until the monstrous waste and the shocking profits in the defense budget have been eliminated and our country starts to use its strength, its tremendous resources, for people and peace, not for profits and war."

Chisholm was reelected to Congress in 1971. A year later she achieved another "first," becoming the first African-American to seek the presidential nomination on the Democratic ticket.

Although her presidential bid was unsuccessful, she remained in the House for another decade, fighting for civil rights and women's rights. In 1983 she retired from politics. There was little she could do within Congress, she had concluded, to change the way the political system worked. Change would come only when the "have-nots" of all races and colors joined together to wake the conscience of the nation.

I did not come to Congress to behave myself and stay away from explosive issues so I can keep coming back. Under the circumstances, it's hard for me to imagine I will stay here long. ...

Most Americans have never seen the ignorance, degradation, hunger, sickness, and futility in which many other Americans live. Until a problem reaches their doorsteps, they're not going to understand. They won't become involved in economic or political change until something brings the seriousness of the situation home to them. Until they are threatened, why should they change a system that has been fairly beneficial for a fairly large number of people? It is going to have to be the have-nots—the blacks, browns, reds, yellows, and whites who do not share in the good life that most Americans lead—who somehow arouse the conscience of the nation and thus create a conscience in the Congress. My role, as I see it, is to help them do so, working outside of Washington, perhaps, as much as inside it. ❖

Botpipèl

Félix Morisseau-Leroy

Félix Morisseau-Leroy was born in Haiti. He was exiled in 1959 after François Duvalier came to power, and has worked in Africa and the United States. He lives in Miami, where he writes plays and poetry in Haitian Creole.

"Boat People" touches on key events in Haitian history. It recounts the capture of Africans and their sale at the notorious Bossal slave market in the French colony of St. Domingue. It notes the impact of the Haitian Revolution—"we stamped our feet, the earth shook ..." The Duvalier regimes are evoked in the mention of Fort Dimanche, an infamous prison in Haiti that housed political prisoners. "Krome Avenue" is the Krome federal detention center in Miami, where U.S. immigration authorities have jailed many Haitian refugees.

"Botpipèl" appeared in DYAKOUT 1,2,3,4 (Jamaica, N.Y.: Haitiana Publications). © 1990 by Félix Morisseau-Leroy. English translation by J. Knapp, M. Racine and C. Sunshine. Used by permission of the author.

Nou tout nan yon kannòt k ap koule
Sa te rive deja Sen Domeng
Se nou sèl yo rele botpipèl

Nou tout nou mouri depi lontan
Sa k rete ankò ki kab fè nou pè
Kite zòt rele nou botpipèl

Se jodi n ap goumen ak lamizè
Nan zile sou lanmè toupatou
Se zòt ki rele nou botpipèl

Agawou di long kou lannuit long
Wè pa wè fòk jou louvri kanmenm
Nou pa janm di nou pa botpipèl

Nan Ginen yo te kenbe n ak chen
Met chenn nan pye n anbake n
Sa k pou te rele nou botpipèl

Mwatye kagezon an te peri
Yo vann rès la mache Kwa Bosal
Se zòt ke rele nou botpipèl

Jou nou frape pye n tè a tranble
Jouk Lalwizyàn jouk Venezwela
Sa k te vin rele nou botpipèl

Yon move tan pase sou peyi n lan
Grangou fè chen manje rakèt
Yo pat ankò rele nou botpipèl

N al bouske djòb ak libète
Yo boure n nan kanntè DPM
[Dirèk pou Miyami]
Zòt tonbe rele nou botpipèl

Nou tap kouri pou Fò Dimanch
Nou vin echwe nan Kwòm Avni
Se zòt ki rele nou botpipèl

Chalè Miyami wete nanm nou
Fredi Chikago pete fyèl nou
Botpipèl botpipèl botpipèl

E poutan an wetan Vyenvyen an yo
Ki meriken ki pa moun vini
Se nou yo vle rele botpipèl

Nou pa pote dwòg nan dyakout nou
Nou pote kouray nou pou n travay
Botpipèl se sa menm botpipèl

Nou pa vini pou n bay traka
Nou vini ak onè respè nou
Se zòt ki rele nou botpipèl

Nou pap pale fò ni rele twòp
Men tout botpipèl egal ego
Tout botpipèl yo se botpipèl

Yon jou n a leve n a frape pye n
Kou nou te fè nan San Domeng lan
Y a konnen kilès ki botpipèl

Jou sa a kit se Kristòf Kolon
Kit s Anri Kisinjè y a konnen
Kilès nou menm nou rele pipèl
❖

Boat People

We are all in a drowning boat
It happened before in St. Domingue
We are the ones they call boat people

We all died long ago
What else can frighten us?
Let them call us boat people

We've struggled a long time with poverty
On our islands, the sea, everywhere
It's they who call us boat people

Agawou, the spirit, says: However long the night,
Daybreak must surely come
We never said we are not boat people

In Africa they chased us with dogs
Shackled our ankles, loaded us on ships
Who then called us boat people?

Half the cargo perished
The rest were sold at Bossal Market
It's they who call us boat people

We stamped our feet and the earth shook
Up to Louisiana, down to Venezuela
Who would call us boat people?

A harsh season came upon our country
The hungry dog eats thorns
They didn't call us boat people yet

We set out in search of jobs and freedom
Piled on cargo boats—direct to Miami
They began calling us boat people

We fled in fear of Fort Dimanche
But wound up at Krome Avenue
It's they who call us boat people

Miami heat deadens our souls
Chicago cold rips our entrails
Boat people boat people boat people

Except for the Indians
What American isn't an immigrant?
But it's us they call boat people

We don't bring drugs in our bags
But courage and strength to work
Boat people—that's us, boat people

We don't come to make trouble
We come with honor and respect
It's they who call us boat people

We don't raise our voices or scream
But all boat people are equal, the same
All boat people are boat people

One day we'll stand up, stamp our feet
As we did at St. Domingue
Then they'll know who these boat people are

That day, be it Christopher Columbus
Or Henry Kissinger—they will know
Whom we ourselves call people
❖

> **Agawou:** one of the spirit figures of vodou,
> Haiti's popular religion
> **the hungery dog eats thorns:** a Haitian
> proverb
> **honor and respect:** traditional Haitian
> greeting

Poems of Exile

Lourdes Casal

Lourdes Casal (1938-1981) was born in Cuba and emigrated to the United States in 1962. She taught at City University of New York and Rutgers University, and was known for her sociological studies of black Cubans. This research was set in the context of Casal's larger interest in the dynamics of the transition to socialism in Cuba.

Casal was one of the first exiles to make return visits to Cuba. She is remembered for her pioneering efforts to bring about improved relations between Cubans in Cuba and those in the United States. She moved back to the island shortly before her death from illness in 1981.

Casal's poetry explores the experience and emotions of exile. "Para Ana Veldford" was written for her friend Anna Veltfort, an American who had lived in Cuba.

(continued on next page)

Para Ana Veldford

Nunca el verano en Provincetown
y aún en esta tarde tan límpida,
(tan poco usual para Nueva York)
es desde la ventana del autobús que contemplo
la serenidad de la hierba en el parque a lo largo de Riverside
y el desenfado de todos los veraneantes que descansan sobre ajadas
    frazadas
de los que juguetean con las bicicletas por los trillos.
Permanezco tan extranjera detrás del cristal protector como en aquel
    invierno
—fin de semana inesperado—
cuando enfrenté por primera vez la nieve de Vermont
y sin embargo, Nueva York es mi casa.
Soy ferozmente leal a esta adquirida patria chica.
Por Nueva York soy extranjera ya en cualquier otra parte,
fiero orgullo de los perfumes que nos asaltan por cualquier calle del
    West Side
marijuana y oler a cerveza
y el tufo de los orines de perro
y la salvaje vitalidad de Santana
descendiendo sobre nosotros
desce una bocina que truena improbablement balanceada sobre una
    escalera de incendios,
la gloria ruidosa de Nueva York en verano,
el Parque Central y nosotros,
los pobres,
que hemos heredado el lago del lado norte,
y Harlem rema en la laxitud de esta tarde morosa.
El autobús se desliza perezosamente
hacia abajo, por la Quinta Avenida;
y frente a mí el joven barbudo

que carga una pila enorme de libros de la Biblioteca Pública
y parece como si se pudiera tocar el verano en la frente sudorosa del
    ciclista
que viaja agarrado de mi ventanilla.
Pero Nueva York no fue la cuidad de mi infancia,
no fue aquí que adquirí las primeras certidumbres,
no está aquí el rincón de mi primera caída,
ni el silbido lacerante que marcaba las noches.
Por eso siempre permaneceré al margen,
una extraña entre las piedras
aún bajo el sol amable de este día de verano,
como ya para siempre permaneceré extranjera,
aún cuando regrese a la cuidad de mi infancia,
cargo esta marginalidad inmune a todos los retornos,
demasiado habanera para ser newyorkina,
demasiado newyorkina para ser,
—aún volver a ser—
cualquier otra cosa.

❖

Three poems are presented here in the original Spanish from Casal's collection *PALABRAS JUNTAN REVOLUCIÓN* (Havana: Ediciones Casa de las Américas). © 1981 by Ediciones Casa de las Américas. English translations by Catherine Sunshine.

For Ana Veldford

Never the summer in Provincetown
and even on this clearest of afternoons
(so rare for New York)
it's from a bus window that I contemplate
the serenity of the grass in the park along Riverside
the ease of the vacationers resting on rumpled blankets
of the cyclists weaving down the bike paths.
I'm just as much a foreigner behind this protective glass
as I was that winter
—that unexpected weekend—
when I faced snow for the first time in Vermont.
And despite it all, New York is my home.
I'm fiercely loyal to this acquired hometown.
Because of New York I am a foreigner anywhere else
fierce pride in the scents that assault us on any West Side street
marijuana and the smell of beer
the stench of dog urine
and the savage vitality of Santana
descending upon us
from a loudspeaker perched precariously on the edge of a fire escape
the raucous glory of New York in summer
Central Park and us,
the poor,
who've inherited the lake on the north side,
and Harlem rows through the lassitude of this lingering afternoon.

The bus snakes lazily
downtown, along Fifth Avenue;
and in front of me this young bearded man
carrying an enormous pile of books from the Public Library
and you could almost touch summer on the sweaty brow of the cyclist
riding latched on to my window.
But New York wasn't the city of my childhood,
it wasn't here that I acquired my first convictions,
the corner of my first fall isn't here,
nor the piercing whistle that filled the night.
That's why I will always inhabit the margins
a stranger among the stones
even under the friendly sun of this summer day.
Then, now and forever I will remain a foreigner,
even when I return to the city of my birth,
I carry this marginality inside me, immune to all returns,
too *habanera* to be New Yorker,
too New Yorker to be
—even to become again—
anything else.
❖

habanera: native or resident of Havana

Mi Barrio — Versión No. 2

La tintorería Prompt
se ha transformado en una agencia de pasajes
—y en la vidriera,
prominentemente desplegado,
hay un anuncio que dice:
"Puerto Plata ..."
Cuando la carnicería kosher
que estaba casi en la esquina de Broadway y 161
se convirtió en una venta de cuchifritos,
y la sinagoga,
al doblar de la esquina,
en un templo de testigos de Jehová,
comprendí que todo,
absolutamente todo,
se había consumado.
❖

My Neighborhood — Version No. 2

Prompt Dry Cleaning
has turned into a travel agency
—in its window, boldly displayed,
an advertisement for "Puerto Plata" ...
When the kosher butcher
that was right by the corner of Broadway and 161st
turned into a *cuchifritos* shop,
and the synagogue around the corner,
became a Jehovah's Witness kingdom hall
then I understood that all,
absolutely all,
was complete.
❖

Puerto Plata: resort town in the Dominican Republic
cuchifritos: fried snacks

Hudson, Invierno

Este paisaje irreal
la danza de los árboles
la iglesia que se vuelve, en la bruma, castillo,
y el río que renuncia a su fluir
y adopta
la rigidez y el brillo de un joven granadero.
Todo aquí te recuerda
el cielo siempre gris
los árboles, las piedras,
el río y el acero
Mundo que languidece pues no le has sonreído
tristemente te espera.

Ahora sé
que la distancia es tridimensional.
Es falso que el espacio entre tú y yo
pueda medirse en metros o pulgadas
come si las calles pudieran cruzarse impunemente,
come si fuera fácil extender una mano.

Esta distancia es sólida, robusta,
y la ausencia es total,
inexpugnable:
a pesar de la ilusoria disponibilidad
del teléfono,
tiene espesor, y longitud, y anchura.
❖

Hudson in Winter

This unreal landscape
the slow dance of the trees
the church turned castle in the mist
and the river, its flow arrested,
as rigid and glinting as a young grenadier.
Everything here reminds me of you
the sky permanently gray
the trees, the rocks
the river and the steel
A world that languishes because you have not smiled on it
sadly awaits you.

Now I know
that distance is tridimensional.
It is false that the space between you and me
can be measured in meters or inches
as if the streets could be crossed with impunity
as if it were easy to reach out a hand.

This distance is solid, strong,
and the absence is total,
unassailable:
despite the illusory ease
of the telephone
it has thickness, length, and width.

❖

Remembering Lourdes Casal

Roy S. Bryce-Laporte

Roy S. Bryce-Laporte was born in Panama of West Indian ancestry. He has written and edited numerous works on Caribbean immigration to the United States and Central America. He is currently MacArthur Professor of Sociology at Colgate University in Hamilton, N.Y.

Lourdes Casal has left us, the community of engaged Caribbean-immigrant scholars, a challenge of conscience and a legacy of activism. Born in Havana in 1938, Dr. Casal was educated at Cuban universities. She came to the United States in the first years of the Castro regime, one of a small number of black intellectuals to leave at a time when when the exodus was still mostly white and middle- or upper-class.

She obtained her doctorate in social psychology from the New School of Social Research and later taught at Brooklyn College and Rutgers. As a black Hispanic woman, Lourdes was affected by the social movements of the sixties and by a trip she later took to Africa. She began to reevaluate her ideas about the situation of revolutionary Cuba, particularly as it affected blacks.

Returning to her homeland in 1973, she was one of the first of her peers to make the trip, and one of the few to be permitted repeated entry to Cuba. She pursued comparative studies on the well-being of Cuban blacks in the island and in the United States, especially Miami. She also pressed the Cuban authorities to continue to improve the situation of blacks, to treat them fairly and absorb them in important structures and programs of the country.

Here in the United States she dared show her sympathies toward some kind of rapprochement between the two countries. She spoke of the promises and advances she saw in the Cuban revolution in general and more particularly for women, blacks and working people. Lourdes helped to found the Antonio Maceo Brigade, the Circulo de Culturo Cubana, and *Areíto* magazine. All were involved in reinforcing links of culture, identity and commitment to Cuba among Cubans now living in the United States.

Lourdes was a worker, *una trabajadora*. As a dedicated cultural worker she left us, among other works, a body of thoughtful poems. To appreciate them we must see Lourdes above all as a talented immigrant mind—in search of a universally understandable, yet personal way to bridge time and distance and transcend boundaries. Like so many immigrants, she never stopped seeking ways to make sense of her life, love and experiences through her changing places of residence and evolving identity.

Lourdes was also a fighter, *una luchadora*. Stricken with illness when still in her forties, she was committed to struggle not only for her life, but for the causes and convictions she developed. She returned to Cuba near the end of her life and died there, but her spirit and her vision live on. ❖

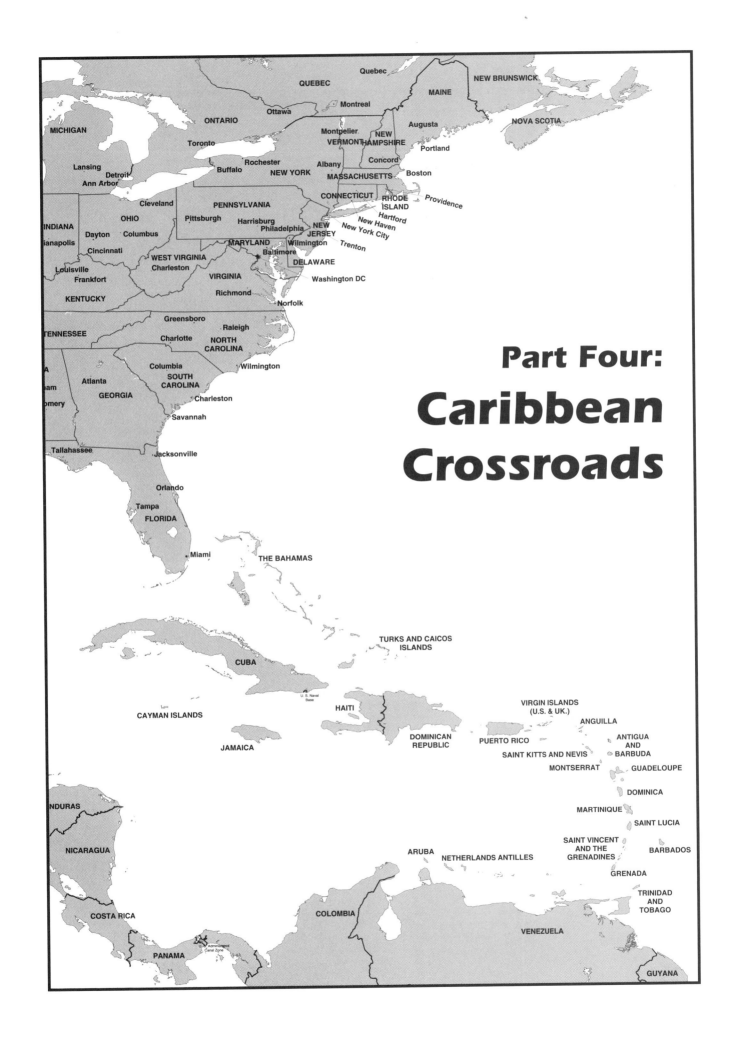

Part Four:

Caribbean Crossroads

Playing bingo at the Little Havana Community Center on Calle Ocho in Miami.

MIAMI

During the 1960s and 1970s, the arrival of thousands of Cuban exiles transformed the city. The part of southwest Miami where the Cubans initially concentrated came to be called Little Havana. Eighth Street became *la Calle Ocho,* a busy thoroughfare of Cuban-owned stores, restaurants and social clubs. "Before the Cuban exodus began," writer Gustavo Pérez Firmat recalls in his memoir, "Eighth Street had been a quiet, out-of-the way street between Downtown Miami and Coral Gables. By the late sixties it had developed into the hub of a thriving community of energetic and ambitious exiles."

As in other large cities, new immigrants typically found housing in inner-city areas that established residents had vacated on their way to suburban living. Some of the original residents stayed on, however, as the neighborhood changed around them. The Dillons are an "Anglo" family that has lived in Miami for several generations. In this 1988 reflection, Thomas Dillon describes how his grandmother, Nana, reacted as her neighborhood became Little Havana.

In the years since this essay was written, Little Havana has continued to change. Many of the original Cuban residents have themselves moved to the suburbs. The neighborhood is now home to recent immigrants of many different ethnic groups. ❖

Nana and the Cubans

Thomas Dillon

Thomas Dillon lives in Miami and teaches in the Miami-Dade County public schools. Nana, his grandmother, died in 1993 at the age of 92. Reprinted by permission from AREITO magazine, December 1988. © 1988 by Thomas Dillon.

Nana's 86. For 65 of those years she has lived in a small Dade Pine frame house. The house is both shelter and a metaphor for Nana. Both are strong internally but showing wear on the outside. Both are much aged and weathered yet hold on tenaciously to an independent existence. Both are the last of their kind in their environment.

Nana is Scotch-Irish, American-born, in other words really "Anglo." She is conservative and fiercely independent by nature, by heritage and in politics. She thinks and frequently speaks in aphorisms and clichés such as:

A penny saved is a penny earned.

Never a borrower nor a lender be.

It's the straw that broke the camel's back.

She firmly believes that she (and everyone else) should be self—sufficient. She reluctantly gave up driving last year. She is generous of heart—the Irish; and tight with money—the Scot.

The Depression caused her to squeeze eight people into her little house. Now, she vehemently insists on living alone.

Two of her most memorable shocks are the 1926 hurricane and the invasion of the Cubans. The hurricane was an act of nature that she cannot rile against, but that ingrained a fear of hurricanes in general. She fights this fear by boarding up the house and moving to higher ground at even the mention of a hurricane watch. The invasion of the Cubans was a different matter.

Nana's small bastion exists in a section of Miami that the city has named Little Havana. Despite the fact that Nana's house is now sur-rounded by apartments filled with Cubans, she stubbornly knows her part of Miami wasn't always Little Havana.

The "invasion" came in the sixties—hers and the decade's. Her old neighborhood that had been quiet and familiar became loud and foreign. The old cat lady's house to the east and the eccentric inventor's house to the west were torn down and replaced with apartments. Into the apartments came foreigners—Cubans.

Nana, who had chosen to have one child, who never remarried after being widowed, who never moved from her wedding house, was not

Nana's house

ready for the rebirth of her neighborhood.

As more and more Cubans filtered into Nana's neighborhood, Nana felt assaulted. On the streets she heard sounds she did not understand. The local stores became Cuban—never mind that the storefront groceries hadn't been open for years. They were now bodegas. Her downtown, her very neighborhood, became foreign territory. She was asked "Donde está el buzón?" and answered with the Spanish phrase she still knows best, "No comprende," which ironically means, "You don't understand."

In her yard (she has the only yard and garden on the block) she found children playing. When they picked her flowers she chased them with a broom, shouting, "Get out!" One or two would return to battle by pelting the house with stones.

The parents were equally incomprehensible in language and behavior. They would put *their* trash on *her* pile and park *their* cars in front of *her* house. As if to add insult to injury, these invaders received assistance from the government—her government. This woman who eschewed her own Social Security checks, who felt welfare was support to the lazy, resented the free peanut butter mounting on the shelves in the homes of the invaders.

She was in all senses surrounded. The apartment buildings dwarfed her house and the foreignness of the neighbors made her cringe. Though all the rest of her kind of neighbors were dying or running away, Nana wouldn't or couldn't retreat. She has stayed on.

Nana is closing the seventh decade in her house; she is closing her third decade with the invaders. She has changed. She can't remember just how the change came. Nana remembers, at 86, anecdotes.

One day, one of the worst rock-throwers knocked on her door. She answered his knock and with her old lady's bravado said "Yeah! Whadda ya want!" Timid, ashamed, the boy said, "Miss Helen, I'm sorry I threw rocks at your house." Nana remembers the apology well, yet she cannot say that was the turning point.

The children who had been stealing flowers and throwing rocks began to touch the front door with new requests. "Can I take this gardenia to my mother?" "Of course," said Nana.

"Can you help me with my English homework?" Nana, never the teacher, gave them the funnies from *The Miami Herald* and told them to read. She showed them the 1939 edition of the Encyclopedia Britannica and said "Look it up."

Little by little, the children began to conquer Nana. Her new protegés would bring her a piece of cake from one of their birthday parties. Nana, somewhat embarrassed that she had not known, would give them a dollar in lieu of a present. The children were delighted and Nana was softened.

The children began to help fill Nana's days; she began to look forward to their intrusions. She began to make little deals. With Little Emilio: "I'll give you the sports section if you'll watch out for robbers." Emilito was quick to assure her, "Sure, Missy'elen, I already do that."

In no time, four or five of the young "enemy" were in front of Nana's color TV on Saturday nights. Instead of hitting them with a broom she held out the program selection, demanding only Lawrence Welk.

As the years rolled on, Nana was invited to all the parties and went to quite a few. At the parties she met the parents. With hands, broken English and translations by the children, she broke new ground with the adults. The adult "enemy" became humanized, too.

Everyone in the neighborhood knows or knows of her. Everyone shares in her life. The kids who

Nana's new neighbors

were enemies have had her to their weddings, parties and graduations. She is revered and treated with much love and respect.

Now, the ex-enemies bring their grandchildren from the suburbs to visit their grandparents and Nana in Little Havana. Now, instead of an argument over the trash, one of the ex-enemy parks his car in her driveway. Another, every month, borrows $10 for a week until the next Social Security check, and in an uncommon ritual, repays it in order to borrow it again.

Her vocabulary has expanded to include "buenos días" and "adios" and her ear has become attuned to the once-strange sounds of the foreigners. Just the other day, when one of the kids asked her for an "escalera," though she heard "escalator," she understood the child needed a ladder because she listened to the rest of what the child had to say.

Nana's once-foreign neighbors now preserve, protect and honor her as if she were on the near-extinction list and they were life members of the Audubon Society. Last year Nana had an operation. Nothing big—but while she was recuperating every family in the neighborhood stopped by in a slow procession. Each had something to give and all offered to do whatever was necessary. The fruit she ate but the paella went untouched—too spicy.

This year Nana needs another operation and it has been a battle of a very different kind. The neighbors want her to have the operation in Little Havana, be nursed in her own house in Little Havana. Her family, my family, has politely said no and taken her away—temporarily, we assure them. She is after all *one of us* but it is also clear that Nana is not *just* ours. Gringa, Anglo, and still very stubborn, she can't remember that she ever resented her second families. She has been assimilated. ❖

At Negril restaurant on Georgia Avenue NW, customers choose from a menu of Jamaican specialties such as beef patties, codfish cakes, jerk chicken, oxtail stew, sorrel and ginger beer. The Jamaican-owned restaurant, near Howard University, is popular with students.

WASHINGTON, D.C.

Together with its Maryland and Virginia suburbs, Washington, D.C. is one of the most ethnically diverse areas in the nation. Among groups of Caribbean origin, West Indians are particularly well represented. Beginning in the 1940s, Howard University attracted students from the English-speaking islands. Many remained in the area after graduation, and the neighborhoods around Howard became home to Washington's early West Indian community.

Immigration from the English-speaking Caribbean increased rapidly after 1965. The newcomers worked in a variety of occupations, ranging from housekeeping to nursing to professional work at the many international agencies headquartered in Washington.

West Indians in the Washington area today are estimated at anywhere from 30,000 to 70,000, with Jamaicans and Trinidadians the most numerous. Although some still live in the city, the area's West Indian community is now concentrated in the Maryland suburbs of Washington. ❖

"The show links people to each other ..."

Interview with Von Martin

Von Martin came to Washington from Trinidad and Tobago in 1967. He has hosted the CARIBBEANA (CaribbeANa) radio program on WPFW-FM for the last 20 years. He was interviewed by Catherine Sunshine on April 19, 1997.

How did Caribbeana get started?

When I arrived in Washington in 1967, the city's Caribbean community was growing fast. We had dances and parties, but there was no radio program or newspaper to bring Caribbean people together. We connected with each other by word of mouth.

The first Caribbean-oriented radio program in D.C. was called *Calypso Kid,* and it became a rallying point for us. When that program went off the air, I saw a need to find some way we could reach each other. Also there was a lot of antagonism between African-Americans and West Indians, and I felt that was happening because they simply didn't know us. We had to find a vehicle to learn about each other.

In 1972 I joined forces with John Blake, another Trinidadian, and we developed a program on the Howard University station, WHUR-FM. I stayed with that until 1975, then I got my own four-hour program on WPFW called *Caribbeana.* It's been going strong for two decades now.

Can you describe a typical show?

When the program first started we treated each different genre of Caribbean music with some kind of evenness. So you would hear calypsos, reggae, cadence, pan music, a little soft bolero-type music. These days I play mostly music from the English-speaking Caribbean— calypso, reggae, soca—as well as music from Haiti.

You get your news from the Caribbean and you get your community announcements. When people want their parties or events announced, they call our community calendar. It's a major link for them to each other.

The show is done in a style that makes people feel at home. It's like an extension of themselves. As the host, my voice, my accent, my Caribbeanness all contribute to that feeling. In the early years of the program I would sometimes talk in dialect, which is what most working-class Caribbean people are used to speaking. Then I would switch to standard English, which is what the middle class prefers. I would get a lot of flak from the middle class for not speaking "properly." That was life, and I had to deal with that.

Who listens to Caribbeana?

We have a large and diverse listening audience: black, white, Latino. In the early days we were locked into the Caribbean community because other people hadn't been exposed to much Caribbean music. I used to come after the 'Bama [a popular African-American radio host]. Oh, it was rough! Because when he signed off, people would just leave me! But over the years that changed, in part because I played American music sung by Caribbean artists. When Americans hear one of Smokey Robinson's songs done in a reggae tempo, they would say, Hey, I didn't know Caribbean music did that! They would stay and listen.

What music is most popular in the English-speaking Caribbean community?

The major forms are calypso, steelband and reggae. The calypsos are songs of social commentary. Every year in Trinidad and Tobago and some of the other English-speaking islands, they have a Carnival. The calypsonians are a major part of it. They compose new songs for each year's Carnival, and these songs would be hard, satirical, *picong* on the government. They hit on the major issues that affect the country, and they become very popular. The best songs are also very hot in terms of dance. David Rudder is always very popular.

Steelband is an instrument made from a 45-gallon oil drum. Its history is similar to that of calypso since they both come out of struggle by working-class people. During colonial times, slaves in the Caribbean islands used drums to communicate. Even after emancipation the ruling class feared the drums, and drumming was outlawed in Trinidad in 1881. That led to the creation of a new instrument called tamboo-bamboo. This was bamboo reeds with holes at different points that could be beaten together and on the ground, giving a percussion sound.

As time went on people found they could get music out of pieces of metal: hubcaps, dust bins, biscuit tins. They found that by beating in the top of an oil drum until it was concave, they could get musical notes. That was the birth of the steel drum, what we call "pan."

A steelband can play all kinds of music. The different size pans correspond to conventional instruments of the orchestra. A piano's high pitch is compared to the tenor pan. You've got nine base drums. A steelband can play classical or almost any kind of music, but calypso is most typical.

Reggae is one of the later forms of music to be created. It got its first loud outburst around 1972 with Jimmy Cliff and "The Harder They Come." But even before that it was nurtured underground. Coming out of colonialism in the 1950s, Jamaicans were seeking a strong national identity; they wanted a music of their own. So their musicians went in the studio and came up with something called ska. But ska was too fast and it lacked strong lyrics. So they slowed up the pace and out came rock-steady. Rock-steady was a bit softer and was influenced by soul music—Smokey Robinson, Fats Domino. Then they changed it up some more and out came reggae.

The Rastafarians adopted reggae as the vehicle for their message, and as a result the lyrics became stronger. Then Bob Marley came on the scene and the rest is history.

But with Bob's passing in 1980, things changed. Because of the lack of leadership, I feel, there was no sense of direction. The lyrics dropped out of reggae and rhythm became the dominant force, and this was dub music. Then they tried to put some lyrics back in and you got dancehall. Dancehall is a bit derogatory, so after a while you found the old stuff coming back in; religion, spirituality, started coming in to clean the music up, and now you have reggae more in the classic mode of Marley. You have people like Freddy MacGregor, Bernie Ruggs, Michael Rose, Koko T, leading that front.

I don't play as much reggae as I used to, because WPFW now has two all-reggae shows. And then again calypso is the national music of the Caribbean. It's the national music of most of the islands, and it's even played a lot in Jamaica. So therefore I would tend to play a little more calypso.

Soca is a hybrid form out of Trinidad and Tobago. It's a rhythm pattern with a four-by-four timing that blends cadence music with calypso. Cadence comes out of Dominica. It was created in Haiti, but Dominica developed its own reflection of cadence, what they call cadence-lypso. Exile One Band with Gordon Henderson was one of the first to start it. A Trinidadian musician named Ras

Von Martin

Shorty spent a lot of time in Dominica and when he came back in 1975 he came out with the first album that's called soca music. The Eastern Caribbean islands do good soca with strong lyrics. In Trinidad they do it more for party. Not solid lyrics, you know, but "wine and jam" and that kind of thing.

What's your favorite music?

I love message music. It's one way that the artist can influence the society. In Trinidad the calypsonian around Carnival time is one of the most listened-to individuals. You could compare him historically to the griot in Africa, or to the town crier. He gets away with criticism that others can't. In fact this year the new prime minister of Trinidad and Tobago, Basdeo Panday, has said that some of the calypsos are too indecent and he wants to bring these people under check.

How is music important to Caribbean people in the United States?

I call it a survival mechanism, because you're living in an alien world. The music is a constant reminder of where you came from and where you are today. When someone from Jamaica or Trinidad or Dominica hears their music, they go right back home, and they're able to move away from the daily struggles of immigration, of bills, of having to get to work on time, all those kinds of stress. They go into their music and they're transformed.

People want to hear songs that are popular in the Caribbean right now. They want to hear what the folks back home are hearing, because they're talking to the folks by telephone. People enjoy hearing a good strong calypso, what the man says about the prime minister, that kind of thing. They like to hear good solid reggae, and I think this is why Bob Marley continuously becomes more important, because Bob's music is like a perennial cycle in people's lives.

Does music help to create a Caribbean consciousness among immigrants from the different islands?

It does and I'll tell you why: back home, when you live in your country, you're just simply national. In Trinidad we don't hear much music from Dominica or Haiti or so. We live wrapped up in the insular world of calypso, with influences from American music. When we come here we become conscious of calypso, we become conscious of reggae, as our *own*. It also depends on the size of the Caribbean population in a given city. If you're a smaller population you gravitate together. Everybody will hear everybody's music, because you depend on each other for survival.

How is radio important to the Caribbean community here?

In the Caribbean, in fact throughout the Third World, radio is *it*. TV may be popular, but radio is the most important medium. Even here in this country, radio's still the most popular. Wherever you're going, if you're at work or at home, radio is right there with you.

People want to hear news from the Caribbean. We get our sources direct from the region; I work on it every day. I have access to CANA, the Caribbean news service. And when I talk to radio stations in the Caribbean they give me information. When a crisis occurs in the region the people here want to be on top of it. When elections are held, they want to be in on it. The past five elections in the Caribbean I have broadcast live. We go on the air and link up with the island that's having the election, and we give people the election results. They don't have to wait until tomorrow to find out by telephone.

So Caribbean radio programs help maintain the link to home?

Exactly, exactly, that's the whole idea. I travel down to the region and I broadcast from there to here. I let people know what's happening at Carnival time, or election time, or some other special time. If there's a hurricane, I link up with the people there so the folks here can raise funds or send material aid.

We deal with serious political and social issues that are happening in the region. Right now the problem between Petit Martinique and the government of Grenada is controversial. When we did an interview with Petit Martinique people, the ambassador of Grenada got upset and wrote me a stinging letter. So I said, well hey, you have equal time! Come and talk. And he gave his side.

Do you deal with issues that concern Caribbean people here in the United States, as well as issues at home?

For example, take the immigration question and the campaign to have immigrants become citizens. We try to sensitize people that they need to look at that. We want them to realize that their votes here are important. There are a lot of Caribbean people who are U.S. citizens and their votes in U.S. elections can make a difference on issues that concern the Caribbean. You still identify as being Caribbean whether you're a U.S. citizen or not, and therefore it is important that you seek that interest.

When you say "Caribbean," are you defining it as the English-speaking Caribbean, or something broader than that?

When I say Caribbean I mean the wider set, from Cuba all the way down south to Trinidad. We define the Caribbean as that. I play music from Haiti and I play cadence. In the early years I used to play a little music from Cuba or Puerto Rico, but as time went on we've focused on the English-speaking Caribbean. One reason is the time factor; there are already Spanish programs on the air. It also has to do with how we were brought up, as English, keeping away from the Spanish and the French.

Why make the crossover to Haitian music, and not to music from the Spanish-speaking islands?

One, I like Haitian music, and two, it's much closer to calypso and soca than salsa and merengue are. I think we in Trinidad have a closer link to the French. Even the calypso music, when you check the rhythmic beds of some of it, you get that French influence.

Do you encourage Caribbean people to move away from their national loyalties and form a broader community?

I think the fact that *Caribbeana* has existed for 20 years is testimony to that. Because *Caribbeana* reflects all that is Caribbean, and we do something on every Caribbean island. It may not be a song played, but it will be a word or a statement on every island. So everybody can identify. That's what I demonstrate: that we are all one and we need to be together. And I think we are one: the *people* are Caribbean. For example, although I was born in Trinidad, my grandfather on my mother's side came from Barbados and my grandfather on my father's side came from St. Vincent. So there's a lot of cross-pollination taking place.

Do other cities have Caribbean radio programs?

They are all over the place. In North America there are 46 cities that have Caribbean-style carnivals, so that tells you something. There's a Caribbean population in all those cities. In Florida alone you have about eight carnivals. In Canada you have 12. New York state would have four or five: New York City, Rochester, Buffalo, all have their own carnivals. Once you have a carnival, you're going to have a radio program there. Because it means that there's a budding Caribbean community there and that community is moving.

I think Washington, D.C. has the best Caribbean radio shows. I'm not saying that because of me, I'm saying it because of my knowledge of good radio. With *Caribbeana* on WPFW and John Blake's program, *The Caribbean Experience,* on WHUR, we have the best. New York has a lot of shows, but they are much more commercial and very different.

Is there anything you want to add?

Radio—I love it, I've always loved it. You are able to create images in another person's mind with song, with voice, with sound, music, ambiance. You have TV and you have newspapers, but radio is freer, so much more creative and more genuine. That's its beauty: you touch the person one on one. ❖

picong: satire; witty criticism
Rastafarians: religious/cultural group that originated in Jamaica
wine and jam: dancing and partying
griot: traditional singer/storyteller
Petit Martinique: the smallest of the three islands that comprise the country of Grenada
salsa: hybrid music developed in New York City by musicians of various Latin American and Caribbean backgrounds
merengue: popular dance music of the Dominican Republic

"You can let your imagination run wild ..."

Interview with Marjorie Smith

Caribbean-style carnivals are held in various cities in the United States, with the largest in New York City every year on Labor Day. Washington's smaller carnival is held in June. The city has a dedicated community of costume designers who take their creations to Caribbean festivals all along the eastern seaboard.

The popular name for Carnival, "mas," reflects its origins as a masquerade. Work on costumes begins months ahead of time. Costume makers gather in workshops called "mas camps," typically in someone's garage or basement, to build their fantastic creations. On Carnival day, bands of costumed revelers dance their way through the streets to the rhythm of steelband and calypso music.

Marjorie Smith came to Washington from Trinidad and Tobago in 1965. When not designing costumes, she is an office manager at the World Bank. She was interviewed by Keith Q. Warner on May 19, 1997.

How did you get into costume making?

I came to the United States to study psychology and business administration at Catholic University in Washington, D.C. Afterwards I started working and decided to stay in the area. I always thought I would go back, but then I got married and started raising a family. When you have children, you really have to choose the proper time to uproot them, to take them home. So I'm still here.

I do want my children to maintain their roots. We have all types of Caribbean music, and the children love it. I made sure the children went home to Trinidad every year when they were young so they could meet members of our family and appreciate our culture. In doing this, we have gotten more involved as a family in that part of our culture that a lot of people can relate to—namely Carnival.

I only took part in Carnival once or twice when I lived in Trinidad. I grew up in a very strict family where I had to devote my time to books, books, books—no Carnival. But my husband, whom I met here, dealt with Carnival in Trinidad before he came to the United States. And that's how I got deeper and deeper involved in the costumes: designing, making and displaying them.

What's involved in making costumes?

We have a group, or band, called the Trinidad & Tobago Masqueraders. First we get together and decide what the theme will be. My husband is the leader of the band and also the designer, so he does the art work. He and I conceptualize what each costume is going to look like and he creates a drawing. For example, let's say we're going to do a butterfly. If you're going for authenticity, there's only so much you can do. It must be an exact replica. But when you use fantasy, you can let your imagination run wild and do many more things.

The drawings are put on display at various locations around the area, such as Caribbean restaurants, so the public can view them. We also advertise on Caribbean radio programs and hold parties to launch the band. People sign up for whichever costume they like and pay the cost,

Marjorie Smith in one of her creations, a giant butterfly.

A costume is typically about 20 feet high—starting from the shoulders of the person who wears it—and 20 feet wide. There is also a train about 25 feet long. It can weigh anywhere from 125 pounds up to about 250 pounds. If a costume is extremely heavy, we construct it with a base made of steel rods with wheels so the person can pull instead of carry the weight.

Some of the costumes are very extravagant. For example, we made a fantasy version of an enchanted fan that was 15 feet high by 20 feet wide. It was made from bridal satin, sequined braid, hand-made jewelled patterns, glass beads, loose sequins and lots of feathered boas and ostrich plumes.

How do you display the costumes?

The costume is really art in motion. They are made to be collapsible for ease of transport. This art is taken to Caribbean carnivals in various cities. Washington, D.C. has a carnival on the last Saturday of June each year, and of course we participate. We have also gone to carnivals in New York, Baltimore, Miami and Tallahassee, to name just a few. In the Brooklyn Carnival on Labor Day 1996 I won the competition for best individual costume as well as the most prestigious award, Queen of the Carnival Bands. I'll be participating again this year.

It's costly and time-consuming. Why do you do it?

The United States is made up of a multitude of cultures and we do Carnival to show what our country has to offer the world. We want to show those who can't go to the Caribbean what we have there.

from around $50 for a very simple costume to about $150 for a more elaborate one. Most of the people who join our band are from various islands in the Caribbean, but we've also had Americans, Asians and others. Anybody can join with us and play mas.

The larger costumes, or pieces as they are called, are built by my husband and three or four of us. The others help make the smaller ones. All this is done in what we call a mas camp, the place where we gather to build the costumes.

From the drawing board we decide on the colors and materials we will use, taking into consideration which materials will flow most freely. We use materials like bridal satins, lace, leather, nylon net, lamé and organza, with feathers and sequins. Then we have to think of the right colors, bright, to catch the sun and the eyes of the spectators. Then we just add and add, a little change here, a little change there, until we get the desired product.

I see people sway to the music as I go by. People ask to join in, or we invite them to do so. What is really nice is when young American children ask us questions about the costumes. Is it heavy? What does it show? When you explain it to them, you can see the excitement in their eyes, so you know they really appreciate and love your culture.

For us, Carnival is our escape mechanism. It brings home to those who can't go home. I use Carnival as my stress-buster. After all the frenzy of work, I look forward to Carnival times.

I certainly don't do it for the money. My group and I do it for the culture and the enjoyment, for we can never really make a decent return on our outlay. I usually have a very extravagant costume, the cost of which I can never recoup. I feel happy knowing I have brought joy to people, so that makes up for the financial loss. I have won lots of competitions, too, so I have all those trophies to show.

I hold on to my costumes for at least a year because they are so elaborate, but after that I have to build a new one. I can recycle parts, but not too much, because every year it's a different theme. Maybe some of the braid, some parts of the frame, but probably not the feathers, because they take a beating.

It's really a labor of love. You love your culture, and you want other people to enjoy it, too. ❖

Joséito

Children view their North Philadelphia neighborhood through a camera lens in photography classes run by Taller Puertorriqueño.

PHILADELPHIA

When Caribbean people come to the United States, they enter a society that views immigrants and minorities with ambivalence at best and violent hostility at worst. Some may be exempted by virtue of their European appearance and/or privileged background. But for many, the road to acceptance in U.S. society is long and rough. Issues Caribbean immigrants and migrants have faced include:

▶ The struggle for economic advancement in an intensely competitive society;

▶ Schools hostile or indifferent to the children of immigrants and poor people, especially those who speak little English;

▶ Racial discrimination and police brutality;

▶ Lack of power within the political system.

Throughout this century, Caribbean immigrants and their U.S.-born descendants have addressed these issues in a variety of ways. Each group's experience has been distinct. The efforts of Puerto Ricans stand out, however, in part because their U.S. citizenship and their numbers make them a potential political force in some of the nation's largest cities. The greatest strides have been made in New York, which has the oldest and largest Puerto Rican community in the country. But Puerto Rican political activism also has deep roots in Chicago and Philadelphia, which have the nation's second- and third-largest Puerto Rican populations.

In all three cities, early migrants organized hometown clubs and other cultural, political and labor groups specifically representing Puerto Ricans. They were also active in mainstream trade unions and political parties, especially local Democratic Party structures. However, this participation did not automatically translate into political influence or even a vote. Until 1965, an English literacy test was required before casting a ballot. Democratic party "machines" in the big cities were controlled by white ethnic groups and generally sought to exclude blacks and Latinos from power. Political districts were often drawn in such a way as to split the votes of African-Americans and Latinos.

As the Puerto Rican community in the United States grew more impoverished, a second generation of organizations appeared in the late 1950s and early 1960s. These social service agencies offered programs in education, health, legal assistance and other areas, funded in part with federal War on Poverty funds.

Such services, while desperately needed, did not address the roots of Puerto Rican powerlessness. During the 1960s radical youth groups sprang up, influenced by the African-American civil rights and Black Power movements. They sought to confront poverty and racial discrimination with tactics ranging from legal action to rallies, marches, sit-ins and rent strikes. In the process, young radicals often challenged older Puerto Rican community leaders who had worked within the Democratic Party and were seen as too close to the "powers that be."

The radical groups eventually disbanded, but their impact was lasting. They helped form a new generation of Puerto Rican activists who have continued to work for change through grassroots organizing, legal strategies, and the ballot box.

These efforts have gradually resulted in greater Puerto Rican representation on school boards and city councils, and in state assemblies. They have fed into coordinated efforts by African-Americans, Latinos and others to loosen the grasp of the machines on urban politics. As Juan D. González recounts, Puerto Rican voters in Philadelphia were an important part of the coalition that defeated a racist mayor, Frank Rizzo, in 1978. In Chicago, Puerto Rican, African-American and Mexican-American voters together helped elect Mayor Harold Washington in 1983 in defiance of the white-dominated Democratic machine.

"The Turbulent Progress of Puerto Ricans in Philadelphia" was written in 1987. In the years since then there have been further struggles and gains for Philadelphia's approximately 90,000 Puerto Ricans. There continues to be one Puerto Rican on the city council—Angel Ortiz, first elected in 1984—and one in the state assembly. The political influence of Latino voters in the city, 75% of whom are Puerto Rican, is gradually increasing. More Latinos are becoming involved in local Democratic Party structures, which has helped to bring out the vote. A political struggle over redistricting in 1990 led to the creation of a North Philadelphia district where Latinos are a plurality and a crucial swing vote.

A police civilian review commission has been created to respond to concerns about police brutality. An advisory body with little authority of its own, the commission nonetheless has helped focus public attention on the behavior of the police in Philadelphia communities.

Despite these developments, the potential of Puerto Rican political involvement has not been fully realized. Further progress will depend on education to raise the consciousness of potential voters and increase voter turnout. It will require the continuous formation of new leadership, especially women and young people, and the building of coalitions with other groups that share similar goals. ❖

The Turbulent Progress of Puerto Ricans in Philadelphia

Juan D. González

Juan D. González is a columnist with the NEW YORK DAILY NEWS. Born in Puerto Rico, he lived in Philadelphia for 15 years. He is a founder of the Young Lords Party and was the first president of the National Congress for Puerto Rican Rights.

This article is adapted from CENTRO, the bulletin of the Centro de Estudios Puertorriqueños, Hunter College, Winter 1987-88. © 1987 by Juan D. González. Used by permission of the Centro de Estudios Puertorriqueños and Juan D. González.

During the past two decades the city of Philadelphia has spawned the third-largest Puerto Rican population in the continental United States, smaller only than the Puerto Rican *colonias* of New York City and Chicago, and slightly larger than that of Newark, New Jersey.

It is a community that is both geographically compact and socially complex. Like all of our colonias in this land of the dollar bill and the winter coat, it has had to struggle in obscurity for its survival, occasionally erupting into the consciousness of the rest of the city, only to be forgotten and neglected again.

But hidden from view—even from many of us who live here—has been a constant though turbulent progress toward our collective dream of a better life than the one our parents left us.

Our community was created from two streams. One is the migrant workers who came from Puerto Rico to toil in the lush farmlands of southern New Jersey, or in Pennsylvania's Chester County or Lehigh Valley. The other consists of Puerto Ricans raised for a time in New York City, who then left the Big Apple in search of jobs and of a life with less frenzy and crime.

The two streams converged in eastern North Philadelphia, the poorest and most dilapidated neighborhood in one of the oldest and largest cities in the United States.

A Divided City

There are probably few cities as racially divided as Philadelphia. Generally, most whites live in the eastern sections of the city: the Northeast, Kensington, Port Richmond, South Philadelphia. Most African-Americans, on the other hand, live in the western parts of the city: Central North Philadelphia, West Philadelphia, Southwest and Northwest.

Philadelphia's black population, which makes up 40 percent of the city, has battled white racism for generations. Long before slavery was abolished, Philadelphia had the largest free black population in the nation. The African-American community has a proud history and a developed middle class, which in 1983 gained control of the city's

Joséito

Faces of North Philadelphia (pages 176–177): Puerto Rican children and teens involved in Taller Puertorriqueño, a cultural center offering art, dance, photography, ceramics and creative writing classes.

Left, Catalina Ríos, a poet who directed the Taller's youth program.

political superstructure when W. Wilson Goode was elected the city's first black mayor.

Today, most of the major administrative positions of power in the city are held by blacks. The mayor, the city council president, the superintendent of schools, the managing director, the city solicitor, and many other city officials are black. Yet racism continues to flourish. The leaders of the predominantly Irish, Polish and Italian working and middle classes that controlled the political structure previously have yet to reconcile themselves to the loss of power. Meanwhile, the heads of corporations and banks that wield the predominant power in the city—many of whom actually live in the suburbs—seek to control economic policy no matter which group of leaders holds political power.

Puerto Ricans, meanwhile, are a buffer between whites and African-Americans. The main Puerto Rican colonia stretches several miles from South Philadelphia north through the neighborhoods of Northern Liberties, Ludlow, Lower Kensington, Fairhill, Hunting Park and up toward the more solidly working-class area of Olney.

The first Puerto Rican neighborhood was Spring Garden. There, bounded by the art museum on the west, Center City on the south, and Broad Street on the east, the first major Puerto Rican community began developing in the 1950s. Today, the only

Puerto Ricans left in Spring Garden are those who live in the scores of city-owned apartment buildings that real estate speculators have been unable to

Joséito

Joséito

Rojas, Mike Rodríguez, Irma López and others. It catapulted into the city's awareness in a short time and broke with the more mainstream, less confrontational approach of the earlier social agencies.

While those agencies sought assistance from the government for Puerto Ricans, the Young Lords *demanded* that assistance as a right. But the group, like Young Lords chapters in other cities, was short-lived. While it could inspire young Puerto Ricans to action, it was too divorced from the everyday life of Puerto Rican workers, and too unclear about where to concretely take that awakening movement, to attract a consistent following.

Through the mid-1970s, predominant influence in the social and political life of Puerto Ricans was wielded by the Concilio de Organizaciones Hispanas [the Council of Hispanic Organizations]. Headed by businessman Candelario Lamboy, reputedly the city's richest Puerto Rican, the Concilio became a bulwark of the administration of then-Mayor Frank L. Rizzo. During the Rizzo years, from 1972 to 1980, the Concilio received large sums of money from the city administration in return for delivering the Puerto Rican vote, what there was of it, to Rizzo.

seize. Over the past 15 years, gentrification has devoured all privately-owned buildings in the area, pushing Puerto Ricans further east and north along a thin corridor separating white Philadelphia from black Philadelphia.

Between the 1950s and the 1970s, our community was virtually ignored. During the early period, our numbers were few. Even fewer were those of us who participated in the political process. However, Puerto Ricans built dozens of social clubs, baseball leagues, and the first Hispanic social agencies. Among them were La Fraternidad, el Concilio de Organizaciones Hispanas, el Desfile Puertorriqueño, el Club de Leones, Puertorriqueños en Marcha, and the Office of the Commonwealth of Puerto Rico, which has always been a center for the gathering of Puerto Rican leaders.

The Young Lords

In the late 1960s, as the black liberation and anti-Vietnam War movements awakened a generation of youth in America, Puerto Ricans formed the Young Lords Party. This revolutionary youth group emerged first in Chicago and New York. The Philadelphia branch of the Young Lords was formed in 1970, led by Juan Ramos, Wilfredo

Joséito

Fighting Discrimination

In those same years, however, Philadelphia police established a virtual police state. A U.S. Justice Department study in 1980 found that during the Rizzo years, Philadelphia police shot unarmed, non-assaultive suspects fleeing from them at a rate that was 3,700 percent higher than in New York! Major victims of that police terror were African-Americans and Puerto Ricans.

The established Puerto Rican leadership, centered in the Concilio, largely ignored cases of racial discrimination and police violence against Puerto Ricans. Meanwhile, young activists, some of them associated with the Young Lords, played a major part in helping the Puerto Rican community defend its rights.

In 1973, five Puerto Ricans were arrested and charged with the sensational rape and murder of a young white woman and her boyfriend near the art museum. In the city-wide hysteria that followed, all the Puerto Rican defendants were convicted and sentenced to life imprisonment. Paul Valderrama spent five years in jail before Juan Ramos and other activists were able to prove that Valderrama had been in Puerto Rico at the time of the crime. Valderrama's conviction was overturned. Miguel Rivera spent nine years in jail in the same case before a series of investigations by the *Philadelphia Inquirer* caused his conviction to be overturned as well. Fourteen years after his original conviction, Rivera was acquitted in a second trial.

Also in 1973, young Julio Osario, a handicapped junior high school student, was thrown into the Delaware River and drowned by some white youths. Several years later, six people died when the Santiago family home in Feltonville was firebombed by whites who did not want Puerto Ricans in their neighborhood.

In 1977 a Puerto Rican youth, José Reyes, was shot to death by police in circumstances that outraged the community. A group of Puerto Rican activists organized a campaign that resulted in the city settling a lawsuit out of court with the Reyes family.

Throughout all of these atrocities against Puerto Ricans, the dominant Puerto Rican leadership grouped around the Concilio failed to act to defend our rights. Instead, an internal battle within the Concilio consumed much of the group's time. This eventually led to the formation of a new agency, the Congreso de Latinos Unidos.

A turning point in the Puerto Rican community's history came in 1978. Rizzo, in his second term as mayor, tried to change the city's charter to eliminate the two-term limit and become "mayor for life." Such a change would have to be approved by the voters in a referendum. A stop-Rizzo movement gained momentum among white liberals and African-Americans in the city.

The old-line Puerto Rican leaders united around Rizzo. But there was a new leadership developing. The former Young Lords of a decade earlier, the enemies of the Concilio, along with many new Puerto Ricans who had moved to Philadelphia from New York in recent years, came together in a coalition called Puerto Ricans United Against Rizzo.

The coalition launched a massive voter registration drive in the community. Before 1978, an estimated 5,000 Puerto Ricans were registered voters. With the registration drive, that number doubled to around 10,000. The small Puerto Rican electorate had voted in the majority for Rizzo in the two previous mayoral races, but in the referendum more than 60 percent of Puerto Ricans voted against him.

The Puerto Rican Alliance

A few months after Rizzo's defeat, in April 1979, the coalition held a Puerto Rican convention in the city. More than 500 people attended. The convention formally launched the Puerto Rican Alliance, a mass-based civil rights organization, with Juan Ramos as the first president and myself as vice-president. Within two years the Alliance had a paid membership of 700.

There has probably been no organization that so quickly changed the consciousness of this city about Puerto Ricans, and of Puerto Ricans about themselves, as the Alliance did between 1979 and 1983. In a few short years, the group led a housing squatters' movement; organized Puerto Rican workers in several major factories; and supported or led the Fogel Refrigerator strike, the Moritz

Embroidery strike, and the Glencoe strike. The Alliance's education committee organized parents against abusive principals and in support of bilingual education programs. Its justice committee led the campaign to bring to trial the policeman who killed José Reyes. Its political committee began for the first time to organize candidate forums and insist that all political candidates come before the Puerto Rican community for scrutiny.

Housing was a major focus of grassroots organizing. Low-income Puerto Ricans and African-Americans were severely squeezed by the lack of affordable housing in the city. Meanwhile, thousands of houses seized by the federal government as a result of foreclosures stood vacant and boarded up. A squatters' movement developed with the goal of turning these abandoned dwellings into homes for people in need.

In 1979, Puerto Ricans shocked the city when more than 150 tenants of the Philadelphia Housing Authority conducted a sit-in at Independence Hall, birthplace of the U.S. Constitution. The tenants were led by the Alliance. Police had to carry every protestor out of the building.

The Alliance conducted its most stunning action in April 1980. On the eve of the Democratic primary election in Pennsylvania, which saw Edward Kennedy in a virtual dead heat with President Jimmy Carter, squatters led by the Alliance took over Carter's campaign headquarters, where all his records and materials for the next day's primary were kept. Our demand to the President was simple: direct the U.S. Department of Housing and Urban Development to grant the squatters title to 100 vacant HUD-owned houses, or we will ruin your election bid. After a day and night of negotiations, including visits by President Carter's main Hispanic liaison from Washington, as well as by Congressman William Gray, the Alliance won its demand. The squatters received their titles.

Meanwhile, Alliance members were pressing forward with Puerto Rican activists around the country to found a national Puerto Rican civil and human rights organization. That goal became a reality in 1981 when the National Congress for Puerto Rican Rights was founded at the first national Puerto Rican convention in the South Bronx.

Puerto Ricans Take Office

While carrying out direct actions, the Alliance also became involved in electoral politics. In 1979 the Alliance supported the campaign of Ralph Acosta for state representative and that of Juan Ramos in 1981. These races were unsuccessful, but the process had just begun.

After 1982, the Alliance experienced internal divisions that eventually weakened and destroyed it. But it had already served as a catalyst for political change that would continue. In 1984, the Puerto Rican community proudly saw its first city councilman, Angel Ortiz, take office, and in 1985 Ralph Acosta was elected to the state legislature. The board of education gained its first Puerto Rican member, Christina Torres-Matrullo.

In Ortiz and Acosta, we have two of the most committed and politically progressive elected officials of any Puerto Rican community in the nation. They join Common Pleas Court Judge Nelson Díaz as the only Puerto Ricans holding elected office in Philadelphia. This is no accident; it is a direct result of the struggles of the past 15 years.

In addition to Ortiz and Acosta, many other Puerto Rican leaders in Philadelphia today were in the leadership of the Alliance in its early days. They include Irma López-Salter, director of the Mayor's Commission on Puerto Rican and Latino Affairs; Efraín Roche, editor of *Community Focus* newspaper; Danny Rodríguez, director of the Hunting Park Community Development Corporation; Raúl Serrano, president of Spring Garden United Neighbors; Roger Zeppernick, director of Centro Claver; Carmen Bolden, director of Congreso de Latinos Unidos; Socorro Rivera, director of Borinquen Credit Union; Josefina Benítez, assistant director of María de los Angeles Health Clinic; and public school principal Nilsa González.

Today, more than 30,000 Puerto Ricans and Latinos are registered to vote in the city, 600 percent higher than we had ten years ago. Nonetheless, the economic and social conditions of the vast majority of our people have not changed. We have yet to translate that budding electoral participation into political power or into more genuine social and economic equality.

But we are on the road. And there is no turning back. ❖

Travel agencies, shippers and money-transfer offices line commercial streets of Washington Heights and Inwood.

NEW YORK CITY: Washington Heights

By 1998, the estimated Dominican population of New York City reached half a million. Although Dominicans have settled in every part of the city, their favored destination is Manhattan's Washington Heights / Inwood section, where 80 percent of new immigrants are from the Dominican Republic.

How do Dominican New Yorkers live? How do they maintain the link to their homeland while making new lives in New York? To answer these questions, researchers from the Dominican Studies Institute at City College of New York took a close look at a single block in Washington Heights. Five researchers—three of them Dominican college students living in Washington Heights—took a census of households on the block. They visited homes, interviewed residents and observed the rhythm of daily life.

In Washington Heights, they found, people can speak Spanish, buy Dominican newspapers, eat Dominican food, and surround themselves with reminders of home. There is a constant back-and-forth movement between New York and the Dominican Republic, and networks of family and friends span the two countries. Washington Heights, the study concludes, is a "transnational" neighborhood—one with ties to two countries and two cultures at the same time. ❖

Quisqueya on the Hudson

Jorge Duany

Jorge Duany, born in Cuba, teaches in the Department of Sociology and Anthropology at the University of Puerto Rico. This essay is adapted from "Quisqueya on the Hudson: The Transnational Identity of Dominicans in Washington Heights" (CUNY Dominican Studies Institute, 1994). Used by permission of the CUNY Dominican Studies Institute.

On our block, street vendors sell oranges, corn, flowers, music cassettes, and the tropical ice cones that Dominicans call *frío fríos*. On hot summer days, small carts selling frío fríos appear on street corners. Children open fire hydrants and play with water on the sidewalks.

Speaking Spanish, the men listen to merengue, call out *piropos* to young women passing by, play dominoes and drink Presidente beer. They play the lottery, talk about Dominican politics and read Dominican newspapers such as *El Nacional, El Siglo* and *Listín Diario*. Women take their children out in strollers, shop at the *bodegas*, and talk with neighbors in front of their buildings. Teenagers walk in groups to the local public school, bathe in the area's swimming pools, or listen to rap music on huge cassette players. Some people in the streets look and sound Mexican or Central American, but most of the area's residents are Dominican immigrants.

181st Street Scene

With easy access to the George Washington Bridge, 181st Street is the neighborhood's transportation and commercial center. The old subway tunnel and elevators at the 181st Street station are badly rundown, and have been the object of recent protests by local residents. In the mornings, most residents take the subway to work in downtown Manhattan, returning uptown in the afternoons. Others ride the bus to factories across the Hudson River in New Jersey.

Near the subway station, many businesses specialize in sending remittances to the Dominican Republic, such as the Banco Dominicano. Gypsy cabs from the Dominican-owned Riverside Taxi Agency criss-cross the streets looking for customers. A newsstand at the corner of 181st Street and Saint Nicholas Avenue carries ten Dominican newspapers flown in daily from the island.

Small businesses offering private telephone services to the Dominican Republic have proliferated. A single Dominican entrepreneur from the town of San Francisco de Macorís owns 12 of these places, and plans to open 50 more in the near future.

Many cafeterias and restaurants sell typical food from the Dominican Republic. Traditional items include main courses like *mangú, carne guisada, sancocho, mondongo, cocido,* and *cabeza de cerdo*; side orders like *arroz con habichuelas, empanada de yuca,* and *tostones*; drinks like *jugo de caña* and *batida de fruta*; and desserts like *pastelillos de guayaba, yaniqueque, dulce de coco,* and *pan dulce relleno*. Grocery stores offer tropical staples ranging from plantains to *mamey*, and Dominican drinks like Cola Quisqueya, Refrescos Nacionales, and Cerveza Presidente.

Although primarily residential, our block has ten stores on the ground floor: two bodegas, two beauty salons, two bars, a restaurant, a bakery, a liquor store and a hardware store. Dominicans own seven of these businesses. The immediate vicinity also has other bodegas, convenience stores, *botánicas*, travel agencies, car shops and other small stores. Several business owners complained about the stiff economic competition in such a reduced space. "People aren't buying now because they have no money," said an ice cone seller. In addition, rising rents threaten to force many store owners out of the market. In our block, merchants pay between $1,700 and $2,315 a month to lease very small commercial spaces.

Most employees of Dominican businesses are Dominican, although many stores employ other Hispanics as well, especially Ecuadorans, Mexicans and Salvadorans. Many store owners display their ethnic origin by blasting music to the street, usually merengue and salsa, sometimes *bachata* and *bolero*. Some businesses are local subsidiaries of enterprises in the Dominican Republic, such as Nitín Bakery.

Commercial signs attest to the strong presence of immigrants from the Cibao region, such as Acogedor Cibao Supermarket, Cibao Vision Center, Cibao Meat Products, and Hielo Cibao. A Dominican immigrant who planted corn and black beans on Broadway Avenue and 153rd Street longed to have his "own little Cibao" in Washington Heights. During our fieldwork, a young man walked down the street with two roosters, a common sight in the Dominican countryside. Some Dominicans refer to their neighborhood as "El Cibao" or "La Platanera", much as Puerto Ricans call Spanish Harlem "El Barrio" or the Lower East Side "Loisaida."

Private social clubs from the Dominican Republic abound in Washington Heights. Dozens of recreational associations are based on hometown origins, such as those from the towns of Esperanza, Tamboril, Moca and Baní. Club members dance merengue, play dominoes and baseball, watch Spanish soap operas, exchange information about jobs and housing, and raise funds to send back to their country. Some groups select a beauty queen and participate in New York's Dominican Day Parade. Although most clubs are still oriented primarily toward the Dominican Republic, they are increasingly concerned with the day-to-day problems of the immigrant community. The clubs help to receive newly arrived immigrants as well as to reaffirm the cultural roots of the established ones.

Despite its large Dominican population, Washington Heights is a multiethnic, multiracial and multilingual neighborhood. Near Yeshiva University on 186th Street, middle-class Jews have occupied newly renovated buildings. Hasidic Jews occasionally walk by the neighborhood on Saturdays on their way to the synagogue. Jewish-Dominican relations have often been tense.

Dominican contacts with other Hispanics have mainly been cordial. On several buildings, Puerto Rican flags hang from the windows days before and after the Puerto Rican Day parade in June. This symbolic gesture suggests that some residents are Puerto Rican and that Dominicans also celebrate the parade with their Puerto Rican friends and neighbors. Physical traces of a large Cuban immigration remain in the neighborhood, especially businesses with Cuban names such as Restaurante Caridad, Cafetería El Mambí, Havana Bar and Restaurante Sagua. But many Cubans have left the neighborhood for New Jersey and Florida. Our block also has Greeks, Chinese, Italians, Nicaraguans, Peruvians, African-Americans, and other ethnic groups among its merchants and tenants.

Behind Closed Doors

Tenants keep their doors tightly closed and rarely meet in the hallway, except for a few newly arrived Dominican immigrants. Interethnic contacts are limited, especially among people of different

On 164th Street in Washington Heights.

physical appearance. The buildings' physical layout does not foster social interaction, lacking the open, public spaces to which Dominicans are accustomed in their home country. The block lacks a common meeting area, except perhaps for the bodegas and nearby parks.

When they are not at work, the tenants' daily life takes place mostly behind closed doors, in the privacy of their apartments. Many express fears of crime and a few are afraid of being deported by immigration authorities. "Neighborly relations don't exist here as in Santo Domingo," complained Freddy. "My neighbors are Anglos and in four years I haven't talked to them." Only once did we see children playing in the hallways.

Nonetheless, some residents have managed to forge a small community by means of a frequent exchange of favors, mutual aid and emotional support. In one building, tenants take care of their neighbors' children, take their trash down to the basement, share food, or buy them plantains at the marketplace. Each building has several major networks of social interaction, giving the place a

sense of a self-enclosed little town. Long-time residents tend to know most people on their floors and some on other floors as well.

Most immigrants maintain their cultural traditions at home. Some tenants place Spanish stickers on their apartment doors, especially with religious messages like *"Jesús Cristo unica esperanza," "Cristo cambiará tu vida,"* and *"Construyamos la paz con Cristo"* ["Jesus Christ is our only hope," "Christ will change your life," and "Let us build peace with Christ"]. Inside their homes, Dominicans often hang religious prints on the walls with images such as the Sacred Heart and the Last Supper.

Some families hang calendars with a painting of the Virgin Mary, obtained in a local bodega. Others stick a Dominican flag or coat-of-arms in a visible place in the living room. Many Dominican homes have plastic-covered furniture, plastic tablecloths, and plastic flowers as their main decoration. Some display the faceless ceramic dolls typical of the Dominican Republic, as well as plates painted in bright colors with folk themes from their country, usually a rural landscape, a peasant scene, the Cathedral of Santo Domingo, or a tropical beach. Such objects graphically recreate a Dominican atmosphere in Washington Heights. Decorating homes with folk items from their country is common among Puerto Ricans and other transnational groups in New York.

Many Dominican homes and businesses have small shrines with images of Catholic saints and the Virgin Mary in a corner of the hall or a private room. These humble altars are usually surrounded by flowers, lighted candles, food, and glasses filled with fresh water, wine, and other alcoholic beverages. Although the most popular figures are the Virgin of Altagracia and Saint Lazarus, the altars represent a wide range of religious images: Saint Claire, Saint Anthony of Padua, Saint Barbara, the Holy Child of Atocha, the Sacred Heart, the Holy Family, and the Virgin of Fatima, among others. Even an Irish-American woman had an altar dressed in typical Dominican fashion with the help of an immigrant friend.

Like other Hispanic Catholics, many Dominicans believe that the saints will protect them from misfortune and help them to advance economically. One Dominican woman who wore a necklace with a medallion of the Virgin of Altagracia explained: "When you're away from your country, you need protection. And your country needs it too." ❖

merengue: popular dance music of the Dominican Republic
piropos: suggestive remarks or compliments
Presidente: popular brand of Dominican beer
bodega: small grocery store
mangú: green plantain, boiled and mashed
carne guisada: grilled meat
sancocho: stew of meats and root vegetables
mondongo: tripe
cocido: stew of meat and potatoes
cabeza de cerdo: pig's head cooked in various styles
arroz con habichuelas: rice and beans
empanada de yuca: patty made from cassava
tostones: green plantain, sliced and fried
jugo de caña: sugar cane juice
batida de fruta: fruit "smoothie"
pastelillos de guayaba: guava pastries
yaniqueque: fritters
dulce de coco: coconut pastry
pan dulce relleno: sweet bread with a filling
mamey: a tropical fruit
botánica: store where religious articles are sold
salsa: hybrid music developed in New York City by musicians of various Latin American and Caribbean backgrounds
bachata: traditional dance rhythm from the Dominican countryside
bolero: ballad-style music
Cibao: central region of the Dominican Republic

"The Factories Moved Out ..."

Interview with Victor Morisete

In Washington Heights, a variety of organizations cater to the needs of the Dominican community. They include social clubs and hometown clubs, as well as organizations that provide social services and advocate on behalf of immigrants. Two major organizations of the latter type are Alianza Dominicana and ACDP, the Asociación Comunal de Dominicanos Progresistas. Through their day-to-day work with residents of Washington Heights/ Inwood, staff members of these organizations have come to know the community and the social issues it is facing.

Victor Morisete emigrated with his family from the Dominican Republic to New York in 1982. He has lived in Washington Heights since then, and is executive director of the Asociación Comunal de Dominicanos Progresistas (Community Association of Progressive Dominicans). He was interviewed by Catherine Sunshine on July 29, 1996.

How and when did Washington Heights acquire its Dominican character?

This has been an immigrant neighborhood since the 1800s. At first it was mostly Irish, Italian, Jewish and Greek. By the mid-1960s these older immigrant groups began leaving. Many of them moved out of the city to New Jersey or Westchester County. Their kids went to college, improved their position in society, and moved out of Washington Heights.

African-Americans were the largest group in the neighborhood for a while. After 1965, Dominicans began coming in. There was a massive migration of Dominicans to New York, and they clustered in Washington Heights. While the Dominican community has continued to grow, recently new ethnic groups have also been arriving. For instance we now have large numbers of Mexicans and Russian Jews settling in this community.

Why have so many Dominicans come here?

Two reasons: politics and economics. The Trujillo regime ruled the Dominican Republic for 31 years and completely blocked any democratic process. After Trujillo was overthrown, an elected government headed by Juan Bosch governed briefly. It was overthrown by a military coup. There was a civil uprising to restore Bosch to power, and the United States invaded the country.

That's when a large number of people began leaving the island. They left because of political instability and because of the economic problems they faced. The United States government encouraged them to go, in part to get rid of people who had supported the Bosch government.

Why did so many choose New York? In some cases they already had ties here. Economically well-off Dominicans would travel back and forth between the island and New York for business. Another reason was the presence of an established Puerto Rican community, which offered a Latino cultural base in the city.

As to why they settled in Washington Heights, it's difficult to say. One reason, though, was that most of the garment factories were in midtown

Manhattan. People could commute by subway and be at their factory jobs in 25 or 30 minutes.

Many of the Dominicans were garment workers. When we came to New York my brother, who was 17, worked in a garment factory. Entire families would come here and find employment in the garment industry. And although the wages were low by U.S. standards, it was much more than most people could earn in the Dominican Republic.

You've lived in Washington Heights for the last 15 years. How has the neighborhood changed during that time?

In the late 1970s the garment industry started to move out of New York. By the mid-1980s it had almost disappeared. That was when we began seeing many of the problems that the immigrant community faces today.

Some of the factories closed down. Others moved to New Jersey, to the South, or overseas. New York had become a very expensive city in which to do business because of the congestion, the high taxes, the high cost of labor. So they moved their factories to places like Haiti, Mexico, the Dominican Republic, and some Asian countries. It was a major shift. In the past, industries recruited people from other countries to work here for cheap wages. Now they have moved the actual production overseas to take advantage of even cheaper wages in those countries.

The immigrant community that had worked in the factories was stranded, more or less. Most didn't have the skills necessary to shift to other job opportunities. People began to fall into dependence on welfare and other government benefits. That's when we began to see the drug problem in Washington Heights explode.

People who traditionally would have worked in a factory had to find another way to make a living. Some have turned to selling drugs. Many more have found work in street vending, in the delivery industry, or driving gypsy cabs. That's true not only in Washington Heights but in other immigrant communities in New York.

By the mid-1980s you saw the Dominican community making a major move into the small grocery business. Many of the *bodegas,* the little groceries, used to be owned by Puerto Ricans or Cubans. But their children didn't necessarily want to continue in the grocery business. So many of the stores were bought by Dominicans.

Although there are fewer job opportunities, you still have many Dominicans coming in.

Yes. One reason is the chain migration. People want to reunite their families and so they petition to bring their family members here. But the single most important reason is economics. However difficult life is here in New York, living conditions in the Dominican Republic are far worse for most people.

The Dominican economy used to depend on agriculture, especially sugar cane. For a number of reasons, agriculture has declined and the country has moved toward an economy based on tourism, manufacturing and services. But workers who have been working in the sugar cane for years or farming other crops don't always have the training to find jobs in the new industries.

In the 1970s and 1980s it was primarily an unskilled labor force coming in. By the late eighties you began to see more people immigrating with higher education and professional skills. These people also face limited opportunities in the Dominican Republic. They may graduate from a university and find no jobs are available unless they're connected to a political party or some other network that can help them. Many of these people migrate, only to find that opportunities are scarce here as well. Lack of English is often an issue. And good jobs are hard to find these days even for people born and raised here. So you find Dominican teachers, doctors, nurses and engineers in New York who are working in grocery stores or driving taxis.

What is life like for young people in this area?

Young people growing up today in Washington Heights face very difficult circumstances. There is a lack of incentive for them to achieve. Sadly, many of our young people have come to believe that education might not be the best way for them to get ahead. They see somebody who grew up on their block and is a professional, working for a company on Wall Street, making $30,000 a year; while the guy next door is getting his money the wrong way and driving a Mercedes. They make the comparison and ask, "What kind of lifestyle do I want? Do I want to be a professional and not have these luxuries, or do I want to make a lot of money quickly?"

We are trying to convince young people that, yes, these are real problems, but the only solution for them is to get an education. Because that is the only everlasting thing that they can hold on to for the rest of their life. And some do.

There is a severe lack of employment opportunity. This year we had five thousand kids from the immediate area who applied for summer jobs. We were only able to place 912. Only 912 out of 5,000 had a shot at seven weeks of employment in federally subsidized jobs. The economic base of the city doesn't support opportunities for youth and that is hurting all of us.

Our goal isn't just for that first 912 to get a job. It's for them to see that job as an opportunity, to decide to struggle and break away from the vicious cycle that is entrapping many of our youth.

Are there kids who are making it in spite of everything?

Absolutely. We see examples every day among the young people who come to our center. They're focused on college, and they're making it through hard work and through community involvement and family involvement in their lives. I know one child who comes to the center every afternoon after school, and the first thing he does is his homework. We encourage that by giving kids a place to study. Then we try to help them get jobs for the summer, so they see the value of being involved with a community center. The parents are very supportive. They may not have the education, but they understand the need.

Many of the Dominicans who do go to college enroll in the City University of New York. It's the most accessible, in location as well as economically. A large number have to work part-time while they are going to school. That in itself is a challenge—to work and go to school. For example, I've worked since age 16. I had no choice, because my family

Josefina Báez

A fourth-grade student recites in a Washington Heights classroom.

didn't have enough money to support all the children in the family. I packed groceries in a supermarket while I went to college, and I continued working part-time until I graduated.

You find the same thing happening every day out there. The kids who are making it are doing so despite their families' economic circumstances. They are highly motivated and have strong values.

How does this community center respond to these needs?

To begin with, we keep this center open seven days a week with sports and recreation programs. We have basketball, baseball, and volleyball leagues, as well as karate and weight lifting. We have the two huge swimming pools you see out that window. Five years ago this whole facility was closed. It was run down, and the city didn't have any money for programs. So we said, give us the facility and we'll run the programs. We managed to raise private funding to keep it open for the community.

We offer classes in English as a second language, computer classes, and preparation for the GED. We have an after-school homework assistance program for children. And we give people referrals to mental health services and other types of social services.

Part of our mission is to train youth to become community leaders. We offer entrepreneurship seminars to help high school students develop self-esteem, leadership ability, and essential life skills. The goal is for them to go on to college and hopefully focus on a professional or a business career. Then they can come back to the community, understand its problems and needs, and give something back in a positive way. ❖

Martha Cooper

This Brooklyn grocery is named for the original inhabitants of Puerto Rico, the Taíno.

NEW YORK CITY: Brooklyn

With 2.3 million residents, it could be the third-largest city in America. Indeed, one hundred years ago the City of Brooklyn—then independent—was the country's fourth-largest, a hub of shipping and manufacturing where factories made everything from sugar to hats and ships unloaded goods of all descriptions at the bustling piers. Brooklyn merged with Manhattan, across the East River, in 1898. Linked to Manhattan by the Brooklyn Bridge and later by subway, it became part of a consolidated New York City that also includes the Bronx, Queens, and Staten Island. Today, Brooklyn is the city's most populous borough.

Successive waves of immigration have made this population extraordinarily diverse. The first inhabitants of the area were, of course, Native Americans. In the 1600s came Dutch, French and English settlers, with Africans imported as slave laborers. Later, a community of free African-Americans emerged.

Beginning in the mid-nineteenth century, heavy foreign immigration turned Brooklyn into a complex mosaic of neighborhoods and ethnic groups. Puerto Rican and Cuban merchants settled in the city as early as 1830; in the late 1800s they were joined by political exiles and workers from the two Spanish colonies. During the period from 1840 to the 1920s, waves of immigration from Europe transformed Brooklyn. Irish and German working people poured into the city, followed by Italians and Eastern European Jews. Smaller immigrant groups included Swedes, Norwegians, Danes and Poles.

The first half of the twentieth century saw a major influx of African-Americans from the South. Puerto Ricans meanwhile continued to arrive, along with small numbers of West Indians and Haitians. Following the immigration reform of 1965, the number of incoming West Indians and Haitians rose rapidly, and Dominican immigration also surged. Many people also came from Asian countries and from what was then called the Soviet Union.

By this time, the economy of Brooklyn was changing. As in other northeastern cities, the borough's industrial base eroded in the 1950s. Shipping moved to more modern facilities in New Jersey, while manufacturers went in search of cheaper land and labor. They left behind closed factories, empty warehouses and abandoned piers. The developing suburbs meanwhile attracted many established residents, especially middle-class families. As older residents died and their children moved away from Brooklyn, new immigrants came to occupy vacant housing.

Today, the old waterfront neighborhoods of Sunset Park and Industry City are largely Hispanic—Puerto Rican, Dominican, Mexican, and Cuban—and Chinese. Immigration into the central Brooklyn neighborhoods of Crown Heights, Flatbush and East Flatbush is dominated by Haitians and by people from the English-speaking Caribbean, especially Jamaicans, Guyanese and Trinidadians. Nine of the top ten groups settling in Flatbush in the early 1990s were Caribbean (including Panama, since many of the Panamanians in Brooklyn are of West Indian descent).

People from the Dominican Republic are the largest group coming to many east Brooklyn neighborhoods. Only south Brooklyn, where immigrants from the former Soviet Union and Asia predominate, lacks a strongly Caribbean flavor.

Caribbean-Americans are among those Brooklyn residents who have been working to revitalize the borough since the 1970s. They are buying and renovating old housing, starting businesses and small industries, founding and joining civic organizations. Poverty and joblessness are still much in evidence: there is a continuing outflow of more prosperous residents, while many of the newcomers start from the bottom economically, as did earlier immigrants. But today just as years ago, Brooklyn's rich cultural life and economic vitality are in large measure the achievement of immigrants, with those from the Caribbean playing a central role. ❖

A Taste of Caribbean Brooklyn

Lyn Stallworth and Rod Kennedy, Jr.

Dee Dee Dailey owns a catering business in the Sheepshead Bay section of Brooklyn. "I have roots in both the Spanish- and English-speaking Caribbean," says Dee Dee Dailey, "and my roots are also Southern and Native American." Much of Dee Dee's cooking blends spicy Caribbean and African-American flavors. (She prepares Mediterranean food as well.) "This dish is an adaptation of a recipe my mother, Margaret Lynch Dailey, gave me. Her grandmother was born in Cuba, and the heavy use of garlic and olive oil is part of the African-Hispanic cultural legacy."

Dee Dee Dailey's Pigeon Peas and Rice
1/2 pound dried pigeon peas (gandules)
3 to 4 tablespoons olive oil
1 large onion, chopped
4 cloves garlic, minced
1 small green bell pepper, chopped
1 teaspoon dried oregano
1 tablespoon dried basil
2 ounces salt pork, cubed (optional)
1 large bay leaf
1 pound long-grain rice
Salt (preferably sea salt) and pepper to taste

1. Pick through the pigeon peas, removing any stones or dirt. Cover them with water by 2 inches and let soak overnight.

2. Heat the oil in a large heavy stewpot and cook the onions, garlic, bell pepper, oregano, basil and salt pork (if used) for about 2 minutes, stirring. Add the drained pigeon peas and stir in for 1 minute, to blend. Add water (or chicken or vegetable stock) to cover, and the bay leaf. Cover, bring to the boil, then reduce the heat and simmer for 1 hour, or until the peas are almost tender. Add a little boiling liquid, as needed.

3. Stir in the rice, and enough liquid to cover. Season with salt and pepper. Simmer the dish for about 20 minutes, or until the rice is cooked and the peas are tender. Let stand for 15 minutes before serving. *Serves 8.*

Mavis George is from Trinidad, and now lives on Eastern Parkway in central Brooklyn. "We cook callaloo on Sundays," she says. "We serve it as a side dish, with curried chicken or goat, and rice." The kind of pumpkin called *calabaza* is sold by the piece in markets catering to Caribbean and Hispanic people, as are the green leaves called callaloo or dasheen.

Mavis George's Callaloo

1/2 pound fresh okra, cut into 1/4-inch rounds
1 1/2 cups water
1 1/2 pounds callaloo (dasheen) chopped, or 1 package frozen chopped spinach, defrosted
1 large onion, sliced
1/2 pound of pumpkin (calabaza), peeled and cut into chunks
1 tablespoon vegetable oil
1 cup unsweetened cream of coconut, at room temperature
Salt and pepper to taste
Goya seasoning salt
1 hot fresh or dried pepper

1. Put the okra and water in a large saucepan and bring it to the boil. When the okra seeds turn pink, add the callaloo or spinach, onion and pumpkin. When the liquid returns to the boil, add the oil. Add the coconut cream, salt and pepper, a dash of Goya seasoning, and the hot pepper. Simmer for 1/2 hour, or until the vegetables are soft.

2. Remove the pepper, put the contents into a blender jar or food processor bowl, and puree. *Serves 4.* ❖

Donna DeCesare, Impact Visuals

Thanksgiving Day, Haitian style: Lily Cérat, a Haitian-American school teacher in Brooklyn, shows her daughter Tania how to stuff a Thanksgiving turkey. This turkey is stuffed with coconut, a recipe from Lily's Jamaican stepmother.

All Ah We Is One:
Caribbean Carnival in New York

Patricia Belcon

At summer's end, central Brooklyn comes alive in a dazzling explosion of color, fantasy and music. The West Indian Carnival, modeled on Trinidad and Tobago's famous celebration, now draws crowds of two million to Brooklyn each year on Labor Day. Attracting press and politicians along with revelers and visitors, it is a dramatic statement of the growing Caribbean presence in New York City.

Patricia Belcon calls herself a "New Yorker Trinbagonian." Born in Trinidad and Tobago, she came to New York in the late 1960s and has lived in the Crown Heights section of Brooklyn and in Queens. A sociologist, she is on the faculty of the State University of New York at Geneseo. She also coordinates a yearly conference of scholars concerned with Carnival at Medgar Evers College of the City University of New York.

Carnival has gone international. From Trinidad and Tobago, the Carnival capital of the Caribbean, emigrants have transported their carnival model to Europe, North America, and other parts of the world. Bringing together people of diverse Caribbean nationalities in the diaspora, these carnivals symbolize the potential of Caribbean unity and identity. They also reflect the rising importance of Caribbeans as a cultural, economic and political force in their adopted countries.

At least 40 cities in the United States hold Trinidad-style carnival celebrations every year. They include, among others, Atlanta, Baltimore, Boston, Detroit, Hartford, Houston, Miami, New York, Rochester, San Francisco and Washington, D.C. Major carnivals are also held in London, England, and Toronto, Canada.

The Carnival celebration on Labor Day weekend in Brooklyn, New York, is the largest outside Trinidad. Over two million people, mostly Caribbeans, descend on Eastern Parkway each year for the event. They "play mas"—don a costume and join the parade—or simply enjoy the spectacle with family and friends. Many are New Yorkers, but others come from elsewhere in the United States, the Caribbean, Canada and Europe. Hundreds of Trinidadians fly up to participate in Brooklyn's Carnival on Labor Day weekend, just as West Indian New Yorkers fill chartered planes to Trinidad at its mid-winter Carnival time.

By reaffirming Caribbean culture and identity, the Brooklyn Carnival serves the same social function for Caribbean-Americans that the St. Patrick's Day Parade does for Irish-Americans or the Puerto Rican Day Parade does for Puerto Rican New Yorkers. Celebrants and spectators alike merge into a movement of social and political solidarity that symbolizes "Caribbeanness."

Roots in Europe and Africa

Trinidad and Tobago is a twin-island republic at the southern tip of the Caribbean island chain. Its people are of African, East Indian, European, Chinese, and indigenous Amerindian descent. All these cultures contributed to the development of Carnival, with the major influences from Africa and Europe.

Costumes worn by Carnival-goers dazzle the eye in fuschia, orange, red, blue, green and gold.

The word "carnival" comes from the Latin *carne* and *vale*, meaning "farewell to the flesh." In medieval Europe, Catholics engaged in feasting and revelry before the yearly fast of Lent that begins on Ash Wednesday. These traditions came to the Caribbean with the French colonists who settled in Martinique, Guadeloupe and Haiti. Some French moved to Trinidad, which was then a Spanish colony, after the 1787 "Cedula of Population" invited non-Spanish Roman Catholics to settle in that island. Ten years later, Trinidad was conquered by the British.

After emancipation in 1834, Trinidad's majority population of African descent began to participate in Carnival and soon became the dominant element. African-derived traditions of parading and masking blended with the fancy masked balls of the Catholic Lenten festival. Carnival took on aspects of social protest as the poor and powerless majority, descendants of the freed slaves, took to the streets. The colonial authorities tried to suppress the festival on various occasions, notably

in 1884. Since Trinidad's independence in 1962, however, the Trinidad government has given Carnival official recognition and financial support as an expression of national culture and a major tourist attraction.

Carnival in Trinidad and Tobago is held the week before Ash Wednesday, which usually falls in February. It combines three central elements: steelband, calypsoes and masquerade.

▶ Steelband, also called "pan," was created in Trinidad and Tobago in the 1940s. Large metal oil drums are heat-fired and tuned to produce a wide range of notes. Once associated with street gangs in urban shantytowns, pan is now the national instrument of Trinidad and Tobago.

▶ Calypso, or "kaiso," traces its roots to the griots of Africa, whose songs praised or criticized community leaders. West Indian calypsonians compose witty, often ribald lyrics commenting on social issues and personalities of the day. New calypsoes are released each year in time for Carnival.

▶ In "mas," the Carnival masquerade, bands of costumed revelers parade through the streets on Carnival Monday and Tuesday, performing exuberant and sensual dance steps. The bands are open to anyone who wishes to play mas and can afford a costume. The elaborate costumes traditionally include such stock characters as sailors, devils, stilt-walkers and minstrels; in recent years they have grown increasingly fantastic. Bands may have as many as 4,000 masqueraders costumed along a single theme. Lavishly costumed special characters, typically a king and queen, are the centerpiece of each band. The "King and Queen of Carnival" competition pits the kings and queens of the various bands against each other in a contest of costume design and choreography.

From Trinidad to Brooklyn

The beginnings of Carnival came to New York City with immigrants from Trinidad and other West Indian islands in the 1920s. In Harlem, where many of the early immigrants settled, islanders would get together for their annual pre-Lenten festivities in mid-winter. They organized events in houses and ballrooms similar to the ones held back home in the Caribbean.

By the 1940s the Harlem celebration had become extremely popular. On one occasion over 5,000 revelers filled the Renaissance Ballroom on 138th Street, while many others were turned away for lack of space. The overcrowding problem led the organizers to plan an outdoor festival during the warm-weather months. The first such street carnival was held in Harlem on Labor Day in 1947.

After the permit for the Harlem parade was revoked in 1964, Rufus Goring, a Trinidadian, organized a carnival in Brooklyn, where many new West Indian immigrants had settled. Beginning on Fulton Street, the parade later moved to Eastern Parkway, a broad boulevard through Brooklyn's Crown Heights section. Since then, the West Indian–American Day Carnival Association led by Carlos Lezama, also a Trinidadian, has successfully organized the Labor Day event in Brooklyn each year.

From a simple parade, the Brooklyn Carnival has expanded greatly. The Brooklyn Museum on Eastern Parkway is the center of "Carnival City,"

where an almost week-long program includes concerts of pan, calypso, soca, reggae and other Caribbean music. Competitions are held for King and Queen of Carnival, best steelband, and Kiddies Carnival. Vendors sell Caribbean foods like roti, cook-up rice, jerk chicken and curry goat, along with crafts made of coconut, bamboo or wood. The celebration culminates in the day-long parade down Eastern Parkway on Labor Day Monday.

A few blocks from the museum, Medgar Evers College, part of the City University of New York, holds an annual conference on Carnival the weekend before Labor Day. Scholars from the Caribbean, the United States and elsewhere meet to share their research on the meaning and practice of Carnival.

Unity and Strength

The Brooklyn Carnival is an important source of pan-Caribbean unity in New York. Although Trinidadians are the main organizers, the event brings together immigrants from all the English-speaking Caribbean countries, including those that have a Carnival tradition and those that do not. Crossing the language barrier, Haitians too join in. On Eastern Parkway there are no Jamaicans, no Bajans, no Trinidadians—we are all "Caribbeans." We benefit through our solidarity as we learn to leave parochial squabbles behind.

In a city of many ethnic parades and festivals, Labor Day Carnival is now the largest annual street celebration. As such, it spotlights the burgeoning size and potential political weight of New York's West Indian community. In recent years dozens of state and local politicians have attended the event, with the mayor and the state governor heading up the Carnival parade. In an election year the various candidates make appearances as well.

By attracting visitors to the city, Carnival has been a successful revenue earner for New York. Sadly, this is not reflected in the amount of attention or resources devoted to the city's Caribbean community. This is one of the battles still to be fought.

Carnival's symbolic presentation of West Indian strength and unity has made it a focal point in the rough-and-tumble of local ethnic politics. In Brooklyn, this has often involved relations between Caribbeans and the ultra-Orthodox Hasidic Jews

The calypsonian Crazy, from Trinidad, comes up every year to take part in Brooklyn's Carnival.

who also live in Crown Heights. In August 1991, a few days before Carnival, tensions erupted in Crown Heights when a car driven by a Hasidic man struck and killed a West Indian child. The black community, both West Indian and African-American, was outraged, and later that night a young Jewish man was stabbed to death in apparent retaliation. Rioting went on for several nights as a thousand police officers tried to restore order and the mayor appealed for calm.

With a million people expected in Crown Heights for Carnival, there were fears that the violence would escalate. Instead, Carnival helped to defuse the tensions. On Sunday morning before Labor Day, Carlos Lezama, head of the Carnival association, met with leaders of the Hasidic community and invited them to march down Eastern Parkway with the parade. Governor Cuomo of New York and Mayor Dinkins of New York City also worked to mediate the conflict. On Carnival Monday morning Lezama stood side by side with Hasidic leaders on the Carnival reviewing stand, and that year's Carnival was one of the most peaceful ever.

In 1994, for the first time, the Carnival parade date coincided with Rosh Hashana, the Jewish New Year. At the behest of the Hasidic community, the police commissioner asked that the parade be moved to Sunday instead of the traditional Labor Day Monday. The Caribbean community, out of respect for their Hasidic neighbors, agreed instead to end the parade at 6:00 PM Monday, well before sundown. This concession was empowering to the Caribbean community because it gave them an opportunity to show their neighbors that they could respect the cultures of others. They did so with dignity and a new resolve.

Link to Home

Carnival artists have become goodwill ambassadors for the Caribbean. They present Caribbean culture in the global "market." An editorial in *The Caribbean-American* in 1996 said it well: "The spirit of Carnival is beyond one people and one culture. It is our Caribbean gift to the world."

Equally important, Carnival creates a link to home for West Indians in the diaspora. It provides a channel for cultural innovation to flow in both directions. Carnival artists bring the latest inventions from Trinidad to West Indian communities abroad. Innovative costume designs, popular new calypsoes, and other trends in Carnival art are studied and incorporated by Carnival artists in the United States. At the same time, carnivals in the diaspora have a reverse cultural impact on Carnival art in the Caribbean. New ideas, practices and techniques developed in the diaspora are exported to the Caribbean, and the resulting changes are reflected in the various carnivals in the region.

Caribbean people are empowered, both politically and socially, by the globalization of their culture. This is important, but the most important thing is the joy that Carnival brings. Carnival has brought the Caribbean to people around the world, and in the process, brings Caribbean people together wherever they may live. ❖

soca: soul-calypso
roti: wrapped sandwich introduced to the Caribbean by immigrants from India
cook-up rice: rice cooked with meat and spices
jerk chicken: spicy grilled chicken
Bajans: Barbadians

Mas in Brooklyn

The Mighty Sparrow

From his initial triumph in 1956, The Mighty Sparrow has dominated the calypso world. A master of both lyrics and melody, he has been crowned "Calypso Monarch" eight times and is undoubtedly the calypsonian best known in and outside the Caribbean. Born in Grenada (his given name is Slinger Francisco), Sparrow grew up in Trinidad and now divides his time between Trinidad and New York.

He is a long-time participant in New York City's Carnival. Years ago, the Sparrow and his friends would gather at a restaurant called Myra's Cook Shop in Harlem to watch the revelers. These memories surface in Sparrow's 1976 calypso, "Mas in Brooklyn."

Let me tell you something
About Labor Day in Brooklyn
Everybody jumping
Labor Day in Brooklyn
Every West Indian jumping up like mad
Just like a Carnival day in Trinidad
Yankee and all listening to the steelband beat
Rolling in canal just like on Charlotte Street

Chorus:

And if you hear them with
Mas, play mas
Mas in you' mas, play mas
Even though I feeling homesick
Even though I tired roam
Just give me my calypso music
Brooklyn is my home

Early in September
That is fete to remember
When they say Labor Day
That is New York Jouvert
All the people from the Virgin Island
Jump in the streets of New York like wild Indian
Ah mean fungee and fish with rice and peas by Myra
And 116th Street in Harlem on fire

Chorus: And is mas, play mas ...

Night time in Manhattan
Now things start to happen
When the boat ride over

The Mighty Sparrow performing in a Brooklyn calypso tent.

Man have to run for cover
Twenty woman to one man in New York
Ah mean a man like a piece o' gold anywhere he walk
When they drink up their booze
You better run 'way quick
Otherwise you go have to beat them off with a stick

Chorus: When they start with mas, play mas ...

You could be from St. Clair or from John John
In New York, all that done
It ain't have no who is who
New York equalize you
Bajan, Grenadian, Jamaican, *tout moun*
Drinking they rum, beating they bottle and spoon
Nobody can't watch me and honestly say
They don't like to be in Brooklyn on Labor Day!

Chorus: It is mas, play mas ...

❖

jump up: dance with loose abandon
Yankee: a (white) American
Charlotte Street: street in downtown Port-of-Spain, Trinidad
play mas: wear a costume in the Carnival parade
fete: a party
Jouvert (pronounced zhu-VAY): Literally "open day," the beginning of Carnival in the predawn hours of Carnival Monday
fungee: boiled cornmeal, like polenta
rice and peas: rice and pigeon peas, a traditional Caribbean dish
St. Clair: wealthy section of Port-of-Spain
John John: poor section of Port-of-Spain
Bajan: Barbadian
tout moun: French Creole for "everyone"

"Battling" crews compete with fancy breakdance moves in a playground on Manhattan's Upper West Side.

NEW YORK CITY: Hip-Hop

A s people from different cultures set down roots in New York City, their musical traditions meet and interact. Popular new music and dance styles have emerged from the melding of African-American, Afro-Caribbean, and Latin-Caribbean cultures in the crucible of New York. In the 1940s there was Afro-Cuban jazz on the Fania Records label. The mambo dance craze of the 1950s combined Afro-Cuban percussion and big-band orchestra music. Rhythm and blues, doo-wop, bugalú, Latin soul and salsa all draw on African and Latin musical roots.

The hip-hop culture that first emerged in the streets of Harlem and the South Bronx in the 1970s springs from similar origins. Its creators were young African-Americans and Latinos, the latter mainly Puerto Ricans born in New York (some-times called Nuyoricans).

Despite their differences, these two groups had much in common. Their parents and grandparents

had come from rural backgrounds: African-Americans from the southern states and Puerto Ricans from the island. Born in New York or arriving there at a young age, African-American and Puerto Rican teenagers found themselves sharing schools, workplaces, tenement buildings and street corners. They shared, as well, the bitter experience of poverty and racial discrimination in a white-dominated society (Puerto Ricans can be any color, and many are black). Drawing on African, Afro-Caribbean and Latin musical traditions, these youths created an inner-city street culture that was constantly experimenting with new styles.

Hip-hop has three basic elements: rapping, breakdancing, and graffiti art. Rap music features strongly rhythmic and rhyming verse that showcases a rapper's ability to improvise. Lyrics often project a social message: rappers make up songs about themselves, their neighborhoods, and about life and struggle in the city. Rap draws on the

African-American blues tradition and on Jamaican reggae, but also fits well with Puerto Rican musical forms such as *plenas* and *décimas*.

Hip-hip culture in the 1980s revolved around the "crews," loosely organized groups of youth that included both African-Americans and Latinos. Crews would throw street jams of rapping and breakdancing with music from a boombox or a DJ and turntable.

As rap developed and became more complex, Latino rappers began to experiment with bilingual English, Spanish, and "Spanglish" rhyming. Around 1990 Latino rap emerged as a distinct style. Mellow Man Ace (of Cuban heritage), Kid Frost (Mexican-American), El General (Panamanian), and Latin Empire (New York Puerto Rican) have led the way in gaining recognition for this dynamic new music. ❖

Puerto Rican in the USA

A rap by KMX Assault

¡BRINCANDO! ¡TRABAJANDO!
Tryin' to make good,
puro Boricua born and raised in the 'hood.
Boy to a man with a plan! Understand!
Tryin' to do the best that I can.
Pop is dying a slow bleed
killing himself on a job that don't fulfill his needs.
Mi abuelita, 62
still works sewing in a sweatshop but what is
    she to do.
Boricuas puros, trabajan duro
el futuro no se ve tan seguro.
Just lotta work luggin' boxes all day
what can I say, a lotta work, little play.

Yo, there's gotta be a better way
for Puerto Ricans in the USA.

Gunshots bust out in succession.
Another brother lettin' out aggression.
People look around and think it's a bad scenario
Yo, by the way, welcome to mi barrio.

I take a stroll and roll upon my Homeboy Rick.
Once Cock Diesel, now terminally sick.
Jumped without a jimmy when he got laid
no se cuidó and now he's dyin' of AIDS.
¡Bendito! You know the — is hard, bro
but that's my boy and I give props in that regard, yo.
I give him five, a hug to let him know I'm on
    his side ...
then I continue my ride.
So profound's my frustration,
parks are empty lots and there's no education ...

Boricuas are a tribe, hard to describe
Bass in time with rhythm to make you realize
that we go with the flow, yo
in every size, shape and color of the human rainbow.
We do our thing with much respect,
we speak two lingoes and one dialect.
In effect, don't you know
we swing low con mucho orgullo.
Despierta Boricua, defiende lo tuyo.

Mi abuelita says la vida es dura.
¡Levántate, Boricua! Wakin' up es la cura.
Orgulloso, proud of my heritage
Echar pa'lante with my people is my imperative.
This Boricua will endeavor to be clever,
got to succeed to make our kids' lives better.
We need this new breed to lead the way
for all Puerto Ricans in the USA. ❖

Boricua: Puerto Rican
abuelita: grandmother
trabajan duro, el futuro no se ve tan
seguro: they work hard, but the future
looks doubtful
mi barrio: my neighborhood
no se cuidó: he didn't take care of himself
con mucho orgullo: with great pride
despierta, defiende lo tuyo: wake up, take
pride in what is yours
la vida es dura: life is hard
levántate: get up
echar pa'lante: to move forward

"It was always Latinos and Blacks ..."

Interview with KMX Assault

KMX Assault (Jenaro Díaz) is a DJ, producer and rapper who lives in the Bronx. He has been involved in hip-hop music since its inception. Explaining his name, he says: "K is what they used to call me when I was out in the streets. It stands for Krazy or Kamikaze. MX means mixing music and Assault stands for the assault I intend to do on the media."

KMX Assault was interviewed by Blanca Vázquez, Juan Flores and Pablo Figueroa. A longer version of this interview appeared in CENTRO, the bulletin of the Centro de Estudios Puertorriqueños at Hunter College, City University of New York, Winter 1992-93. Used by permission of Centro de Estudios Puertorriqueños.

Tell me about your family. Where were you born and raised?

I was born in 1961 on the Upper West Side of Manhattan. Then we moved to the South Bronx. From 1968 to around 1972, that's when I started getting into the music. I started hearing James Brown, New Birth, a lot of the records that were basically the foundation for what people now call hip-hop. Music was probably what kept me out of jail because instead of stealing cars, going to rumbles and starting fights, all of a sudden I was at home. I really got into music and deejaying especially. Instead of hanging out on the street drinking beer, we would go into the studio, go into the sound room and start playing music.

There was no such thing as a rap record yet. Everything was still out on the street. DJs would come out with mixers and turntables and steal electricity from a light pole, especially on University Avenue. The only time the cops would hassle us was when we really started booming it late at night. We got together in playgrounds and projects, in between project buildings, sometimes right in the middle of a block. It was very impromptu. It was similar to guys bringing out congas and playing out in the streets. That's really how I started learning to rap.

What's the distinction between rap and hip-hop?

Rap was what spearheaded the whole hip-hop culture. Hip-hop is basically the whole culture—graffiti, politics, the music, the values, 'cause hip-hoppers have their own set of values.

It was always Latinos and blacks. Of the Latinos, the majority were Puerto Ricans. Since we grew up listening to a lot of R&B-based music, a lot of the music that the DJs used to scratch to was what people would consider black music. But it wasn't exclusive because there used to be a band I remember called the Average White Band and we used to scratch to that. There were really no barriers to the music. We would rap over congas too and that would be considered Latin music. It didn't really matter as long as you had a groove. As long as you had a rhythm to roll with, you were okay.

Most of the rappers were black but not all of them were black. Some of them were black Puerto Ricans. Grandmaster Caz, you looked at him, yeah, he was black, but he was Puerto Rican.

How was the relationship between Puerto Ricans and African-Americans?

You lived next door; you shared the same cockroaches; you lived in the same building. We used to all get together and jam out on the street. There may be fights but it had nothing to do with it being racial. Maybe it was a neighborhood rivalry, something like that.

Whether you're black or Puerto Rican, you can get kicked by a cop, you can get chased down, you can get shot by a stray bullet, you can meet a girl and fall in love, you can party together and the whole nine yards. And what happens is that you experience the same things, so you have a certain type of camaraderie.

Let's face it, this whole rap thing is now considered black. And it was never a black thing, it was an *urban* thing, it was a *B-boy* thing. There were mostly blacks and Puerto Ricans, but I remember whites, I remember Chinese coming up and chillin' with us. It was never a racial thing—it was an inner-city thing.

As rap went from its street form to a commercial form, it changed. At this point was when I believe that blacks were thinking ahead and were really looking at the potential of this. They were willing to take chances and invest in the music.

Later on what happens is that they started to make subdivisions of rap. You got Latin rap, you got hard core, you got gangsta, you got underground, you got pop rap. I don't consider that a bad thing. My point of view as a Puerto Rican and a Latino hip-hopper is that we got to learn to do our own thing. And maybe not just in hip-hop but in everything. You gotta first be able to build your foundation and from there create. Because that's one thing about hip-hop: hip-hop got no kind of prejudices whatsoever. If it's fat and it works, it's gonna get played. It's not the type of thing where you're gonna be discriminated because you're Latino. But I think in anything you have to have your own base, you have to have something you start, and it's got to be rightfully yours. ❖

rumble: fight between gangs
DJ: disk jockey, the person who cuts and mixes background music for a rapper
congas: drums
B-boy (or B-girl): original term for breakdancer

"We are breaking barriers ..."

Interview with Latin Empire

Latin Empire is one of the pioneers of Nuyorican rap. Its members are KT (Tony Boston); Puerto Rock (Rick Rodríguez); and DJ Corchado, their manager. Rapping bilingually in Spanish and English, Latin Empire is building bridges between the street world of Spanglish and the commercial world of records, videos and media recognition.

When they gave this interview, the members of Latin Empire had just returned from a trip to Puerto Rico and the Dominican Republic. They reflect on how the interaction between New York and island rappers enriches the music of both.

Latin Empire was interviewed by Juan Flores, professor of black and Puerto Rican studies at Hunter College, City University of New York. A longer version of this interview appeared in CENTRO, the bulletin of the Centro de Estudios Puertorriqueños, Hunter College, Spring 1991. Used by permission of Centro de Estudios Puertorriqueños.

Is rap from Puerto Rico any different than rap from here?

There's a difference between here and there because here we've got to adapt it to the style of rhyme music of New York, which has more finesse, more flair. There they are still more monotone, and basically more limited. The first time we went there a few years ago, it was like they were learning from us. They couldn't believe the style we had, but in Spanish. You see over there they hear the New York style, but in English. They heard us in Spanish, and it was like a whole different thing, you know.

So there was no Spanish rap down there yet?

There's Spanish rap over there, but not with the style that we have over here from New York. So they are basically coming along. Now they are getting more and more of the finesse in their style.

Did you rap any Spanglish down there, or English rap?

We sang English, Spanish, Spanglish.

How did they respond to all those languages?

They are all trying mixing styles and languages too. They've heard the other groups like Mellow Man Ace and Kid Frost. They are all trying to do Spanglish now. There's also a guy called General. He came out with reggae rap in Spanish. You see, over there the trends change. Whatever's in style they'll do. Like rap with house music they're doing now. Styles come from everywhere you can say, more or less. But they make their own. Puerto Rico got their own style, because that Spanish rap is crazy-big over there.

By people down there?

Yeah, they're cool people. Some of them were born here and went over there. So they basically got exposed to rap here and then brought it with them. Rap, they caught on to it by videos and all of that, you know. They got motivated, plus with us doing New York style in Spanish. That's more or less where they get steps, dance steps, fashion trends. That's how they

Puerto Rock and Krazy Taíno (Rick Rodríguez and Tony Boston) of the rap group Latin Empire

keep up to date. Instead of traveling back and forth, because not all of them can be traveling back and forth, they just watch TV and catch on to the videos.

And then they work with that?

Yeah. Then they derive. They get their own style from it. And they have a whole different technique.

So how do you find that the groups start down there? How you guys got together?

Like the same thing over there as here, in the streets. That's how we started off. Even before rap records came out on the radio, we were rhyming in the streets. In the Bronx, on every street corner there were DJs, crazy jams they called them, groups that were real well known even before records came out.

And Puerto Ricans were part of it all along, right?

Right. And by now, even Queen Latifah just came out with a Spanish song, it's got salsa mixed

into it. That's like the main jingle to the main chorus, it's bad!

And you've been exposed to a lot of salsa, right?

Our parents, you know, family, all they do is play salsa, merengue ...

How did they respond to you doing rap?

In the beginning it was all in English and they thought you were American. They considered it noise. "Ay, deja ese alboroto!" you know. We said, let's try to do it in Spanish so that they can understand it, instead of complaining to us so much.

How did it go over when you started rapping in Spanish?

They liked it! They was like, "Oh, mi hijo"! Every time they saw us they would try to encourage us to do more, "Say that rhyme again" to their friends and neighbors next door.

Were there some people who don't know Spanish and liked the Spanish music?

We used to walk around with the tapes and the big radios and the black people behind us, "Yo, man, that sounds dope, that's fly!" They be like "Yo, I don't understand it, man, but I know it's rhyming and I hear the last word man, that's bad, yo!" Then I used to try to do it in the street jams and the crowd went crazy. We had experience first performing it in the streets, street jams, house parties.

Mostly Puerto Ricans or mixed?

Anything. We perform in any type of crowd. We have different routines too, but we also try our Spanish routines even if there's just a black crowd to let them know more or less we ain't got nothing to hide, we're not afraid to let them know about our culture. Yeah, they like it.

One of the things people are interested in is how you use the language, how you mix, alternate Spanish and English.

And make it make sense at the same time and rhyme. It's complicated. In the competition rounds, we have one in Spanglish that we are working on. Listen, it starts off like this:

When you play with fire,
  you're bound to get burned with candela
That's what you get for trying to make a novela ...

So you know when to put the Spanish part and when to put the English. Now let's say, "When you play with fire, you're bound to get burned with candela," cause candela is more or less fire, but it's Spanish, so it fits in cool. Then it goes: "That's what you get for trying to make a novela." That's street slang which means stop making movies, you know, you're overreacting, something like that. Imagine saying it in English: "That's what you get for trying to make a soap opera." Novela is more comical. Spanglish gives that, so we choose depending what it sounds like, according to the subject and all of that. If the Spanish sounds like not too hot, we be like Yo the English sounds one crazy fly, let's say it in English. Or if not, we mix it up, and if it sounds even better in Spanish, we stick with that.

One rhyme is called "Puerto Rican and Proud." It mentions a lot about Puerto Rican style. It goes:

I am so bad, people say I am the MC bandit
Here to rock in Spanglish
Though you may not understand it
See I wasn't going to do it
But that's what you have demanded
Now we are here to let you know
The Puerto Ricans have landed
Live on the scene if you know what I mean
As we get a little busy with our Spanglish routine
Since I like Pedro Navaja
And Willie Colón
Don't watch novelas
But I bet you watch Iris Chacón
Man, forget the Pepsi challenge
And Coke is it
For that we'll have a Coco Rico
Word, forget that sh —
I can do for a piragua
But prefer me a coquito
And if there's no Cafe Bustelo
Man, you better get El Pico
Man, don't go to Burger King
Mickie Dee's, c'mon negrito
For that you come with me
Where to? The cuchifritos

And we got slang, we even use slang from Puerto Rico, like "Nítido." We go over there, we learn the slang from Puerto Rico and pure Puerto Ricans, and we bring it into our little raps too. And they be, "Oh, that's Puerto Rican slang." Like Mellow Man Ace used Cuban slang, Ah man *jalaboa, salao,* whatever, and these guys Kid Frost have their slang from the Chicanos and all that, *vatos, cholos.* It's good, I like it. I consider it an art, the whole thing of hip-hop, I consider it crazy art. Like graffiti, breakdancing, the fashion trends, everything. The music of rap and everything, music by itself just helps bring all the different types of culture together.

It's the same thing with reggae in Spanish, it makes the Spanish people listen more to reggae and reggae people, Yo, what's up with that Spanish? Now whenever they hear reggae even if it's English they like it. You know because there are certain people that stick to their certain one thing. "Yo we rap and that's it. We don't like free style, that's Whack!" So if we do rap with merengue they be like, "Oh!" Then they start to listen to more merengue and they start to like it, like us. We're rappers but we adjust to all kinds of music. We wind up rapping to house, to free style, to slow jams, everything. You know we've got comedy rap, serious rap, all subject-type raps, political, etc.

On the positive tip, on the lyrics and all of that, it's the awakening up of the youth, how they be lost in their little trend. We don't wear gold, we prefer not to because we know that there's too much violence going on as it is. If we wear gold, kids will want to be the same way, but they can't afford it. They'll try to get it through any means possible. So we wear beads and it's affordable and it's nice and it still catches the eye. That's what's in now, anyway, more or less. All the rappers are catching onto that, too.

'Cause you walk through the streets and the little kids they idolize the rappers and they see all the rappers with those big gold chains, then they don't have a job to get that type of money. So what they see in the streets, "All right I'll sell drugs, and if I rob somebody I probably can be like my idol, the rapper." But they get it and they don't realize that some other kid wants the same thing, so then they get into problems. Instead of pushing the youth in that direction, you might as well help them to progress, motivate, be positive, use your mind.

Certain rappers, you know, instead of helping each other, they try to knock each other off, competing, to keep each other down. We're not like that, we're willing to get so-called competition ... We don't consider it competition, we're glad that there is a lot of it. Rappers finally, for Latinos, finally! It's all about helping each other out, instead of trying to keep each other down. The way we see it, we are breaking barriers for other Latin rappers to follow.

All the Puerto Ricans here, they want to buy English stuff. But as more Latin rappers come out doing Latin reggae, Latin this, Latin that, hopefully they'll start to have Latin sections in certain stores and everybody will be proud again of speaking their language. You know some of them speak Spanish and they play it off and conversate with you, "Yo, I don't speak Spanish," and play the role. You be like, come on, man! What's up with your culture? See, if you don't speak Spanish, learn it. I was trying to learn, because I was feeling funny being Puerto Rican and not speaking much. But now I speak more than ever, I'm getting more fluent as time goes by.

And being down there in Puerto Rico must have helped, right?

It helped a lot. You had to speak more Spanish. When you said something wrong, they corrected you. There's some things I still say wrong, but hey, what do you expect? I'm from New York. But I'm getting into it, learning more and more.

Did you see anything they were doing in Puerto Rico that you felt you could learn from, some new thing that hadn't occurred to you?

They've got customs they do over there around Christmas time. They call it *parranda*. So we did that and it was like a whole different experience and we are planning on using that now in one of our raps. Like there's one that goes: "Vámonos, vámonos, vámonos que la parranda se acabó!" We are going to use that same rhythm more or less, working on the hip-hop tip, talking about a party like it was over and then we are going to do like the neighbors are complaining, "You know, it's late, it's two in the morning, it's time to end the party." And we be like [sings]: "Que no, que no, que no, que no me da la gana! Que no me voy de aquí hasta por la mañana!" You know with the rap and all of that.

Is there anything else you picked up down there? Even things that the rappers themselves were doing?

Their slang. We've got to catch up some more on their stuff. Because some of it we don't understand. Since they're brought up over there, they are up to date with it. Their Spanish, you can't learn that thing in school. You go to school and you learn, what kind of Spanish? Spaniard Spanish. And it's like, Cómo está usted? PRs don't say that. We've got to get it up to date with the hip-hop slang. And then with the New York flavor!

What about in the Dominican Republic? Are there rappers there?

Yeah. They've got some groups coming out. Dominicans from over there. You can tell 'cause they come out with their own unique style. There's this guy, Boruga, he's got this comedy rap called "Mi País, Que País." He's talking about his country.

How were you received in the Dominican Republic?

They went crazy over us. 'Cause they knew us from MTV International. In three days we did like twelve TV shows. And now they invited us for March to do a concert over there with some other rappers from PR. They are going to do a big concert over there, like a Latin rap. That's bad!

Did they call you Latin Empire before you started doing rap?

No. We worked with a few different trend names, all of us. And then I wound up coming up with Puerto Rock, and I like that one. That's the one that clicked the most. The Puerto Ricans that are into the trend of hip-hop and all of that, they call them Puerto Rock. It's trying to be down with hip-hop.

Is it black people that say that?

Yeah, to the Hispanics. They used to see the Hispanics dressing up with the hat to the side and all hip-hop down and some assume that we're just supposed to stick to our own style of music and friends. They thought rap music was only a black thing, and it wasn't. Puerto Ricans used to be all crazy with their hats to the side and everything. So that's why they used to say, "Oh look at that Puerto Rock, like he's trying to be down." They used to call them Puerto Rocks, so that was a nickname, and I said, "I'm going to stick to that. Shut everybody up." That's cool though.

And MC KT is his name, because before Latin Empire we were called the "Solid Gold MCs," and KT stood for Karat like in gold. Now MC KT, we finally found the best name that will fit our image. Instead of Karat Gold, KT stands for Krazy Taíno.

How did you get "Latin Empire"?

Riding around in our car with our manager, DJ Corchado, we were trying to think of a Latin name.

We didn't want to limit ourselves with Puerto Rican something … We wanted Latin something to represent all Latinos. We came up with "Latin Imperials," "Latin Alliance." And then one time we were driving along the Grand Concourse and my manager's car happened to hit a bump when I had told him, "The Latin Employees." Joking around, we were just making fun and when the car hit the bump my manager thought I said, "Empire." I was like, what? "Latin Empire!" I was like, yo, that's it! As soon as they said it, it clicked. It's a strong title. It's more or less like the Zulu Nation. "Latin Empire," it's like a strong title, like, Oh snap! ❖

DJ: disk jockey, the person who cuts and mixes background music for a rapper
Spanglish: mixture of Spanish and English
Queen Latifah: African-American rapper
salsa: hybrid music developed in New York City by musicians of various Latin American and Caribbean backgrounds
bad: (slang) admirable, terrific
merengue: popular dance music of the Dominican Republic
Deja ese alboroto: Quit that racket!
Pedro Navaja: character in a song
Willie Colón: Puerto Rican salsa star, born in the Bronx
Iris Chacón: well-known dancer
Coco Rico: soft drink sold in Latino groceries
piragua: snow-cone
coquito: drink made from coconut and rum
Cafe Bustelo, El Pico: brands of Latin-style coffee
negrito: affectionate term for a dark-skinned person
cuchifritos: fried snacks
reggae: popular music of Jamaican origins
parranda: Puerto Rican tradition of house-to-house serenading at Christmas
vámonos que la parranda se acabó: let's go, the parranda's over
que no me da la gana/no me voy de aquí hasta por la mañana: I don't feel like it, I'm not leaving here until morning
mi país, que país: my country, what a country
Taíno: orginal inhabitants of Puerto Rico
Zulu Nation: influential South Bronx "crew"

The Fugees: Hip-Hop's Haitian-American Pioneers

Anthony Ng

When their second album, THE SCORE, topped the charts in 1996, the Fugees were hailed as having expanded the boundaries of hip-hop. Their creative combination of singing, rapping and instrumentation have made the Fugees one of the hottest groups in hip-hop today.

The three-person band— two Haitian-Americans and an African-American—has strong Caribbean links. Influences on their music include Jamaican reggae and Haitian Creole music. While THE SCORE was racking up sales (it would go on to win the 1997 Grammy Award for best rap album), Wyclef Jean, the most charismatic vocalist and composer of the group, recorded six songs in Haitian Creole and released them in Haiti. This helped to create a groundswell of support in Haiti for the Fugees and inspired Wyclef to include some songs in Creole on his solo album, WYCLEF JEAN PRESENTS THE CARNIVAL.

(continued on next page)

auryn Hill, Wyclef Jean and Prakazrel Michel are injecting new life into hip-hop music. The three members of the celebrated rap group known as The Fugees, they also present a perfect example of how Haitian-Americans across the country are making extraordinary professional breakthroughs.

Their second and current album, *The Score*, has become a spectacular success. It has gone multi-platinum, and as of May 19, 1996 was the number one album on the Billboard charts. Since March, it has remained one of the top five selling albums in the country, a rarity for rap albums. Record sales have been driven by the group's hip-hop remake of Roberta Flack's 1973 single, "Killing Me Softly." Additionally, the group manages to command respect from the core urban audience that reveres hard-core hip-hop acts such as the WuTang Clan and Mobb Deep, and at the same time, has gained major mainstream success.

The group calls itself The Fugees to bring attention to the fact that Jean, age 26, and Michel, 23, are of Haitian descent. Fugees is short for refugees, a term that can have derogatory connotations for Haitians and second-generation Haitian-Americans. The group, however, wears its name like a badge of honor, and refers to their production company and their "peoples" (hip-hop slang for close friends and family) as their "Refugee Camp."

Jean's family emigrated from Haiti when he was nine years old. Like Jean's parents, Michel's are Haitian immigrants, although he himself was born and raised in the United States. The two performers, who are cousins, grew up in Brooklyn, New York, and later Newark, New Jersey, and both have fathers with strong religious ties. Jean's dad is a pastor and Michel's is a deacon. Lauryn Hill, a 21-year-old African-American, met her two collaborators while attending Columbia High School in South Orange, New Jersey, an institution also attended by Prakazrel Michel.

To appreciate how the distinct talents and cross-cultural musical influences of each Fugee member coalesce to form the Fugee sound, one needs to see them live.

Marc Baptiste, SONY Music

The Fugees: (l-r) Wyclef Jean, Lauryn Hill and Prakazrel Michel.

In 1997 the Fugees performed a "Coming Home Concert" in Port-au-Prince. The homecoming was a huge event in Haiti, as the country all but shut down to welcome them. A crowd of some 65,000 packed the concert, which was billed as a benefit for Haitian refugees expelled from the neighboring Dominican Republic.

Anthony Ng has written for underground music magazines as a freelance hip-hop music critic. Born in Hong Kong and raised in Brooklyn, New York, he recently graduated from the Massachusetts Institute of Technology with a master's degree in city planning. This article is reprinted from HAITI INSIGHT, the bulletin of the National Coalition for Haitian Rights, June/July 1996. © 1996 by Anthony Ng. Used by permission of National Coalition for Haitian Rights.

Live performances of most rap groups simply include the DJ (disc jockey), the rappers themselves, and much macho posturing, including pacing from side to side. The Fugees perform with Jean on guitar or piano, a DJ named Leon, drummer and fellow Haitian Donald Guillaume, and bass player Jerry Duplessis, who is also Jean's cousin and co-producer of *The Score*.

A typical Fugees show begins with Jean and Duplessis playing the breaks (instrumentals) of classic and popular hip-hop songs. As this occurs, DJ Leon comes in with the actual 12-inch (vinyl single) of the song. A blending of the acoustic and recorded versions is created and this often throws the crowd into a joyous frenzy. Throughout the rest of their show, the Fugees do their hit songs, perform a few raps in Creole (to stress their ethnic pride), toast (a type of cadence used in delivering reggae lyrics) in a dancehall style, do covers of reggae songs and when possible, bring popular, contemporary reggae acts on stage to perform with them.

The Fugees' connection to reggae music is more intimate than other rap groups because of Jean's and Michel's Haitian-American heritage. Reggae music is ubiquitous within the West Indian communities in the New York City area, and serves to remind Jamaicans, Haitians and Trinidadians of their Caribbean and African ancestry.

In addition to reggae, the Fugees incorporate elements of African-American music genres such as soul, funk, and rhythm & blues into their performances. Not only does *The Score* contain Hill's soulful remake of "Killing Me Softly," it also includes a cover of Bob Marley's "No Woman, No Cry"; "Zealots," which samples the Flamingoes' 1959 hit "I Only Have Eyes for You"; and Jean's "Mista, Mista," which is an acoustic ballad about a drug addict. The music that the Fugees sing, croon and rap to on the remainder of *The Score* is full of hip-hop beats, keyboard sounds of moody horns, whirling, ascending and descending organ chords and acoustic guitar riffs. Their intelligent, clever and metaphor-filled raps comment on topics such as police brutality and the half-truths that image-conscious people invent about themselves.

The Fugees' creative fearlessness removes the barriers that many current hip-hop groups place on themselves when it comes to creating new material. While a handful of rap groups have incorporated instruments and other music genres into their hip-hop, no group until the Fugees has done it as successfully or has been so fearless in taking it on. They have shattered the notion that a hip-hop group can't use live instruments, do hip-hop remakes of classic soul and reggae songs, or sing ballads. The doors for other rap groups to experiment in a similar manner have been swung wide open. By understanding how the Fugees' diversity of musical tastes has affected their hip-hop, one can fully appreciate their courage and hope that other hip-hop artists become just as brave. ❖

DJ: disc jockey, the person who cuts and mixes background music for a rapper

CONNECTICUT

Although the nation's big cities have been poles of attraction for immigrants, the Caribbean presence in this country is far broader. For decades, people have migrated directly to smaller cities, towns and rural areas, mainly in response to job opportunities. As they are joined by relatives, the Caribbean population in these smaller communities grows. Meanwhile, a substantial number of immigrants whose first stop was a major city eventually move to an outlying suburban area or smaller town—to find work, to be with relatives, or simply to enjoy a more tranquil life.

Caribbean people have come to Connecticut in all these ways. They have settled in every part of the state. Caribbean influence is felt not only in the large urban centers of Hartford, Bridgeport and Stamford, but also in smaller cities and towns and in the countryside. ❖

Connecticut's Caribbean Communities

Ruth Glasser

Ruth Glasser was born and raised in Brooklyn, New York. A former fellow of the Centro de Estudios Puertorriqueños of Hunter College, she is the author of MY MUSIC IS MY FLAG (University of California Press, 1995), a study of Puerto Rican musicians in New York. Her most recent book is AQUÍ ME QUEDO: PUERTO RICANS IN CONNECTICUT (Middletown, Conn.: Connecticut Humanities Council, 1997). She lives in Waterbury, Connecticut.

For more than a century, the farms and industries of Connecticut have beckoned to people from other lands. The Old Yankee communities of this small New England state were transformed first by waves of immigrants from Ireland, and later by people from southern and eastern Europe.

These groups are long established, woven into the ethnic tapestry of the state. Immigration today is mainly from the Americas, above all from the territories in and around the Caribbean Sea. The vast majority of Connecticut's Caribbeans are Puerto Ricans—who are U.S. citizens—followed by Jamaicans, Haitians, and smaller groups of English- and Spanish-speakers.

Numbers alone cannot tell the story. There are fewer Caribbeans in Connecticut than in some larger states nearby, notably New Jersey and New York. But people of Caribbean background, especially Puerto Ricans, make up an impressive share of the population in many Connecticut cities and towns. And the state's Caribbean population is growing at a dramatic rate.

Caribbean people have been coming to Connecticut for more than a century, but the majority have arrived during and since World War II. Many of the wartime migrants came to work on farms or in factories; such jobs were plentiful in the state through the end of the 1960s. Jesús Marmol, a Cuban immigrant who came to Bridgeport in 1952, remembers that immigrants readily found work in the city's steel and metal products, appliance, car, and coat factories. "The day after you arrived at the airport, you were working. They would look for you, pull you off the street to work in the factories."

Those who came decades ago—in the Puerto Rican community they are sometimes called *los pioneros*, the pioneers—have put down firm roots. Indeed, the pioneers are often the aristocrats of their ethnic communities, the ones who have bought homes, opened businesses, founded churches and clubs, and even run for office. Their children, for whom the pioneers strived to obtain higher education, have moved in significant numbers into the middle class.

Photos page 211-212: West Indian and Puerto Rican businesses lend a Caribbean flavor to the streets of Hartford, Connecticut. All photos by Jenna Moniz.

Today, it is far more difficult for new immigrants to gain an economic foothold. The economy of Connecticut, and of southern New England in general, has changed. No longer can arriving immigrants count on steady factory income. Most of the older factories have closed or moved; new industries coming to the state are largely high-tech. As a result, there are relatively few opportunities for workers without advanced education or technical skills. The consequences are felt in deepening poverty and joblessness, especially in Connecticut's larger cities.

The more recent immigrants are, in general, still struggling to get established. Some of the pioneers are critical of these newcomers, blaming them for community problems such as drugs and crime. Others realize that these newer immigrants arrive under difficult circumstances, and often with fewer resources to begin with. They face a post-industrial

Connecticut with disappearing farms and factory jobs, expensive and scarce housing, and cutbacks in government programs that help those in need.

Yet they continue to come, driven by desperate economic conditions and sometimes political persecution in their home countries. Many Caribbeans arrive in Connecticut as part of a chain migration, recruited by family members or friends from their hometowns. Others have come on contract to do agricultural or domestic work. Still others move to Connecticut after a short or long sojourn in New York.

Whatever their origins, many say that what they like about Connecticut is precisely that it is *not* New York. Rather, Connecticut is a collection of smaller cities, towns and suburban areas, set amid pleasant countryside. Despite growing problems, especially in the larger cities, it is still easier in

many parts of the state to find a job or an apartment, raise children, and participate in local government. Some Caribbean people find that the hills, lakes and rivers of New England remind them of their homelands, if only for the few warm months of the year!

The nature of this small town and city life, however, makes it particularly difficult to bring together Caribbean people in Connecticut. Whereas Caribbeans in New York City are densely concentrated in a few neighborhoods, in Connecticut they have settled all over the state. Puerto Ricans, who total at least 150,000 statewide, are found in every major city and town, with the largest concentrations in Hartford and Bridgeport, 50 miles apart. At least 20,000 to 30,000 English-

speaking West Indians live in greater Hartford; others live 40 miles away in New Haven or in the more distant southwestern part of the state. Haitians are said to number about 8,000 in the Stamford/Norwalk/Bridgeport area, and about 4,000 in and around Hartford; their actual numbers may well be higher. Cubans and Dominicans are relatively small populations, estimated at 6,300 and 4,000 respectively, and are scattered throughout the state.

Partly because of this geographic dispersion, attempts by Puerto Ricans, West Indians and Haitians to organize statewide have met with limited success. In a state whose 169 towns tend to be feistily independent, immigrants often get absorbed into the lives of their local communities. At times, members of the same ethnic group living in different towns may be unaware of each others' issues, leaders or organizations. Events meant to bring Caribbean people together, such as the Connecticut Puerto Rican and West Indian parades, can end up fostering competition between the ethnic leadership in different towns over which

locale will host the happening. Cities and towns with larger Caribbean populations may overshadow those with more modest ethnic niches.

West Indians and Puerto Ricans, with their larger numbers, publish their own newspapers in the state. In the case of Haitians, Dominicans and Cubans, those in Connecticut often stay informed by keeping in touch with the larger communities of their compatriots in New York, New Jersey, Rhode Island or Massachusetts. Although some local radio and cable television programs serve these groups, they also rely on newspapers published in New York or Miami, or in their homelands.

In Connecticut, as elsewhere, the separate Caribbean groups tend not to identify together as Caribbeans. Puerto Ricans are more likely to socialize with other Spanish-speakers—from the Caribbean or from Central or South America—than with non-Hispanic Caribbeans such as West Indians.

Jamaicans are by far the largest of the English-speaking Caribbean groups in Connecticut. They have usually organized socially and politically either by themselves or within a pan-Caribbean framework that includes other West Indians, and at times, Haitians. In addition, West Indians sometimes have organized successfully with African-Americans. Puerto Ricans and African-Americans, on the other hand, have often found themselves in competition for jobs, housing, and social programs, and as a result, coalitions between these two groups have generally been short-lived.

Yet for all their separateness, the different groups of Caribbean people have intertwined histories in Connecticut. In many cases, for example, labor practices of the U.S. government or private employers have placed immigrant groups in competition with one another. Migrating through employment contracts, Puerto Ricans succeeded Jamaicans in the state's tobacco fields; various groups now work in the much-reduced tobacco sector. Puerto Ricans who once worked in the mushroom farms of eastern Connecticut have been largely replaced by Haitians. Nonetheless, as we will see below, Caribbeans of different nations or territories have gone through—and are going through—many of the same steps in building their new communities in Connecticut.

Whether in cooperation or competition with each other, there is no doubt that the growing Caribbean population in Connecticut has enriched the state. As laborers, shopkeepers, professionals and elected officials, and as organizers of agencies, festivals and social clubs, Caribbeans have brought new ingredients to Connecticut's cultural mix. Their presence has also forced ethnic groups with longer histories in the state to reexamine what it means to be ethnic: to cherish and preserve one's culture while finding a place within the larger society.

Puerto Ricans in Connecticut

Puerto Ricans have lived in Connecticut since at least the nineteenth century; indeed, several Puerto Ricans who lived in New Haven fought in the Civil War! Most, however, have come during the second half of the twentieth century. According to the 1990 census, Puerto Ricans are more than 4 percent of Connecticut's population and still growing. Puerto Ricans account for more than two-thirds of all Latinos in the state, and hold more electoral positions in Connecticut than in any other state except New York.

Connecticut has long been a center of weapons manufacturing, and Puerto Ricans were recruited to work in Bridgeport munitions factories during the Second World War. A few years later, an arrangement between the Puerto Rican Department of Labor and the United States government brought many Puerto Ricans to work in agriculture. Connecticut was one of the states that relied most heavily on this imported work force. From the 1950s to the 1970s, thousands of Puerto Ricans

picked apples, cured tobacco, and cultivated trees for Connecticut's orchards, farms and nurseries.

Conditions in most farmworker camps were poor, with low wages and little labor protection. Some of the farm workers organized jointly with local church groups, the United Farm Workers, and the Puerto Rican Socialist Party to improve conditions for farm workers and form a union. Many eventually chose to "vote with their feet" and move to nearby cities, where factory work was plentiful and paid a good deal better.

Like Irish, Italian and other European immigrants before them, Puerto Ricans found themselves in the dirtiest and most dangerous industrial jobs. From the 1950s onward, Puerto Ricans labored in the foundries of Guilford, Madison and Union City. They worked in poultry processing plants and textile mills in Willimantic, plated metal objects in Wallingford, and sewed clothing in Norwalk and Danbury. Puerto Ricans were an important part of the silver industry in Meriden and the brass industry in Waterbury. They made tools in New Britain, rubber products in Naugatuck, and typewriters in Hartford. And all over, they performed service jobs, working in hotels, hospitals and restaurants.

In the factories and service industries, Puerto Ricans who had left the farms worked alongside others who had come directly from the island, or from New York. Chain migration often brought people from particular towns and regions of Puerto Rico to particular towns in Connecticut. Hartford, for example, attracted many people from the area around Comerío, Cayey and Caguas, while the community in Meriden consisted mostly of people from the town of Aguada. Partly as a result of these different hometown connections, the Puerto Rican community in each Connecticut town developed its own social, cultural and political dimensions. The city of Meriden, for example, had Puerto Rican elected officials by the end of the 1950s. Waterbury, on the other hand, elected its first Puerto Rican official in the mid-1990s.

Despite the differences in their hometowns and host communities, Puerto Ricans coming to Connecticut struggled with many of the same challenges. Most lived at first in small pockets surrounding the downtown and factory areas of

Annual health fair sponsored by the Hispanic Health Council in the south end of Hartford. Community agencies set up tables to provide health education, hearing and vision tests, and screening for conditions such as diabetes and high blood pressure.

each town. Facing a sometimes hostile, sometimes curious community of European-Americans and African-Americans, Puerto Ricans often had difficulty obtaining housing and services. Many responded by creating their own institutions, both to counter discrimination and to meet their particular cultural needs.

Many Catholic churches, for example, were reluctant to accede to the demand for a Spanish-language mass. Those that did for the most part grudgingly allowed the Spanish mass in the church basement. Connecticut's Puerto Rican Catholics responded by creating their own Hispanic parishes, often with the help of a few sympathetic North American clergy. Pentecostal and other Protestant Puerto Ricans also created their own church organizations. These religious institutions became important community resources, providing social services and opportunities for cultural celebrations as well as for worship. Later, they welcomed the

increasing numbers of non–Puerto Rican Latinos coming to the state.

Puerto Ricans also established small businesses, hometown clubs, and social service organizations. They gathered with other Latinos for social activities such as dances or baseball leagues. To some extent these activities brought together Puerto Ricans from different towns or regions of Connecticut. After years of individual town celebrations, the Puerto Rican Parade was established in 1964 as a collaborative effort. But most towns with significant Puerto Rican populations still host their own festivals, saints' day celebrations, and other cultural events.

From the War on Poverty era of the 1960s, a host of new Puerto Rican and Latino organizations worked to bring political power and better living conditions to Connecticut's Puerto Ricans. Some followed the social-service model of the older institutions. Others, notably ASPIRA, emphasized education and leadership training. Some of these groups worked to establish the bilingual education programs that are now a feature of schools in all the major areas of Puerto Rican settlement. The late 1960s also saw the emergence of radical youth groups that sought to confront the roots of Puerto Rican poverty. The Young Lords, founded in Chicago and New York, formed a chapter in Bridgeport that staged rent strikes and organized free breakfast and lead-testing programs for children.

By the 1970s, urban renewal and gentrification were taking their toll on the Puerto Rican population in Connecticut's cities. New highways, office buildings, and luxury apartments displaced thousands of Puerto Rican renters and shopkeepers. While some were able to relocate to other neighborhoods or to the suburbs, many poorer Puerto Ricans found themselves forced into more crowded and deteriorating areas. As other groups, including many African-Americans, moved out of the inner cities, Puerto Ricans remained.

With decades of hard work, some of the pioneers and their children have achieved the "American dream" of home ownership and secure jobs. So, too, have a few of the more recent arrivals, mainly the more highly educated. But this middle class, although growing, is still small. Many of Connecticut's Puerto Ricans remain mired in poverty, especially those in inner-city Hartford and Bridgeport. As factories close and affordable housing becomes ever scarcer, budgets are slashed for social programs that could help to ease the impact.

At the same time, Puerto Ricans have been leaders in creating community groups that are confronting these problems with creative solutions. La Casa de Puerto Rico, emphasizing housing and health care, was one of the first social service and advocacy programs for Puerto Ricans in Hartford. Several groups including the Hispanic Health Council grew out of La Casa. Taino Housing and El Hogar del Futuro work to create affordable housing in Hartford. Casa Otoñal in New Haven serves senior citizens and local schoolchildren. The Puerto Rican Political Action Committee works to assure electoral representation of Puerto Ricans at the state and local levels. Through service, action and advocacy, these organizations and many others

Courtesy of Hispanic Health Council

Child care during a nutrition focus group at the Hispanic Health Council.

like them are helping to revitalize Connecticut communities at the grassroots.

The Hispanic Health Council
One winter day in 1973, a Puerto Rican baby in Hartford fell ill. Her mother, who spoke little English, went to two hospitals and was told to give the child aspirin. Finally she called police. The baby died in a patrol car on the way back to the hospital.

Although this incident was extreme, it was also emblematic of the poor health care local Latinos often received. In the furor following the child's death, the Hispanic Health Council was formed to improve health care for Hartford's Latinos.

The council carries out research on traditional beliefs and health practices among Latinos, and uses this understanding to develop more effective ways of providing health care. For example, council members discovered that lack of prenatal care was contributing to low birth weights and high infant mortality in Hartford's Latino community. But many pregnant Latina women were not comfortable going to hospitals or doctors' offices where they might be misunderstood or stereo-typed. Many were used to rural health care where mothers-to-be are attended by *comadronas* (midwives) and female family members.

To help these women have healthy babies, the council sends Spanish-speaking health workers called "comadronas" to reach pregnant women in stores, churches and shelters, even on the street. Although not midwives, the comadronas visit the women at home and serve as go-betweens with the medical system. The council runs a reproductive health clinic, and the comadronas make sure pregnant women attend clinic regularly, offering transportation and child care if needed.

The Hispanic Health Council has other projects under way or planned on AIDS, domestic violence, hunger and substance abuse. It holds an annual health fair for families where children and adults can receive health screenings and health education.

At the same time, the council engages in advocacy to change public policies on health care. One goal is to ensure that hospitals and clinics have health providers who speak both Spanish and English. In an era of shrinking public programs, the council fights to maintain social services for poor people in Hartford, knowing that poverty and ill health go hand in hand.

Casa Otoñal

By the 1970s many of New Haven's early Puerto Rican migrants were facing the problems of old age. Some lived in deteriorating housing in the city's shrinking low-rent neighborhoods. Many spoke little English and felt unwelcome in the local elderly apartment buildings and senior centers.

Latina community activists and a local Catholic priest began making informal visits to the homes of Hispanic elderly. This evolved into a day program for seniors featuring lunches of their familiar ethnic foods. This was the beginning of Casa Otoñal (Autumn House).

More than twenty years later, Casa Otoñal houses a bilingual and bicultural senior center and 100 apartment units for the elderly. The senior

At Casa Otoñal in New Haven, neighborhood children receive help with homework in an intergenerational after-school program.

program has expanded to include community gardens, crafts, a thrift store, and a singing group called Los Otoñales. In 1993 Casa launched an intergenerational after-school program for senior residents and neighborhood children. Together, young and old work on computer programs and homework, enjoy music and theater activities, participate in Little League, and cook traditional foods with vegetables they grow themselves.

In Casa Otoñal, Latino elders and children have a refuge in one of New Haven's toughest neighborhoods. Casa's employees and residents have created strong links with the surrounding area, buying and renovating blighted properties and building a community center with the help of local unions and technical students. As neighborhood people take part in these programs, they have gained inspiration to fight the area's crime and neglect. Casa Otoñal is not just for the elderly but is an important source of skills, resources, and community revitalization from the grassroots.

Pericas Travel
When Elaine Torres's grandparents came to Connecticut in the 1940s, they probably never dreamed that fifty years later their granddaughter would be running a travel agency with three branches. But Pericas Travel, named after this pioneering couple, is a family business well known and appreciated among Latinos in Bridgeport and New Haven.

Torres's grandparents originally settled in New York. Moving to Stamford and then Bridgeport, the couple started several businesses, including a record store and the first Spanish-language movie theater in Connecticut. As established residents, the Pericases often helped new Hispanic arrivals. They translated documents and helped make travel arrangements for those who wanted to bring family members over. This informal assistance evolved into a travel agency by the early 1960s. The Pericases passed on the business to their daughter, who in turn passed it to her daughter, Elaine Torres.

In accord with Hispanic culture, Pericas Travel does business with *cariño* (caring and affection). In the early days, this meant transporting clients to and from the airport, interpreting for them, and making sure they were not bumped from flights. These days, it means getting to know customers

and giving them patient attention. Among Latinos, Torres says, "when they go to buy a ticket, one person is traveling, but they'll come in with grandma and grandpa, mother, father and the kids. If this happens to be a client that we've known for a long long time, not only do they want to buy that ticket, they want to tell us what they've been doing since the last time they bought a ticket. It may not be the most efficient, but ... And it doesn't matter if they're buying a $99 ticket to Washington, D.C. or a full-blown vacation."

West Indians in Connecticut

West Indians have a long although little-known history in Connecticut. As a result of trade between the Caribbean and New England, West Indian visitors and immigrants have been coming to the state at least since the nineteenth century. People from the island of Nevis, for example, formed a settlement in New Haven around 1900. Edna Carnegie, whose father came from Nevis in 1905, explained that while her forebears stopped at Ellis Island, "they didn't like New York too much, and someone told them there was work up here."

Most of these Nevisians were tradespeople. Carnegie's father was a shoemaker, her mother a dressmaker and teacher. Immigrants from Nevis, along with those from other Caribbean territories who joined them, worked hard to establish careers, businesses, and mutual assistance organizations. Nevisians owned some of the first black shoe stores, funeral homes and restaurants in New Haven. Their Nevis Society collected dues for a fund to help the sick and bereaved. The club later became the Antillean Friendly Society as more immigrants arrived from St. Kitts, St. Croix, St. Thomas, Anguilla, Montserrat, Antigua and other islands.

West Indian immigration increased greatly during World War II as new jobs opened up in factories and on farms. During the war, with labor scarce, Connecticut's Shade Tobacco Growers Association recruited thousands of Jamaicans to help cultivate, harvest and cure the tobacco. Other workers came on contract to Connecticut's dairy farms, vegetable farms and orchards. Jamaicans were the largest group, but Barbados, Guyana, Trinidad, and other territories were also represented.

The St. Lucia American Society and the Trinidad & Tobago American Society share a block of Albany Avenue in Hartford.

When the contract program ended in 1950, some of the farm workers sought permission to stay in the United States. Many settled in the Hartford area, taking jobs in factories, offices or stores. Since a fair number had been office workers or tradespeople in their homelands—not farmers— they used their skills to forge new employment opportunities. Many sought to open small businesses of their own.

The farm workers and other West Indians in Hartford came together to socialize and play cricket, often competing against New York teams. Soon the group founded a West Indian Social Club, as well as an Elks Club and a cricket club.

Many West Indian women came as contracted domestic or child care workers. Those who stayed often sought further training and moved into other areas of work, especially health care. In addition, many nurses and health workers have come directly from the Caribbean to fill jobs in their fields. As a result, West Indian nurses, lab technicians and nursing home attendants are a pillar of health care in the state.

Still other West Indians arrived with advanced education and skills and moved, sooner or later, into professional and managerial jobs. Whatever their class background, virtually all struggled and sacrificed to secure an education for their children.

By and large they have succeeded. Many second-generation Caribbeans, born or raised in Connecticut, have become doctors, lawyers, and other professionals, living comfortable suburban lives.

Today, West Indians in and around Hartford may number as many as 40,000. Although Jamaicans account for some 70 percent, every English-speaking Caribbean nation is represented. This diversity is reflected in an array of social clubs, including the Barbados American Society, the Trinidad & Tobago American Society, the Connecticut Haitian Society, the Guyanese Cultural Association, the St. Lucia American Society, and the Jamaica Progressive League, among others.

These groups host programs for their own nationals, but they also work together in organizations such as the Caribbean-American Society and the West Indian Social Club. The social club is especially active during the week-long West Indian Independence Celebration, started in 1962, which commemorates the political independence of the English-speaking Caribbean nations. Plays, lectures, dances and concerts are hosted by the different nationality clubs, culminating in the West Indian parade through downtown Hartford.

In addition to the clubs, West Indians have founded several organizations concerned with public policy and education. These include the

Center for Urban Research and Training, the Council for West Indian Planning and Development, the West Indian Credit Union, and the West Indian Foundation, together with *The West Indian American* newspaper, all in north Hartford.

West Indians in Connecticut are also active participants in African-American organizations such as the NAACP and the Urban League. Virtually every such organization in the state has members who trace their roots to the English-speaking Caribbean.

Connecticut's West Indians have achieved an impressive measure of economic success. The emerging challenge is to translate this economic and organizational energy into political empowerment, beginning with the election of more West Indians to local office. West Indians have been elected to city councils in Hartford, Windsor and Bloomfield, and there is a state senator from Bloomfield. Further victories will depend in part on success in forging coalitions with other groups in Connecticut around common goals.

West Indian Social Club
As vice-president Marva Douglas relates, the West Indian Social Club was started by farm workers who came to Connecticut to pick apples and tobacco and "felt the need of a homeplace." Members at first held meetings in a church basement, paying dues of 50 cents apiece. Nearly half a century later, the club owns a spacious building in north Hartford and is a vital part of Caribbean life in the area.

The majority of the original club members were Jamaican, but they were joined over time by immigrants from the other West Indian territories. At first the club was for men only. Eventually a Women's Auxiliary formed, and later merged into the club as a whole. Today there is a Youth Auxiliary for teenagers, as well as a West Indian Boy Scout troop.

The 500 active club members enjoy domino games, exercise classes, an African drumming group and a dance troupe. The club hosts parties, fundraisers, and performances of Caribbean theater companies on tour. It is a forum for news from the Caribbean, and sponsors relief efforts for islands that have suffered natural disasters.

An offshoot of the club is the West Indian Foundation, which offers scholarships to promising Caribbean students. The majority of the foundation's members are elected from the membership of the West Indian Social Club. Although the club is non-political, two of its past presidents have gone on to win elective office as city council members. The club provides a leadership forum for members who have been elected to positions in the Hartford area.

Members of the West Indian Social Club of Hartford at the club's 40th anniversary ball in 1990.

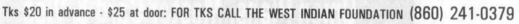

CHALKDUST

The 4-time Calypso Monarch of Trinidad & Tobago
and the reigning World Calypso Monarch

LADY GUYMINE
D'IVAN of Guyana

comes to

SHOW & DANCE, HARTFORD, CT.
West Indian American Centre, 3340 Main St
SATURDAY, SEPTEMBER 13, 1997, 10 P.M.

Tks $20 in advance - $25 at door: FOR TKS CALL THE WEST INDIAN FOUNDATION (860) 241-0379

Presented by THE WEST INDIAN FOUNDATION: airJamaica   AT&T

The West Indian Social Club of Hartford hosts cultural presentations by well-known theater groups and musicians on tour from the Caribbean.

Metropolitan Academy

Education has been key to the steady upward mobility of Connecticut's West Indians. The quality of their children's schooling is therefore an overriding concern for parents. When Dr. K. Alexander Paddyfote founded the Metropolitan Academy of Greater Hartford in 1994, he was responding to the call of community members. West Indian parents in Hartford, dissatisfied with their children's education, asked Paddyfote and other local leaders to help them start their own school.

Metropolitan Academy is the first West Indian–founded school in Connecticut. It serves a small group of students from sixth to twelfth grade, the majority of them from West Indian families. In preparing its students for college and civic life, the school stresses rigorous academic instruction and personal discipline. The school leadership works actively to involve parents and community members, drawing upon them as resources for the students and for help with fundraisers to keep the school going.

Connecticut Cricket League

No sport is closer to the hearts of West Indians than cricket. First played in England centuries ago, the sport spread throughout the British Commonwealth and is an enduring passion in the former British Caribbean. Since the 1960s, West Indian teams have been among the best in the world—a source of boundless regional pride. And West Indians emigrating from the region have taken the game with them wherever they go.

Every fair-weather weekend, the crack of the cricket bat is heard in towns around Connecticut. Some 90 games are played in the state each year, culminating in the finals in early October. Cricket games are played on a grass pitch with ball, bats and two wickets between teams of 11 players each. The rules are complicated and games are long.

The Hartford-based Connecticut Cricket League oversees cricket teams all over the state. Greenwich, Bridgeport, Norwalk, New Haven, New Britain, Waterbury and Hartford all have their own teams, attesting to the strong West Indian presence in these communities. Hartford alone has six teams, including teams specifically for St. Lucians, Barbadians, and Guyanese. The Connecticut Cricket League invites teams from as far away as Canada and Jamaica for matches, although most come from New York, New Jersey, Washington, D.C., Maryland, and other eastern seaboard areas.

Haitians in Connecticut

Significant Haitian migration to Connecticut dates to 1957, when exiles began fleeing "Papa Doc" Duvalier's regime. Most of these early immigrants settled in Hartford. While a fair number were highly educated and skilled, it was nonetheless difficult for them to find jobs at their level or in their fields, in large part because of the language barrier. Many had to take jobs in local hospitals and restaurants, in factories, or as domestics.

Connecticut's southwestern city of Stamford also had a few 1950s immigrants, but the Haitian community there really developed during the 1970s and 1980s. During those years, new waves of refugees fled Haiti to escape the repression of the Jean-Claude Duvalier government and post-Duvalier military regimes. At the same time, a significant number of Haitians were leaving New York City in search of jobs; many headed for nearby Stamford.

Despite its late start, Stamford quickly grew into the state's largest and most active Haitian community. As late as the 1980s, Stamford still had factory jobs to offer. Haitians kept arriving and bringing other family members.

As factory work has declined, Haitians have worked in hotels, hospitals, restaurants, and fast-food chains, and driven taxis. With the advent of urban renewal and gentrification in Stamford, many Haitians, along with African-Americans, Latinos, and less affluent whites, can no longer afford housing in the city. Many have moved to nearby Norwalk and Bridgeport.

In recent decades, Haitian refugees arriving in Connecticut have been assisted by Catholic Family Services, Interfaith Refugee Ministry, and other church agencies. Through them, immigrants with agricultural backgrounds and little English have been placed in low-skilled jobs such as at Franklin Mushroom Farms in the eastern part of the state.

Haitians who have started off in such jobs have often ended up settling in eastern Connecticut towns such as Willimantic and Norwich.

Others have come from Haiti with more education and resources. They typically spend a few years working in retail or industry before starting their own business or beginning a professional career. Haitians have established restaurants, groceries, limousine companies, hair salons, and other services oriented toward the Haitian community. They are college professors, teachers, lawyers and health workers. Haitian immigrants' children, many of whom have obtained higher education, often go on to professional or managerial careers.

Two main organizations in the state cater to Haitians. In Hartford, the Connecticut Haitian-American Society is dedicated to social events and passing on knowledge of Haitian culture to youngsters brought up in Connecticut. Its members work in cooperation with the local West Indian Social Club, holding a dinner dance with Haitian food and music during the annual West Indian independence celebration. In Stamford, the Haitian Community Center offers immigration counseling, job placement, and other assistance to Haitians of the Stamford/Norwalk/Bridgeport area.

Bilingual classes with Haitian Creole–speaking teachers are increasingly common. A few Protestant and Catholic churches offer services in Creole. An art gallery in New Canaan showcases Haitian art, and a radio station in Norwalk hosts a weekly Creole program.

Haitians in Connecticut maintain strong links to Haiti. Immigrants typically send home part of their earnings to help family members left behind. Haitian groups host fundraising events for material aid to Haiti, such as equipment for schools. They remain keenly interested in political events in Haiti, gathering at Stamford's Lacaye Restaurant to hold unofficial elections for Haitian leaders. Because of its financial resources, skills and education—and its potential access to the U.S. political process—the Haitian-American community wields considerable clout in Haiti's political life. Haitian politicians now make Stamford, as well as New York, a standard overseas campaign stop.

Teacher Marie Jean-Claude Jeune works with students in an after-school program at the Haitian Community Center in Stamford.

Connecticut's Haitians also have voiced their opinions regarding U.S. policies in Haiti through demonstrations and letter-writing campaigns. In 1990 Haitians in Connecticut and New York joined forces to protest federal policies designating Haitians as a high-risk group for AIDS. Shown to be without foundation, the policy was eventually rescinded.

Haitian Community Center
Arriving in Stamford in 1980, Emilio Revolus found his skills in demand. A computer programmer with degrees in law and education, he was soon flooded with calls from other Haitian immigrants asking for help with everything from immigration forms to jobs. Together with other community leaders, Revolus decided to start a center to meet this need. The nonprofit Haitian Community Center opened in 1985 with Revolus as director.

The center's Creole-speaking staff helps newly arrived Haitians find food, clothing and jobs. They interpret for them in court, at the Social Security office, and at other state and city offices. Immigrants—of any nationality—can get help filing for legal status or U.S. citizenship; those who have naturalized can register to vote. The center hosts an after-school program and helps people enroll in English classes, GED classes, computer training and day care. As the liaison between the Stamford public schools and the Haitian community, Revolus has helped to establish and run bilingual programs in English and Haitian Creole.

The center also works to preserve Haitian culture and ties to the homeland. Haitian Flag Day, May 18, brings an annual dinner and parade. At times the center joins in efforts to raise money for needs back home, such as the effort to send a delegation of Haitian priests from New York to build and repair schools in Haiti.

Restaurant Lacaye
Lacaye means "home" in Haitian Creole, and owner Etzner Bocicault labors long hours to make his restaurant feel like home to patrons. This Stamford restaurant serves both restaurant-style Haitian food and Haitian home cooking. Lunches and dinners range from the humble pork *grillot* and conch to a "high-class" shrimp dish that blends French wine with Creole tomato, onions and garlic.

A local Haitian band plays on Friday nights. On special weekends, out come the white tablecloths and napkins, and Bocicault's friends and loyal customers of Haitian, Jamaican, Puerto Rican and Italian descent come to join the revelry.

Bocicault comes from a family of restauranteurs in Haiti. Growing up in Pétionville, a suburb of Port-au-Prince, he helped cook for visitors to the house. He remembers making Creole cake, a simple confection of butter, sugar, eggs and flour that must be beaten by hand for hours. This cake, along with *pain patate* (sweet-potato pudding) is found on Lacaye's dessert menu.

Bocicault arrived in Connecticut with a degree in business administration and experience as a bank inspector. Like many other highly qualified immigrants, however, he at first found only menial work. During some dozen years working at Dress Barn, a clothing chain, he rose to a supervisory position and saved money. In 1994 he realized his dream of opening a restaurant.

His wife, a hospital dietician, enjoys home cooking—at her husband's restaurant. Their young son spends time at Lacaye every day, and his father hopes that the boy will someday inherit the business.

Cubans in Connecticut

Cubans have lived in Connecticut since at least the nineteenth century. A handful of wealthy merchant families settled in the shoreline towns, while upper-class families in Cuba sometimes sent their children to prestigious Connecticut private schools. A few Cuban laborers came to work in the factories of Connecticut's large cities and small industrial towns.

Larger numbers arrived in the 1940s and 1950s, when skilled laborers were attracted by rumors of plentiful work. Cuban men typically took jobs in heavy industry; women in light manufacturing, sewing or retail. Some worked in hotels or restaurants or cleaned offices, while others cultivated tobacco or did other farm labor. As time went on, these early arrivals brought family members. By 1954, Cuban immigrants in Bridgeport had founded their own club, the Liceo Cubano.

Nonetheless, it is really since the Cuban Revolution of 1959 that the number of Cubans has grown in Connecticut, reaching more than 6,000 by 1990. Typically, immigrants arrived in Miami first but found little work there. Some came to Connecticut to join friends or relatives, while others arrived through the sponsorship of Catholic or Protestant church organizations.

Arriving Cubans were quickly incorporated into local Latino life. Many joined Hispanic parishes and other organizations founded by Puerto Ricans.

Quite a few Cuban immigrants have opened their own businesses—in wholesale and manufacturing, the skilled trades, restaurants, groceries, furniture stores, clothing stores, and other enterprises. The most highly educated have pursued careers as doctors, dentists, lawyers and other professionals. These, like Cuban-owned small businesses, often serve a Latino clientele. Still, many of the Cuban immigrants arriving recently in Connecticut, especially the less educated, struggle to find jobs and gain an economic foothold within the state's declining economy.

Points of view on the meaning of the emigration vary among Cubans in Connecticut, depending in large part upon social class, timing of migration, and generation. Some consider themselves political exiles, but others say they left Cuba for long-term career motives or simple economic survival. While some of the older exiles have been waiting for decades to return to Cuba, others feel that their home is now in Connecticut. Most of the immigrants' children, born or raised in the United States, can scarcely envision life anywhere else.

The community is united, however, it its desire to celebrate traditional Cuban culture and keep it alive for the next generations. This is accomplished through ongoing contact with relatives in Cuba, the use of Spanish, cooking and eating favorite Cuban foods, and holiday observances. An important role is played by clubs such as the Centro Cívico Cubano of East Hartford and the Liceo Cubano of Bridgeport, which also reach out to other Latino groups for joint activities. As the state's Cuban population grows, many Connecticut Cubans have gradually become more involved in local social and political life.

Centro Cívico Cubano
Housed in a modest building in an industrial section of Hartford, the Centro Cívico Cubano serves as a hub of Cuban life in the city. Orestes Delgado, the Centro's president, also owns a grocery store on Park Street and is vice-president of

Hartford's Spanish American Merchants Association. He describes the Centro as "a little piece of our homeland in this country." He sees the club as an opportunity for Cuban families to socialize and to "keep ourselves unified for the liberation of the homeland."

Most of the 200 members come from Hartford and nearby towns, including East Hartford, Newington and New Britain. The club hosts parties for baptisms, weddings, birthdays and *quinceañeras*, the coming-of-age party held for Latina girls when they turn 15. The club celebrates the birthday of José Martí, the nineteenth-century Cuban independence leader, and gives gifts to the parents of the first baby born on that date.

The membership includes Cubans who arrived forty years ago as well as those who came virtually yesterday. Long-time members take new arrivals under their wing, helping them find jobs and apartments and orienting them to life in Connecticut.

La Estrella Bakery

When María do Nascimento and her husband decided to open a bakery, they started the business from the floor up. Cuban-born María had spent years working in retail and insurance, while Portuguese-born Carlos worked in construction. The couple saved money and began their bakery in 1975 in a tiny storefront on Hartford's Broad Street.

The now-thriving business offers not only standard bakery fare, but also Latino and Portuguese specialties. Cuban *pastelillo de guayaba* (guava pastries) and Portuguese *pastel de nata* (custard cups) take their places alongside cakes, cookies, doughnuts and muffins.

"You have to be a very tough person to be able to work 18 hours a day, seven days a week most of the time, and still keep your sense of humor and your family intact," observes María. She attributes her ability to maintain this balance to the generations of strong women in her Cuban family—especially María's mother, for whom La Estrella is named. María has virtually raised her own daughter in the bakery, passing on the example of determination and hard work.

Customers are "a little 400-person family" at La Estrella. People of all backgrounds who might not otherwise speak exchange family news and jokes

around the bakery's small tables. In 1986 the do Nascimentos opened a second Hartford location in a diverse area of Latinos, Italians, Portuguese, African-Americans, and Vietnamese. Offering fresh baked goods and a friendly style that respects all ethnic backgrounds, María and her husband have created a small business with a loyal following.

Dominicans in Connecticut

Dominicans are a relatively recent presence in Connecticut, migrating to the state since the late 1950s. Sandwiched between the much larger Dominican communities of New York City and Providence/Boston, Dominicans have a low profile in Connecticut. Even so, their numbers are growing quietly but steadily in all the state's major urban areas. Although the 1990 census showed the statewide population at a modest 4,000, Dominicans believe that the real number may be three times as great.

Many Dominicans in Connecticut have come from larger cities—New York, Boston, Miami—looking for a quieter and safer place to live. Others arrive directly from the Dominican Republic or from Puerto Rico, recruited by relatives here before them. Patterns of settlement reflect this chain migration. While many Dominicans in Waterbury, for example, come from the capital city of Santo Domingo, Dominicans in Danbury are often from rural central towns such as San José de las Matas and Jarabacoa.

Connecticut's Dominican population has a diverse class base. Early immigrants in Danbury, for example, included laborers who toiled on area horse farms and orchards and as well as medical professionals working at Danbury Hospital. Many are skilled tradespeople, or come from agricultural backgrounds. But others are trained professionals such as doctors, lawyers and engineers who were unable to find jobs in their homeland. Although a few in this situation have been able to resume their professional careers in Connecticut, many others find themselves working in menial jobs, at least for the first few years.

In Danbury, Waterbury, Hartford and Bridgeport, Dominicans can be found working in factories and on construction sites, in restaurants and hotels, in government and private agencies, and running their own businesses. Many of the *bodegas* (small Latino groceries) throughout the state are Dominican-owned. In some cases, bodega owners have come up from New York City looking for safer and less competitive places to do business. Once relocated, they recruit workers from among friends and family in New York or on the island.

Dominicans in Connecticut have a few organizations of their own and have also joined clubs, sports leagues, and churches founded mainly by Puerto Ricans. In Waterbury, where the Latino population is still overwhelmingly Puerto Rican, Dominican celebrations of birthdays, baptisms and holidays usually take place in private homes. In the Danbury area, on the other hand, Dominicans are the largest Latino group, numbering up to 8,000 by informal estimates. Dominicans in Danbury have founded a Hispanic Catholic parish, Nuestra Señora de Guadalupe. Although the parishioners reflect Danbury's mix of Spanish-speaking nationalities, Dominicans are the dominant group. The same is true in various Protestant churches in Danbury, including the Iglesia Hispana Unida de Cristo, which has a Dominican pastor.

In response to negative portrayals of Dominicans in the local press, a group of Danbury leaders founded the Dominican Cultural Society in 1991. Through the club, local Dominicans get together to celebrate their country's national holidays, Mother's Day and other occasions. Other initiatives have included a sister-city arrangement between Danbury and the Dominican town of Jarabacoa.

Bridgeport has a Dominican Social and Cultural Club which serves the 60 or 70 Dominican families in the area. In 1996 the club sponsored a float in Bridgeport's Puerto Rican parade. Through a folkloric dance group and other cultural activities, club leaders hope to give Dominican youth raised in Bridgeport a stronger sense of their roots.

Latino Restaurant

This eatery at the corner of East Main and Cherry Streets in Waterbury opened in 1992. Owner and cook Ycelsa Díaz keeps the restaurant going seven days a week, from eight o'clock in the morning until ten or eleven o'clock at night.

Although the restaurant is her first venture, Díaz is no stranger to business, having grown up with a

stepfather who owned a bus line in the Dominican Republic. After moving to Waterbury in 1980 she worked a series of factory jobs while cooking for a large group of family members. When her factory relocated to Norwalk, Díaz decided to go into business for herself rather than face a daily hour-and-a-half commute.

Díaz's customers range from factory workers to government officials. They come not only from Waterbury but also from Bridgeport, New Haven, New Britain, Hartford and even New York. She specializes in affordable home cooking, Dominican style. Always on the menu are meat, beans and rice—the national dish Dominicans call *la bandera* after the red, blue and white of their country's flag. Díaz's other specialties include *mangú,* a breakfast dish of mashed plantains and onions; chicken *asopao,* a thick soup; *mondongo,* or tripe; and *sancocho,* a savory stew of meat and root vegetables.

Dominican Social and Cultural Club

Since the 1960s, a handful of Dominican families in Bridgeport had been getting together in each others' homes to play bingo and dominoes and hold holiday celebrations. But with the rapid growth of the city's Dominican population in the last few years, a club seemed a practical necessity. For area Dominicans, explains Nadir Lajám, one of the club's founders, it is important to have a site that whole families can come to. Perhaps most important, it provides a base for maintaining Dominican culture among quickly Americanizing children.

In 1997 the club celebrated its first anniversary in a spacious location on Island Brook Avenue. Its present emphasis is social and cultural: there is a dance troupe for youth, and halls are rented for special events and parties. But the organizers are working to secure nonprofit status and apply for grants that will allow the club to offer social services to Dominicans and others. After-school tutorials, music lessons, and help with citizenship applications are among the activities planned.

Members of the club's board of directors have a long history of work with other Latino organizations in the area. Some bring years of organizing experience from the Dominican Republic as well. Still, it is an uphill battle. "It's not easy to organize a club," explains president Angel Reyes. "It interferes with the work that each of us does to sustain our family." For a recent immigrant group struggling just to survive, the club's existence and growth attests to a dedication that goes beyond the family to embrace the larger community.

La Brava

At age 29, Dominican-born Manuel Ramírez is probably the youngest Latino radio station president in New England. In little more than a year, *El Príncipe*—the Prince, as he is called—has taken Meriden radio station WMMW and transformed it into a 24-hour Latino station with innovative programming. The station is known as *La Brava*, the brave or fearless one.

Latino broadcasting is becoming a competitive business in Connecticut. New stations and programs abound. But Ramírez has plenty of experience and ideas. Formerly a communications student in Santo Domingo, he migrated to New York in 1989. After a short stint there, Ramírez moved to Connecticut, where he has worked in radio ever since. He served as program director and disk jockey for several Spanish-language stations before buying time for his own shows. When the opportunity came to lease air time on WMMW, he jumped on it.

In some ways WMMW's transformation reflects the population shift taking place in Connecticut's urban communities. To the dismay of an older audience of European descent, the station that once played big band, crooners and polkas now broadcasts entirely in Spanish. For younger Latino listeners, however, La Brava offers an unusual variety—the standard salsa, balada, and merengue are complemented by cumbia, vallenato, bachata, and one English-language pop song per hour. Talk shows highlight issues of concern to the various Spanish-speaking communities in Connecticut. ❖

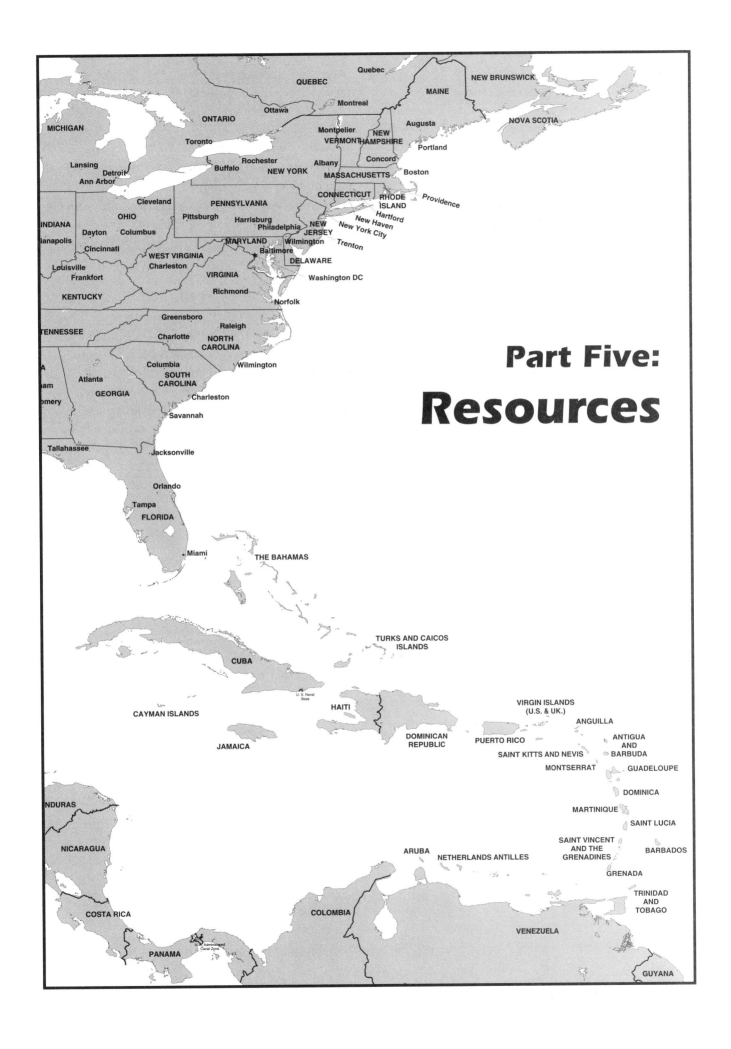

Part Five:

Resources

Caribbean Life in Your Community: A Research Guide

T his guide is intended to help you explore Caribbean life and culture in your town, city or state. This project will vary depending upon where you live. Most major cities along the eastern seaboard have significant Caribbean populations, with various cultural events for you to take advantage of. In a small town, rural area, or city in the West or South, the task will be more challenging. Caribbean cultural influence may not be readily apparent. But you can almost always find small population groups or individuals who came from the Caribbean, perhaps many years ago.

The following are suggested starting points. One contact will lead to another. Design your project well, let your enthusiasm show, and you will find most people delighted to help you delve into the life of their community.

A note about on-line resources: If you have access to the Internet, this can give you a head start. Using a search engine, try key words such as "Caribbean," "West Indian," "Puerto Rican" or "Cuban-American." Much of it will be about tourism, but you can also turn up the Web sites of Caribbean community organizations, student groups and university programs. A few Web sites for specific organizations are listed in this guide.

Personal Contacts

Begin your research by searching for personal connections that members of your class or group may have with the Caribbean. Was anyone in the group born in the region? Does someone have a parent, grandparent or other relative born there? What about friends or neighbors?

If such connections are found, you may want to invite these family members or friends to talk with the group. This could be a single visit or a continuing exchange. You should prepare questions in advance, but also be open to pursuing themes that your guest suggests.

For a longer project, consider doing an oral history. This could be a personal narrative of an individual's life or the history of a neighborhood or a community. The group should prepare by reading other oral histories, learning about oral history techniques, conducting background research, and developing questions. Several resources offer step-by-step advice:

Studying Life Stories in the Classroom: Grades 5–8. Available from the Oral History Center, 25 West St., 2nd floor, Boston, MA 02111. Tel: (617) 423-2722.

Cynthia S. Brown, *Like It Was: A Complete Guide to Writing Oral History.* Available from City Lore, 72 East First St., New York, NY 10003. Tel: (212) 529-1955.

William Zimmerman, *How to Tape Instant Oral Biographies.* Available from National Women's History Project, 7738 Bell Road, Windsor, CA 95492. Tel: (707) 838-6000.

Local Organizations

Social clubs and other civic organizations often serve as a focus of local Caribbean life. Members of these organizations will know the people and events of the local Caribbean-American community and can help you make other contacts.

National associations are social clubs for people from a particular country—Jamaica, Trinidad and Tobago, or Haiti, for example. They offer cultural and social activities, and their members often organize to send material aid or sponsor development projects in the home country. **Social service organizations** provide assistance such as job placement, health care, legal aid or housing referrals. They may cater to a particular nationality, but are usually open to anyone who needs their help. Other groups include **professional and business associations**, **student organizations**, **alumni groups**, **sports clubs** (mostly cricket and soccer), and **Carnival mas bands.** Some cities have one or more umbrella groups that help to coordinate the various Caribbean organizations in the area.

There are thousands of Caribbean-American organizations across the country, and the roster is constantly changing. Groups go out of existence and new ones form. Embassies of Caribbean countries may be able to put you in touch with organizations serving their nationals in your city or state.

Suggested activities:

▶ Contact local organizations and ask them to help you find a speaker to address your class or group. Be specific about the topic you want to cover.

▶ Ask an organization to help you plan a Caribbean cultural day at your school, church or community center. Organizations might provide or suggest workshop leaders, speakers or musicians. A local Caribbean restaurant could be engaged for catering. When the event is planned and a date is set, be sure to send invitations to the organizations that have helped you.

▶ Ask members of a local organization to accompany you as your class or group visits specific neighborhoods or cultural events (see below).

Neighborhoods and Small Businesses

Storefront businesses often give a neighborhood a distinctive ethnic character. Caribbean-owned enterprises typically include restaurants, bakeries, travel agencies, shipping companies, money-transfer offices, groceries, music stores, law firms, medical and dental offices, real estate agencies, and insurance companies. They are often interspersed with Central American, African, or African-American businesses, or with those remaining from earlier immigrant waves, such as Italian or Portuguese.

Suggested activities:
Visit a part of your city where Caribbean businesses are clustered. You will learn more if you ask a member of a local Caribbean organization to accompany you and explain unfamiliar foods, words and customs. Some ideas for your visit:

▶ Walk down a busy commercial street and make a list of Caribbean-owned businesses, with their locations. What goods and services do they provide? What nationality are the owners? (Look for clues like a name, flag or wall poster, or ask.) Afterwards, make a map of the street showing the location and nature of these businesses.

▶ Visit a grocery (in Spanish-speaking neighborhoods, a grocery may be a *bodega, almacén* or *tienda*). Find and learn about different foods used in Caribbean cooking—for example, ackee, callaloo, cassava, coconuts, dasheen, mangoes, okra, oxtail, papayas, pigeon peas, plantains, saltfish, yams.

▶ Eat in an inexpensive Caribbean restaurant. Taste Caribbean specialties like roti, jerk chicken, fried plantains, *sancocho* or *tostones*. Visit a bakery for meat patties, coconut buns and other treats.

▶ Make an appointment to interview the owners of a Caribbean business. Ask how they came to the United States, about their early experiences here, and about how they succeeded in opening a business. A local Caribbean organization may be able to arrange such a visit.

Policy and Advocacy Organizations

A number of national organizations are working to improve policies, laws and social conditions that affect the lives of Caribbean immigrants in the United States. Some also offer legal assistance or other services. Most can provide information about the communities they serve and the work they do; contact them by mail or e-mail, or visit their Web sites.

ASPIRA National Office
1444 I St. NW, #800
Washington, DC 20005
(202) 835-3600
e-mail: aspiral@aol.com
www.incacorp.com/aspira

Caribbean Action Lobby
391 Eastern Parkway
Brooklyn, NY 11216
(718) 773-8351
e-mail: waldaba@undp.org

Center for Cuban Studies
124 West 23rd St.
New York, NY 10011
(212) 242-0559
e-mail: cubanctr@igc.apc.org

Cuban Committee for Democracy
1755 Massachusetts Ave. NW
Washington, DC 20036
(202) 319-0056
www.us.net/cuban/

Institute for Puerto Rican Policy
286 Fifth Avenue, 3rd floor
New York, NY 10001
(212) 564-1075
www.iprnet.org

National Coalition on Caribbean Affairs
820 H St. NE, Suite 200
Washington, DC 20002
(202) 546-7040

National Coalition for Haitian Rights
275 Seventh Avenue, 25th floor
New York, NY 10001
(212) 337-0005
e-mail: nchr@nchr.org
www.nchr.org

National Congress for Puerto Rican Rights
NYC Chapter
P.O. Box 1307
Madison Square Post Office
New York, NY 10159
(212) 631-4263
(also has chapters in Boston, Philadelphia and San Francisco)

National Puerto Rican Coalition
1700 K St. NW, #500
Washington, DC 20006
(202) 223-3915
e-mail: nprc@aol.com
www.incacorp.com/nprc

Puerto Rican Legal Defense
and Education Fund, Inc.
99 Hudson St.
New York, NY 10013
(212) 219-3360

For information about U.S. immigration policy and general migration issues, contact:

Center for Migration Studies
209 Flagg Place
Staten Island, NY 10304
(718) 351-8800
e-mail: cmslft@aol.com
www.cmsny.org

National Immigration Forum
220 I St. NE, Suite 220
Washington, DC 20002
(202) 544-0004
www.immigrationforum.org

Reports on immigration to New York City are available from:

New York City Department of City Planning
Population Division
22 Reade St.
New York, NY 10007
(212) 720-3300

Universities, Research Centers and Libraries

To learn about the history of Caribbean immigration to your community, you will want to take advantage of scholarly resources in your area.

A university may have a department or program that focuses on some part of the Caribbean. More often, Caribbean concerns are addressed within a Latin American Studies or Black Studies department or program. Some universities house specialized research centers or libraries focused on a particular Caribbean population. The City University of New York (CUNY) has several such centers:

Caribbean Research Center
Medgar Evers College
1150 Carroll St.
Brooklyn, NY 11225
(718) 735-1750
(focuses on the English-speaking Caribbean)

Centro de Estudios Puertorriqueños
(Center for Puerto Rican Studies)
Hunter College
695 Park Avenue
New York, NY 10021
(212) 772-5689
www.latino.ssnet.ucla.edu/research/centro.html

Dominican Studies Institute
City College of New York
Convent Avenue at 138th St.
NAC Room 4/107
New York, NY 10031
(212) 650-7496
www.ccny.cuny.edu/dominican/home/html

Haitian Bilingual Education Technical
Assistance Center
City College of New York
Convent Avenue at 138th St.
NAC Room 5/206
New York, NY 10031
(212) 650-6243

Also in New York City is the Schomburg Center, a branch of The New York Public Library:

Schomburg Center for Research in Black Culture
515 Malcolm X Boulevard
New York, NY 10037
(212) 491-2200
www.nypl.org/research/sc/sc.html

Consult your public library for materials on immigration to your state or city. Most public libraries have a local history division.

Local historical societies may have libraries, publications or photo collections that will help you. For example, the Brooklyn Historical Society has resources on Caribbean immigration to Brooklyn. The Rockland County (New York) Historical Society has documented Haitian immigration to that area.

Music and Festivals

Trinidadian steelband and calypso, Jamaican reggae, Dominican merengue, and the hybrid Latin music called salsa all have large followings in the United States. Some U.S. cities have local groups or musicians who perform these types of music. Performers from the Caribbean sometimes visit the United States on tour.

Dozens of U.S. cities have Caribbean-style carnivals organized by local residents. The largest is the West Indian–American Day Carnival held in Brooklyn, New York every year on Labor Day weekend. Hartford, Connecticut recognizes West Indian independence with a week-long celebration in August each year. Puerto Rican Day parades are held annually in New York City, New Jersey, Connecticut, Philadelphia, and other locales. New York City and New Jersey have Dominican Day parades. South Florida has various Cuban cultural events, and a Cuban Day Parade is held in New York City in May.

Suggested activities:

▶ Listen to Caribbean radio programs or check with local Caribbean civic groups to learn of upcoming concerts, festivals and parades. Organize a trip to the event. Before you go, learn as much as you can about the festival or the music.

The Media

Radio is very important to Caribbean communities in the diaspora. There are programs that cater to West Indians, others that serve Spanish-speakers, and still others for Haitians. Most report news from the Caribbean and provide a forum for debate on issues of concern to Caribbean-Americans. Listening is one of the best ways to stay in touch with local Caribbean life and upcoming cultural events.

Some areas have public-access cable television programs catering to particular national groups.

A number of weekly or biweekly newspapers serve Caribbean communities in the United States. One long-established weekly oriented to West Indians is *The New York Carib News. The West Indian American* is based in Hartford, Connecticut.

Caribbean Daylight is distributed free in several cities. There are three Haitian-American weeklies in New York City and several Spanish-language papers, including the daily *El Diario–La Prensa.*

Everybody's Magazine, published in Brooklyn, focuses its coverage on New York but draws a nationwide English-speaking Caribbean readership.

Daily newspapers published in your city or state may have printed articles on Caribbean immigration to the area. Check the newspaper's index (at the library, at the newspaper's offices, or on its Web site, if it has one) under headings such as "immigration," "Caribbean," "West Indian," or "Hispanic," or use the name of a national group, e.g. "Cuban." Most libraries keep back issues of newspapers on microfilm, or you can find them in the newspaper's archives.

Suggested activities:

▶ Visit the offices of a local Caribbean newspaper and talk with the writers and editors about Caribbean life in your community. Be sure to set an appointment and prepare questions in advance.

▶ Write an article about your class's or group's study of the Caribbean and submit it to the paper for publication. You might write about what aspects of Caribbean history and culture interest you, what special projects you have done or would like to do, and your personal or family links with the Caribbean. Discuss ideas with the editors to see whether they are interested before you begin to write.

▶ Arrange for several members of your class to be interviewed on a Caribbean radio show. Discuss with the host in advance what you will talk about (see suggested topics above.)

Embassies and Missions

Embassies and missions of Caribbean governments are located in Washington, D.C. and New York City. They may be able to refer you to other resources such as local Caribbean civic groups or publications. They may also provide or recommend a speaker on topics relating to their country. ❖

Suggested Reading

itles listed here all touch on the theme of migration and Caribbean immigrant experiences in the United States. Works set principally in the Caribbean are excluded, even if their authors have emigrated. The focus is on literature from the past few decades; readers may also wish to explore older writings by Bernardo Vega, Jesús Colón, Claude McKay, José Martí and others.

Only books are included here, and only those suitable for a broad readership. There is an extensive scholarly literature on immigration that may be consulted by those interested.

Novels and Short Stories

Agüeros, Jack
   Dominoes and Other Stories from the Puerto Rican. Willimantic, Conn.: Curbstone Press, 1993.

Alvarez, Julia
   How the García Girls Lost Their Accents. Chapel Hill, N.C.: Algonquin Books, 1991. Reprint, New York: Penguin, Plume,   1992.

Bernardo, Anilú
   Fitting In. Houston: Arte Público, Piñata Books, 1996.

Danticat, Edwidge
   Breath, Eyes, Memory. New York: Soho Press, 1994.

García, Cristina
   Dreaming in Cuban. New York: Knopf, 1992.

   The Aguero Sisters. New York: Knopf, 1997.

Guy, Rosa
   The Friends. New York: Holt, Rinehart & Winston, 1973. Reprint, New York: Bantam Books, 1983.

Hijuelos, Oscar

Our House in the Last World. New York: Persea, 1983.

The Mambo Kings Play Songs of Love. New York: Farrar, Straus & Giroux, 1989.

Hyppolite, Joanne

Seth and Ramona. New York: Delacorte, 1995.

Marshall, Paule

Brown Girl, Brownstones. 1959. Reprint, Old Westbury, N.Y.: The Feminist Press, 1981.

Reena and Other Stories. Old Westbury, N.Y.: The Feminist Press, 1983.

Praisesong for the Widow. New York: Putnam's, 1983.

Daughters. New York: Macmillan, Atheneum, 1991. Reprint, New York: Plume, 1991.

Mohr, Nicholasa

Nilda. New York: Harper & Row, 1973. Reprint, Houston: Arte Público, 1986.

El Bronx Remembered: A Novella and Stories. New York: Harper & Row, 1976. Reprint, Houston: Arte Público, 1991.

In Nueva York. New York: Dial, 1977. Reprint, Houston: Arte Público, 1993.

Felita. New York: Dial, 1979.

Going Home. New York: Dial, 1986.

Ortiz Cofer, Judith

The Line of the Sun. Athens, Ga.: Univ. of Georgia Press, 1989.

The Latin Deli: Prose & Poetry. Athens, Ga.: Univ. of Georgia Press, 1993. Reprint, New York: Norton, 1995.

An Island Like You: Stories of the Barrio. New York: Puffin Books, 1996.

Santiago, Esmeralda

When I Was Puerto Rican. Reading, Mass.: Addison Wesley, 1993. Reprint, New York: Vintage, 1994.

Suárez, Virgil

Latin Jazz. New York: Morrow, 1989. Reprint, New York: Simon & Schuster, 1990.

Havana Thursdays. Houston: Arte Público, 1995.

Thomas, Piri

Stories from El Barrio. New York: Knopf, 1978.

Vega, Ed

The Comeback. Houston: Arte Público, 1985.

Mendoza's Dreams. Houston: Arte Público, 1987.

Casualty Report. Houston: Arte Público, 1991.

Poetry

Agüeros, Jack

Sonnets from the Puerto Rican. Brooklyn, N.Y.: Hanging Loose Press, 1996.

Alvarez, Julia

Homecoming: New and Collected Poems. New York: Grove, 1984. Reprint, New York: Plume, 1996.

The Other Side/El Otro Lado. New York: Dutton, 1995.

Collins, Merle

Rotten Pomerack. London: Virago, 1992.

Espada, Martín

The Immigrant Iceboy's Bolero. Madison, Wis.: Ghost Pony Press, 1982.

Trumpets from the Islands of Their Eviction. Tempe, Ariz.: Bilingual Press, 1987.

Rebellion Is the Circle of a Lover's Hands. Willimantic, Conn.: Curbstone Press, 1990.

Imagine the Angels of Bread. New York: W.W. Norton, 1996.

Esteves, Sandra María

Yerbabuena. Greenfield, N.Y.: Greenfield Review Press, 1982.

Bluestown Mockingbird Mambo. Houston: Arte Público, 1990.

Hernández Cruz, Victor

Mainland. New York: Random House, 1973.

Rhythm, Content & Flavor. Houston: Arte Público, 1989.

Red Beans. Minneapolis: Coffee House Press, 1991.

Panaramas. Minneapolis: Coffee House Press, 1997.

Laviera, Tato
   La Carreta Made a U-Turn. Houston: Arte
   Público, 1979, 1992.

Ortiz Cofer, Judith
   Terms of Survival. Houston: Arte Público, 1987.

   Reaching for the Mainland. Tempe, Ariz.:
   Bilingual Press, 1987, 1995.

Pérez Firmat, Gustavo
   Bilingual Blues. Tempe, Ariz.: Bilingual Press, 1994.

Pietri, Pedro
   Puerto Rican Obituary. New York: Monthly
   Review Press, 1973.

Personal Narratives and Memoirs

Chisholm, Shirley
   Unbought and Unbossed. Boston: Houghton
   Mifflin, 1970.

Levins Morales, Aurora, and Rosario Morales
   Getting Home Alive. Ithaca, N.Y.: Firebrand Press,
   1986.

Mohr, Nicholasa
   *In My Own Words: Growing Up Inside the
   Sanctuary of My Imagination*. New York: Simon
   and Schuster, 1994.

Ortiz Cofer, Judith
   *Silent Dancing: A Partial Remembrance of a Puerto
   Rican Childhood*. Houston: Arte Público, 1990.

Pérez Firmat, Gustavo
   *Next Year in Cuba: A Cubano's Coming-of-Age in
   America*. New York: Doubleday Anchor, 1995.

Rivera, Edward
   *Family Installments: Memories of Growing Up
   Hispanic*. New York: Morrow, 1982. Reprint,
   New York: Penguin, 1983.

Thomas, Piri
   Down These Mean Streets. New York: Knopf,
   1967. Reprint, Vintage, 1974, 1991.

Literature Anthologies

Behar, Ruth, ed.
   Bridges to Cuba. Ann Arbor: Univ. of Michigan
   Press, 1995.

Duran, Roberto, Judith Ortiz Cofer, and Gustavo
Pérez Firmat, eds.
   *Triple Crown: Chicano, Puerto Rican, and Cuban-
   American Poetry*. Tempe, Ariz.: Bilingual Press,
   1987.

Hernández Cruz, Victor, Leroy Quintana, and
Virgil Suárez, eds.
   Paper Dance: 55 Latino Poets. New York: Persea,
   1995.

Hospital, Carolina, and Jorge Cantera, eds.
   A Century of Cuban Writers in Florida. Sarasota,
   Fla.: Pineapple Press, 1996.

Santiago, Roberto, ed.
   *Boricuas: Influential Puerto Rican Writings—An
   Anthology*. New York: Ballentine, 1995.

Suárez, Virgil, and Delia Poey, eds.
   *Little Havana Blues: A Cuban-American Literature
   Anthology*. Houston: Arte Público, 1996.

Tashlik, Phyllis, ed.
   Hispanic, Female and Young: An Anthology.
   Houston: Arte Público, Piñata Books, 1994.

Nonfiction

Boswell, Thomas, and James Curtis
   The Cuban-American Experience. Totowa, N.J.:
   Rowman & Allanheld, 1984.

Bryce-Laporte, Roy S., and Delores Mortimer, eds.
   Caribbean Immigration to the U.S. Washington,
   D.C.: Smithsonian Institution, 1976.

   *Female Immigrants to the United States: Caribbean,
   Latin American, and African Experiences*.
   Washington, D.C.: Smithsonian Institution, 1981.

Glasser, Ruth
   Aquí Me Quedo: Puerto Ricans in Connecticut. Middletown, Conn.: Connecticut Humanities Council, 1997.

Gmelch, George
   Double Passage: The Lives of Caribbean Migrants Abroad and Back Home. Ann Arbor: Univ. of Michigan Press, 1992.

Grasmuck, Sherri, and Patricia Pessar
   Between Two Islands: Dominican International Migration. Berkeley and Los Angeles: Univ. of California Press, 1991.

Haslip-Viera, Gabriel, and Sherrie L. Baver, eds.
   Latinos in New York: Communities in Transition. Notre Dame, Ind.: University of Notre Dame Press, 1996.

Johnson, Fay Clarke
   Soldiers of the Soil. New York: Vantage Press, 1995.

Kasinitz, Philip
   Caribbean New York: Black Immigrants and the Politics of Race. Ithaca, N.Y.: Cornell Univ. Press, 1990.

LaGuerre, Michel
   American Odyssey: Haitians in New York City. Ithaca, N.Y.: Cornell Univ. Press, 1984.

Manuel, Peter
   Caribbean Currents: Caribbean Music from Rumba to Reggae. Philadelphia: Temple Univ. Press, 1995.

Masud-Piloto, Felix
   From Welcomed Exiles to Illegal Immigrants: Cuban Migration to the U.S., 1959–1995. Lanham, Md.: Rowman & Littlefield, 1996.

Morales, Julio
   Puerto Rican Poverty and Migration: We Just Had to Try Elsewhere. New York: Praeger, 1986.

Palmer, Ransford
   In Search of a Better Life: Perspectives on Migration from the Caribbean. New York: Praeger, 1990.

   Pilgrims from the Sun: West Indian Migration to America. New York: Simon & Schuster Macmillan, Twayne, 1995.

Pérez Firmat, Gustavo
   Life on the Hyphen: The Cuban-American Way. Austin: Univ. of Texas Press, 1994.

Portes, Alejandro, and Rubén Rumbaut
   Immigrant America: A Portrait. Berkeley and Los Angeles: Univ. of California Press, 1990.

Rodríguez, Clara
   Puerto Ricans: Born in the U.S.A. Boston: Unwin Hyman, 1989. Reprint, Boulder, Colo.: Westview, 1991.

Sánchez-Korrol, Virginia
   From Colonia to Community: The History of the Puerto Rican Community in New York City, 1917–1948. Westport, Conn.: Greenwood Press, 1983.

Suro, Roberto
   Strangers Among Us: How Latino Immigration Is Transforming America. New York: Knopf, 1998.

Sutton, Constance, and Elsa Chaney, eds.
   Caribbean Life in New York City: Sociocultural Dimensions. New York: Center for Migration Studies, 1987.

Torres-Saillant, Silvio, and Ramona Hernández
   The Dominican Americans. Westport, Conn.: Greenwood Press, 1998.

Watkins-Owens, Irma
   Blood Relations: Caribbean Immigrants and the Harlem Community, 1900–1930. Bloomington, Ind.: Indiana Univ. Press, 1996. ❖

About the Editors

Catherine A. Sunshine is a writer, editor and translator based in Washington, D.C. She edited the previous titles in the Caribbean Connections series published by NECA: *Puerto Rico* (1990), *Jamaica* (1991), and *Overview of Regional History* (1991). She is the author of *The Caribbean: Survival, Struggle and Sovereignty* (EPICA/South End Press, 1985, 1988), an introduction to Caribbean history and politics.

Keith Q. Warner is professor of modern languages at George Mason University in Fairfax, Virginia. Born in Trinidad and Tobago, he previously taught at the University of the West Indies in Trinidad and at Howard University in Washington, D.C. He is the author of *Kaiso! The Trinidad Calypso* (Three Continents Press, 1982), a study of the calypso as oral literature. His most recent book is *And I'll Tell You No Lies* (Calaloux Publications, 1993), a novel of life in Trinidad.

About the Publisher

The Network of Educators on the Americas (NECA) provides resources and teacher training for K–12 anti-racist, multicultural education. A nonprofit organization based in Washington, D.C., NECA offers publications, staff development workshops, speakers and seminars to help parents and educators transform their schools.

NECA publications include the Caribbean Connections series for secondary schools, with readings and lesson plans on Puerto Rico, Jamaica, Haiti, and Caribbean regional history. NECA has recently published a practical guide to multicultural education, *Beyond Heroes and Holidays*. A semi-annual catalog offers a diverse selection of books and audiovisual resources.

In the D.C. metropolitan area, NECA sponsors the Tellin' Stories Project and co-sponsors the D.C. Area Writing Project with Howard University and the District of Columbia Public Schools. NECA also offers staff development courses called Teaching for Equity.

To order more copies of this book or receive a catalog, contact:

NECA
P.O. Box 73038
Washington, DC 20056
phone: (202) 238-2379, (202) 429-0137
fax: (202) 238-2378
e-mail: necadc@aol.com
www.cldc.howard.edu/~neca